Kant's Pragmatic Anthropology

SUNY series in Philosophy
George R. Lucas Jr., Editor

KANT'S PRAGMATIC ANTHROPOLOGY

Its Origin, Meaning, and Critical Significance

HOLLY L. WILSON

STATE UNIVERSITY OF NEW YORK PRESS

Published by
State University of New York Press, Albany

For information, address State University of New York Press,
194 Washington Avenue, Suite 700, Albany, NY 12210-2384

Production by Judith Block
Marketing by Michael Campochiaro

Library of Congress Control Number

Wilson, Holly L., 1957–
    Kant's pragmatic anthropology : its origin, meaning, and critical significance /
Holly L. Wilson.
        p. cm. — (SUNY series in philosophy)
    Includes bibliographical references and index.
    ISBN 0-7914-6849-6 (hardcover : alk. paper)—ISBN 978-0-7914-6850-0 (pbk. :
alk. paper)
    1. Kant, Immanuel, 1724–1804. 2. Philosophical anthropology—History—18th
century. I. Title. II. Series.

B2799.M25W55   2006
128.092—dc22

2005027976

ISBN-13 978-0-7914-6849-4 (hardcover : alk. paper)

10 9 8 7 6 5 4 3 2 1

To my teacher John Compton
in gratitude for having awakened me to the love of philosophy

Contents

Preface

When I was studying Philosophy in graduate school at Penn State, I was impressed with Immanuel Kant when I studied his *Critique of Pure Reason* for the first time under Professor Thomas Seebohm. Later, I approached Professor Seebohm and told him that I wanted to write on Kant. He asked me what I had read by Kant and I answered, "The Critique of Pure Reason." Now as I look back, that does sound pretty pitiful. And it probably did sound that way to Professor Seebohm, because he immediately told me that I had to read everything written by Kant before I could write on him. Now I understand what solid and wise advice I had been given! While I was reading through all of the then translated works by Kant—it was during my independent studies with Professor Seebohm—I discovered the *Anthropology from a Pragmatic Point of View*. I didn't know what to make of the work. It seemed so foreign to me. I had never encountered anything like it before. Today I am very grateful to Professor Seebohm for having me read all of Kant, for I discovered this text for the first time and have over the years struggled to understand it with great fruits of wisdom as my reward.

Rotary International and the National Endowment for the Humanities made it possible for me to spend time in Germany researching the secondary literature on Kant's *Anthropology* while perfecting my fluency in German. While I was in Germany for three years, I was very fortunate to meet and study under Professor Werner Flach at the Würzburg Universität. From Professor Flach I learned to be a Kant scholar and a careful interpreter of Kant's works. He also supported my work on Kant's *Anthropology*. For all of this I am very grateful.

Through the years, attending Kant Congresses and APA Kant sessions, I have been fortunate to meet Kantians who are also interested in the "Other Kant." That these scholars found Kant's non-Critical works of interest encouraged me in my endeavors to make sense of this little discussed work. I am especially thankful that Professor Philip Rossi took the time to read the early stages of the manuscript; he directed me to find the link between the *Anthropology* and Critical philosophy. Hopefully that key will give an opening to philosophical research, which seeks to understand the unity of Kant's Critical philosophy and Philosophies of Experience rather than the disunity of the two.

I am also very grateful for the support of my mother, Marjorie Wilson, and the wisdom she instilled in me. And I am thankful to have a sister, Robin W. Morey, who can engage in philosophical conversation and critical thinking with me. Our conversations are a good test of the success of popular philosophy.

Of course, this book wouldn't have even been a twinkle in my eye if Professor John Compton had not taken me under his Socratic wing during my undergraduate career at Vanderbilt University. He showed me that philosophy is more than just an exercise of sparring concepts, but is really what it claims to be: "the love of wisdom." I never would have become a philosopher had I not been convinced that philosophy was the path toward wisdom. In so many ways, it has shown itself to be that and more.

When I put together an interdisciplinary major at Vanderbilt and entitled it "Philosophical Anthropology," I had no idea Kant's *Anthropology* even existed, let alone any notion that I would end up dedicating my professional research and writing career to this field. Kant made that possible. His "Philosophical Anthropology" not only tells us who we are and where we are going, but also how to live a free life. It is an exciting perspective that could radically transform our thinking about the purpose of life, the education of human beings, the psychological life of human beings, the social existence of human beings, the religious orientation of people, as well as our understanding of our relation to the Earth and animals. It is definitely worthy of study and consideration.

Key to References, Sources, Abbreviations, and Translations

References to Kant's works will be listed with the volume and page number from the original German text along with the page number of the English translation. References to Kant are to *Kant's gesammelte Schriften* (KGS), herausgegeben von der Deutschen (formerly Königlichen Preussischen) Akademie der Wissenschaften, 29 volumes (Berlin: Walter de Gruyter [and predecessors], 1902) [except for the *Critique of Pure Reason* , and the *Lectures on Ethics*] and will be listed with the volume in Roman numbers, and page number in Arabic. In addition, I include the page numbers from the English translation, where that is available. References to the *Critique of Pure Reason* are from the Norman Kemp Smith translation and are referred to using the standard A and B pagination. Many of the quotations have been edited.

Abbreviations are necessary, in order to shorten the footnotes. Where there are no established abbreviations in English, I have tried either to make them as obvious as possible, or I have taken over the German abbreviations. The following abbreviations will be used.

Anth	*Anthropologie in pragmatischer Hinsicht*, in KGS, vol. VII: 117–334; *Anthropology from a Pragmatic Point of View*, trans. Mary J. Gregor (The Hague: Nijhoff, 1974).
Beo	"Beobachtungen über das Gefühl des Schönen und Erhabenen," in KGS, vol. II:205–256.
BzB	"Bemerkungen zu den Beobachtungen über das Gefühl des Schönen und Erhabenen," in KGS, vol. XX:3–192
Col 70	*Collegentwürfe aus den 70er Jahren*, in KGS, vol. XV/2: 657–798.
Col 80	*Collegentwürfe aus den 80er Jahren*, in KGS, vol. XV/2: 799–980.
DoV	*Metaphysische Anfangsgründe der Tugendlehre*, in KGS, vol. VI:373–493; *The Metaphysics of Morals*, trans. and intro. by Mary J. Gregor (Cambridge: Cambridge University Press, 1991).

Ed
Pädagogik, in KGS, vol. IX:437–500; *Education*, trans. Annette Churton, 2d ed. (Ann Arbor: The University of Michigan Press, 1964).

Entwürf
"Entwürf und Ankündigung eines Collegii der physischen Geographie nebst dem Anhange einer kurzen Betrachtung über die Frage: Ob die Westwinde in unsern Gegenden darum feucht seien, weil sie über ein großes Meer streichen," in KGS, vol. II:1–12.

Erdbeben
"Geschichte und naturbeschreibung der merkwürdigsten Vorfälle des Erdbebens, welches an dem Ende des 1755sten Jahres einen großen Theil der Erde erschüttert hat," in KGS, vol. I:429–462.

First Intro
Erste Einleitung in die Kritik der Urteilskraft, in KGS, vol. XX:193–251; *First Introduction to the Critique of Judgment*, trans. Werner S. Pluhar, in *Immanuel Kant: Critique of Judgment* (Indianapolis: Hackett Publishing Co., 1987).

Gr
Grundlegung zur Metaphysik der Sitten, in KGS, vol. IV: 385–464; *Grounding for the Metaphysics of Morals*, trans. James W. Ellington (Indianapolis: Hackett Publishing Co., 1981).

Hauptvorlesung
Die Philosophischen Hauptvorlesungen Immanuel Kants, ed. Arnold Kowalewski (München und Leipzig: Rösl & Co., 1924).

Idea
"Idee zu einer allgemeinen Geschichte in weltbürgerlicher Absicht," in KGS, vol VIII:15–32; "Idea for a Universal History with a Cosmopolitan Intent," in *Immanuel Kant: Perpetual Peace and Other Essays*, ed. and trans. Ted Humphrey (Indianapolis: Hackett Publishing Co., 1983).

Jus
Metaphysische Anfangsgründe der Rechtslehre, in KGS, vol. VI:203–272; *The Doctrine of Right*, trans. Mary Gregor (Cambridge: Cambridge University Press, 1991).

KpV
Kritik der praktischen Vernunft, in KGS, vol. V:1–164; *Critique of Practical Reason*, trans. Lewis White Beck, (Indianapolis: Bobbs-Merrill Co., 1956).

KrV
Critique of Pure Reason, trans. Norman Kemp Smith (New York: St. Martin's Press, 1965).

KU
Kritik der Urtheilskraft, in KGS, vol. V:165–486; *Critique of Judgment*, trans. Werner Pluhar (Indianapolis: Hackett Publishing Co., 1987).

Letters
"Briefe," in KGS, vols. X–XIV.

LoE	*Lectures on Ethics*, trans. Peter Heath (Cambridge: Cambridge University Press, 1997).
Log	*Logik*, in KGS, vol. IX:3–150. *Immanuel Kant, Logic*, trans. Robert S. Hartman and Wolfgang Schwarz. (New York: Dover Publishing Inc., 1974).
Log Blomberg	Logik Blomberg, in KGS, vol. XXIV:1–300.
Menschenkunde	*Immanuel Kants Menschenkunde & Immanuel Kants Anweisung zur Menschen- und Weltkenntnis*, ed. F. C. Starke (Hildesheim/New York: Georg Oms, 1976). Also in KGS, vols. XXV.
Meta L₁	"Metaphysik L$_1$," in KGS, vol. XXVIII
Meta L₂	"Metaphysik L$_2$," in KGS, vol. XXVIII.
Moscati	"Recension von Moscatis Schrift: Von dem körperlichen wesentlichen Unterschiede zwischen der Structur der Thiere und Menschen," in KGS, vol. II:421–426.
Nachricht	"Nachricht von der Einrichtung seiner Vorlesungen in dem Winterhalbenjahre von 1765–1766," in KGS, vol. II:303–314.
PE	"Philosophische Enzyclopädie," in KGS, vol. XXIX.
PP	"Zum ewigen Frieden," in KGS, vol. VIII:341–386; "Perpetual Peace," trans. Ted Humphrey, in *Immanuel Kant: Perpetual Peace* (Indianapolis: Hackett Publishing Co., 1983).
Racen	"Von den verschiedenen Racen der Menschen," in KGS, vol. II:427–444.
Rel	*Die Religion innerhalb der Grenzen der bloßen Vernunft*, in KGS, vol. VI:1–202; *Religion within the Boundries of Mere Reason*, trans. George di Giovanni (Cambridge: Cambridge University Press, 1996).
RzA	"Reflexionen zur Anthropologie," in KGS, vol. XV.
RzL	"Reflexionen zur Logik," in KGS, vol. XVI.
RzM	"Reflexionen zur Metaphysik," in KGS, vol. XVIII.
Telpr	"Über den Gebrauch teleologischer Principien in der Philosophie," in KGS, vol. VIII:157–184.
UnH	*Allgemeine Naturgeschichte und Theorie des Himmels*, in KGS, vol. I:215–368; *Universal Natural History and Theory of the Heavens*, trans. and intro. Stanley L. Jaki (Edinburgh: Scottish Academic Press, 1981).
VzA	*Vorlesungen zur Anthropologie*, in KGS, vols. XXV

Moral and Natural Destinies of Human Beings

PREDISPOSITION	ANIMALITY	TECHNICAL	PRAGMATIC	MORAL
END IN INDIVIDUAL (improvement)	self-preservation physical well-being	culture	happiness	character
MEANS TO END (education)	discipline	skill	prudence	wisdom
NATURE'S PROVISION (in the individual)	inclination to freedom drives	natural talents	feelings	desire
END IN THE SPECIES (progress)	preservation of the species	cultivation	civilization	moralization
MEANS TO END (our performance)	marriage and community	arts and sciences	refinement, virtue, law-constitution	respect for humanity
NATURE'S PROVIDENCE (in society; education of human race)	inclination to sex	inconsistency of dispositions, destructive operations, violence	antagonism competition	

Introduction

By many philosophers, Kantian and non-Kantian, the eighteenth-century German Philosopher Immanuel Kant is considered one of the greatest philosophers that ever lived. A considerable amount of studious and scholarly attention is devoted to Kant. Many articles and books, which appear every year, are concerned with his critical and moral philosophy. The reason why Kant is held in such high esteem is because of his critical and moral philosophy. He is not considered one of the greatest philosophers based on his work on anthropology, education, geography, history, and religion, for these works direct our attention to experience rather than to a priori concepts. These works that are intended to illuminate human experience have not received the attention and accolades that Kant's critical and moral philosophy have received. What is so puzzling about the neglect of these various types of Philosophies of Experience is that Kant himself devoted great amounts of time and attention to these areas of philosophy. For instance, Kant never once taught his *Critique of Pure Reason*, but he taught what later became his *Anthropology from a Pragmatic Point of View* for twenty-three years.

Kant believed he had something to offer his students by offering the anthropology and physical geography lectures every year. This is puzzling: If Kant thought these lectures on philosophy were important, how come we don't? Why has the scholarly attention paid to Kant's *Anthropology* been so sporadic? And then, when scholarly attention is paid to the *Anthropology*, why is so much of it dismissive as though studying philosophy that directs our attention to experience and illuminates that experience is somehow inferior. Some scholars question, Is this even philosophy at all? These are the kind of puzzles that kept me pursuing the *Anthropology* and trying to understand it. Unfortunately, the conceptual apparatus that would help me understand these puzzles was not taught at the university. Thus, it was like a treasure hunt trying to find the key that would unlock the mystery of Kant's *Anthropology*. Why did Kant, a great transcendental philosopher, think that helping his students understand themselves and their experience was so worthwhile?

This book is about my journey through the maze of the *Anthropology* and the scholarship on it. I found I had to first understand what kind of philosophy Kant was doing in the *Anthropology*. Was it empirical psychology or was it philosophy of experience (wisdom) (chapters 1 and 2)? Then I sought to understand if indeed it contained a philosophical anthropology, a theory of human nature. My conclusion was that it did (chapters 3 and 4). Then I had to solve the puzzle of how critical philosophy and philosophy of experience (wisdom) were related because I had to understand how a great transcendental philosopher would train his attention on experience (chapter 5). This is the key to unlocking the final chapter (chapter 6) where I see for the first time how the biases of philosophy, as I had come to understand them, had so blinded me from seeing what Kant was doing in his *Anthropology*. The commonplace and seemingly obvious distinction between rational and empirical made it impossible for me to see that Kant's philosophy does not break along those lines of distinction. It is simply not the case that Kant's critical and moral philosophy are rational philosophy, and his philosophies of anthropology, education, geography, history, and religion are empirical philosophy, and that rational philosophy is superior to empirical philosophy. That distinction and normative dualism obfuscates what Kant is doing in the *Anthropology*. To avoid this confusion I have come to call what Kant is doing in his philosophies of anthropology, education, geography, history, and religion as "Philosophies of Experience," because it directs our attention to experience and attempts to illuminate that experience in a philosophically sound manner. I am not calling it philosophy of experience in the sense that its concepts derive out of experience. Rather I am calling it philosophy of experience because it is directed to experience and is about a systematic and sound way of perceiving that experience.

After the final sentence of the book had been written, I came to another philosophical insight—that the scholarly neglect of Kant's *Anthropology* evidenced a prejudice amongst philosophers for conceptual philosophy over philosophy that points to experience and helps to clarify that experience (wisdom). This bias is not new. Kant was aware of it too. He saw it, he named it, and he didn't agree with it (chapter 6). That is why Kant dedicated his teaching career to doing anthropology. For Kant this was the best and most efficient way to teach students critical thinking. Kant did not simply teach philosophical concepts; he taught his students to philosophize. This is what I call "critical thinking."

Because of this, I came to see philosophy in a totally new light, not as a history of concepts trumping one another, but rather as different paths to the same goal—wisdom. I also started teaching differently and soon saw in my students the results of this change. My students were not simply memorizing concepts to regurgitate back on exams, instead, they were becoming more open-minded. And in the process, more able to see things from another's point of view, more able to give reasons in support of their positions, more able to provide reasons against other positions. Most important of all, however, I saw my students were more prepared to question and challenge their own long held, but heretofore, unchallenged opinions. For me it became of utmost importance that students learn to think for themselves. And for Kant, as his *Anthropology* demonstrates, that is the essence of philosophy.

This book will guide you through this maze and shed light on Kant's *Anthropology*. The first chapter enters into the ongoing German dialogue about the origin of Kant's anthropology lectures. One group of philosophers argues its origin out of the empirical psychology section of Kant's metaphysics lectures. The other group of philosophers maintains that the anthropology lectures arose out of Kant's physical geography lectures. I distinguish between "origin" and "arise": the anthropology lectures arose out of the psychology lectures, but had their origin in the physical geography lectures. Kant's banning of psychology from metaphysics initiated the movement toward an independent series of lectures on anthropology, but the intent and content of the anthropology lectures finds its origin in the physical geography lectures, which were initially given fifteen years prior to the start of the anthropology lectures.

I show that the intent and content of the anthropology lectures ties in with the physical geography lectures even as Kant explicitly ties them together. Kant has produced an anthropology that is cosmopolitan just like the physical geography lectures. Both disciplines are not speculative, but popular. This chapter again addresses the German secondary literature but this time with an eye to whether Kant believed he was doing empirical psychology and if his anthropological thinking can be characterized as empirical psychology. The secondary literature is again divided on this subject. I agree with those who maintain that Kant neither intended to be doing empirical psychology nor did he produce an empirical psychology.

In the second chapter, I will show that Kant produced a pragmatic anthropology not intended to be speculative, but intended to develop the faculty of judgment in his students to bring about prudence and wisdom. Prudence is a type of skill that human beings can develop and its purpose is to bring about happiness in the individual. Kant's use of teleological judgments throughout the *Anthropology* is further evidence of his intent for a pragmatic, not speculative, discipline. The purpose is to bring about better skills at judging human beings, oneself, and the final ends of the whole human species. The use of teleological judgment in the *Anthropology* is also proof that what Kant is doing far exceeds anything Alexander G. Baumgarten had in mind with his empirical psychology. Teleological judgment is grounded in a philosophical methodology not in an empirical science with no a priori guiding principles.

Chapter 3 presents a systematic account of Kant's theory of human nature. This is pieced together from several of his writings, including the *Religion within the Limits of Reason Alone* and the *Education*, along with the *Anthropology*.

First I mention the secondary literature that is relevant to this topic. No one, however, has yet to attempt a systematic interpretation of Kant's theory of human nature. Then I point to the teleological account of providence and unsociable-sociability from the characteristic that inform his theory and make sense of the four natural predispositions: (*a*) predisposition to animality, (*b*) the technical predisposition, (*c*) the pragmatic predisposition, (*d*) and the moral predisposition. Kant argues that human beings develop into humanity from animality, so I lay out his understanding of the difference between animals and human beings. Using evidence from Kant's students' lecture notes, I show that Kant understands human nature as intrinsically communal rather than individual. This is also shown from Kant's *Anthropology*. I argue that the moral predisposition shares some elements of the other predispositions, but it is also unique in that its development does not arise out of the principle of unsociable-sociability. Finally, I demonstrate that Kant's distinction between egoism and pluralism is also evidence that human nature is intrinsically communal. It is wisdom, which tells us that the individual destiny is tied up with the whole human species.

In chapter 4, I lay out the range of each of the predispositions, what they mean, and how we actualize them. Each predisposition has its own means for achieving the ends projected by the predisposition. Nature has provided inclinations, which guide the development of the predisposition to animality. It is through discipline of these inclinations that the ends of animality (procreation, propagation, and preservation) are achieved for the individual human being. It is through the development of technical skills that talents are developed in the technical predisposition. It is through the development of prudence that we actualize our pragmatic predisposition, and finally it is through wisdom that we actualize our moral predisposition. Although I define all the predispositions in chapter 3, in this chapter it is with an eye to how we can, by our own powers, develop the predispositions, rather than how nature is involved in educating the human species. Since it is an account of how we can develop the natural predispositions in children and young adults, that is why I conclude this chapter with Kant's account of pedagogy.

In chapter 5, I argue that teleological judgment is the critical grounding of Kant's *Anthropology*. I maintain that Kant has critically grounded teleological judgment in the Introduction to the Critique of Judgment and in the Critique of Teleological Judgment. It is for the sake of judgment that Kant writes these two texts. It is not for the sake of knowledge, but for judgment. The *Anthropology* is pragmatic and is for the sake of orienting the student to the world and for this they need judgment. Judgement is the skill of being able to choose the appropriate means to contingent and necessary ends. This is what teleological judgment of purposiveness does. Starting with internal purposiveness Kant shows that there are certain a priori principles necessary in order to judge natural organic beings in their purposiveness. This internal purposiveness must give way to external purposiveness as we judge all organic beings in light of their overall purposiveness in nature. Kant argues that if we find purposiveness internal to the organism then we ought to expect it in the whole of nature. He then shows that human beings are not the final end of nature, but merely the last end. If we look within the human being, however, it turns out that the "human being under moral laws" is the final end of nature. This means now that we can subordinate all the contingent ends of our being to the necessary end of being under moral laws. Kant presupposes this in his *Anthropology*. All contingent ends are evaluated implicitly under the final end. That is why Kant says that all prudence must ultimately yield to wisdom or morality. A vast majority of the *Anthropology* is dedicated to teaching how we must relate to our faculties in order to remain free so that we can be moral.

In the final chapter, I begin with the current state of the scholarship on Kant's *Anthropology*. One commentator argues that anthropology for Kant is not philosophy. He seems to hold this view because he is already committed to the idea that the anthropology lectures arose out of empirical psychology. However, Kant explicitly argues that anthropology is a type of cosmopolitan philosophy. It is not scholastic philosophy, and it is not critical philosophy, but it is a type of philosophy. This makes sense if teleological judgment is the grounding of the *Anthropology*, because psychology and biology have absolved themselves of the discipline of teleological judgment. It remains for philosophy to use the method of teleological judgment in order to evaluate the contingent means to the final ends of human existence. Pragmatic anthropology is indeed philosophy and a noble type of philosophy.

It is my hope that this work will shed light on a significant part of Kant's legacy that we have yet to integrate into our views of Kant. He was not simply a great scholar, but a great teacher as well. I believe he found a way to greatness in both areas.

CHAPTER ONE

The Rise and Origin of Kant's
Lectures on Anthropology

Kant published the *Anthropology from a Pragmatic Point of View* at the end of his teaching career after having lectured on anthropology for twenty-three and one-half years.[1] We know from student manuscripts of his lectures that Kant published pretty much the same material that he had been lecturing on during those years. This agreement between the book and his lectures permits the conjecture that Kant's intentions for the book would be consistent with his intentions for his lectures.[2] Fortunately, we have explicit statements about what Kant intended for his lectures on anthropology.

Kant began lecturing on pragmatic anthropology in the winter semester of 1772–73,[3] during the eighteenth year of his teaching at Königsberg University. At that time anthropology was not an independent discipline and Kant was one of the first to lecture on it within the well-established faculty of philosophy.[4] In a copy of one of his earliest lecture notes that we have, Kant claims that "the knowledge of human beings is called by the general name of anthropology, which is not being lectured on in any other discipline [*Akademie*]."[5] He lectured, then, on anthropology consistently for twenty-three and one-half years until he retired. The lecture proved to be very popular, frequented even by Kant's colleagues. He averaged thirty to fifty students a semester with a high of seventy in 1791–92.[6]

Kant's interest in anthropology did not suddenly begin in this winter semester, however. Kant also lectured on the theme of anthropology in his metaphysics lectures as early as 1762.[7] From the Johann Gottfried von Herder papers, which are the notes that Herder took while he was a student of Kant's from 1762–64, we read "Kant's doctrine. . . . The Metaphysic contains 1. Anthropology, 2. Physics, 3. Ontology, 4. The origin of all things, God, and the world, therefore theology."[8] Although by "anthropology" here Kant means little more than empirical psychology, he does call it "anthropology" even then. More decisive, though not the only decisive factor for the formation of Kant's interest in anthropology, were his lectures on physical geography, which he held regularly, mostly in the summer semester, from the beginning of his docent years at Königsberg University in 1755–56. With the exception of one year, winter semester 1758–59, he held this lecture every year inclusive of 1796.[9]

7

In Kant's article "On the Different Races of Human Beings," which appeared as his announcement of his lectures on physical geography in the summer semester 1775, he closely associated the two lectures, physical geography and anthropology, under the name of "*pragmatische Weltkenntnis.*" This *Weltkenntnis*

> serves to procure the *pragmatic* element for all other acquired sciences and skills, through which they become useful not merely for the *school*, but rather for *life*, and through which the accomplished student is introduced to the stage of his destiny [*Bestimmung*], namely, the *world*.[10]

Cosmopolitan knowledge could be gained in a two-part lecture course in which the fields of nature and human beings were covered, first, by physical geography, and, then, by anthropology. The purpose of the two courses was not just to introduce the students to the scientific facts of outer and inner nature, but also to help them orient themselves in relationship to the world as physical and cultural. In other words, the intent was not only to make them scientifically competent, but also to prepare them for social, pragmatic, and practical realities.

THE PHYSICAL GEOGRAPHY LECTURES AND THE ORIGIN OF THE ANTHROPOLOGY LECTURES

Kant explicitly associates his lectures on anthropology with his lectures on physical geography, and so it is illuminating to consider his intent for the physical geography lectures. The intent he had for the lectures will clarify what he means by cosmopolitan knowledge. The *Entwürf und Ankündigung eines Collegii der physischen Geographie* (1757) served as the introduction to Kant's lecture on physical geography, and from a censure mark it has been dated as April 13, 1757.[11] It announced and introduced his lectures for the summer semester 1757. This announcement states Kant's intentions for physical geography as well as his understanding of what is included under the title of physical geography. In this first announcement he wants to make physical geography into a genuine science and the interest in his students' development is not yet stated. In the later announcements, from 1765 and 1775, Kant makes clear that the purpose of the physical geography is to civilize young students to become "citizens of the world." However, we do not find this intention in this first announcement. Nor does Kant refer here to "cosmopolitan knowledge" either:

> The information which is useful here is dispersed in many and great works, and there is still no one textbook by means of which

this science could be made fitting for academic use. For that reason I resolved right at the beginning of my academic career to lecture on this science in special lectures following the direction of a summary sketch. I carried this out to the satisfaction of my students in a half-year course of lectures. Since then I have expanded my plan considerably.[12]

Kant's first intention for the physical geography lectures seems to have been purely scientific, that is, to make a more certain knowledge of believable travel accounts, and to make this into a legitimate academic course of study.[13] Only one year later, however, after one semester of the course, he had learned how interesting it was for the students, how pleased they were, and then he hints that because of this he has extended his plan. This could well refer to his future intention for the physical geography as "cosmopolitan knowledge." The development of physical geography from a scientific interest to a worldly interest was dependent on the reactions of the students. Otherwise, Kant could never have known that it's real nature was to be "popular." When he asserted in 1775 that the two sciences, physical geography and anthropology were popular, it was after two decades of experience with his physical geography lectures and two years experience with the anthropology lecture.

Kant's fascination with anthropology or the nature and characteristics of human beings can already be seen in the *Entwürf*:

> The animal kingdom, in which human beings will be viewed comparatively with regard to the differences of their natural form and color in different regions of the earth. . . . I shall lecture on this first of all in the natural order of classes and finally cover in geographic survey all the countries of the earth, in order to display the inclinations of human beings as they grow out of the particular region in which they live; the variety of their prejudices and types of thinking, in so far as all of this can serve to make human beings more intimately acquainted with themselves; and in order to give a brief idea of their arts, commerce, and science, an enumeration of the . . . products of the various regions, their atmospheric conditions, etc.: in a word, everything which belongs to physical geography.[14]

Kant was not only intrigued by the external differences in the races, and how the various customs arose depending on the specific climates, but also by the inner differences, prejudices, and ways of thinking. This knowledge was not just of scientific worth, but also must be used for the purposes of self-knowledge. Clearly the desire to make "human beings more intimately acquainted with themselves" counts as an interest in making human beings more aware of "knowledge of the world" or cosmopolitan knowledge in the sense that Kant later used it.

Kant communicates his intentions for a course of lectures on physical geography. It will describe the world from its bare natural constituents, typography, and physical characteristics, but all of this must also be from the perspective of a traveler and not just from the perspective of an indifferent scientist:

> Physical geography considers merely the natural constitution of the globe and what is found on it: the oceans, solid ground, mountains, rivers, atmosphere, human beings, animals, plants, and minerals. All of this, however, not with that completeness and philosophical exactitude in the parts which is the business of physics and natural history, but with the reasonable curiosity of a traveler, who seeks everywhere the noteworthy, special, and beautiful, compares the collected observations, and considers its plan.[15]

The popular nature of the physical geography lecture is already fore-shadowed in the description of its guiding interest as that of a traveler's. Travelers can be any one, and travelers are clearly interested in knowledge of the world, and not just in scientific facts that will advance a scientific perspective or hypothesis. The people that would have interest in his lecture would be enlightened, not just scientific:

> The reasonable good taste of our enlightened times has supposedly become so universal that it can be presupposed that only a few people could be found, who would be apathetic about knowing the peculiarities of nature, which the globe also contains in other regions, which is found outside of their horizon.[16]

Scientific interest is of "no small advantage," but Kant mentions this only after the first claim that physical geography ought to be of interest to all enlightened people. Therefore, we can assume that the seeds of his later account of the physical geography and anthropology as "knowledge of the world" are already present even in this earliest of his announcements. Kant's point that pragmatic anthropology should not be from a physiological perspective is foreshadowed here as well. Physical geography is not meant to be a description of the world as a scientist would view it, but rather geography is to be viewed in its purposiveness.

From the *Nachricht von der Einrichtung seiner Vorlesungen 1765–66*,[17] we gather more information about what Kant intended for these lectures in physical geography. According to Kant:

> When I recognized immediately at the beginning of my academic lecture [career] that a great negligence existed among young students, that they learned early to reason, without possessing sufficient histori-cal knowledge, which could take the place of [lack of] experience: I

formed the resolution to make the history of the current condition of the earth or geography, in the broadest sense, into a pleasant and easy summary, which could serve to prepare them for practical reason, . . . I called such a discipline . . . Physical Geography.[18]

Kant not only wrote about the primacy of practical reason within his theoretical scholarship, but he also believed it and practiced it in concrete life. In his teaching, we see Kant concerned about the development of practical reason, and not just theoretical reason, in his students. He originally thought he could best accomplish this through his lectures on physical geography. Later, he realized that knowledge of relations between people was also necessary for the development of practical reason, and he added his lecture on anthropology to the disciplines whose purpose it was to impart knowledge of the world.

For Kant, the discipline of physical geography was not far from what we call "physical geography" today, because it was not only physical, but also moral and political; it dealt not only with the Earth, but also human beings who inhabit the different parts of the Earth. Kant wanted to consider the human being in terms of what differentiated him morally from the manifold of natural properties, but at the same time he wanted to view the human being as an object of experience in the world, and not as the speculative subject, that is suggested by his later critical philosophy.

He wanted to distinguish between the outer physical world and the inner moral world of human beings without being driven into the inner world of psychology. In order to do this he had to avoid using the scholastic distinction between the soul and the body. Instead, he pictured the human being as a natural being who is a member of the world. As G. Gerland puts it, the human being should "be considered only as a natural object, only cosmological-pragmatic, . . . only as an object of outer senses, as an object of experience . . ."[19] In associating the anthropology with his geography lectures, Kant made clear that anthropology did not belong to empirical psychology, or psychology of the inner soul of human beings. Its main concern was with the outer world and outer behavior.[20]

At the time of the writing of the *Nachricht* (1765–66), Kant's interest in anthropology was still developing, but he already had a very strong interest in his students and in their acquisition of pragmatic knowledge of the world. He saw the failing of scholastic instruction in that it taught the students to be clever in the use of reasoning without setting limits to that knowledge or showing how it could be used for life. In the *Nachricht*, Kant referred sarcastically to the "loquaciousness of young thinkers, who are blinder than any other self-conceited person, and as incurable as ignorance."[21] Most of his students would not go on to be academics or professors, and therefore needed to learn to apply what they learned to their future professions, as well as to the society in which they lived. He noticed the problem of application especially in relation to his ethics lectures since

> all instruction of youth has this difficulty by its very nature, that one is obliged to hasten on the years with insight and should give such knowledge, that in the natural order of things can only be understood by a experienced and tried reason, without waiting for the maturity of understanding.[22]

Kant gave his lectures, first, on physical geography and, later, on anthropology, in order to make up for the lack of historical and social experience in his students, since this knowledge can normally only be anticipated in adults with age and life experiences.

The *Nachricht* contains the second announcement of Kant's lectures on physical geography, and it announces his lectures on metaphysics, logic, and ethics as well. In his introduction to the separate disciplines he articulates clearly, for the first time, the problem young students face in the university. They are expected to learn the concepts and ideas way beyond their own emotional and developmental maturity. As a result, they tend to imitate learnedness, but lack the emotional and experiential background that would make this knowledge applicable to their lives.

Kant objected to the imitation of learnedness, because it interfered with real learning. Students learned the scholastic methods and logic all too well, but much too quickly for their slower developing judgment. Teaching methods, in part, are to be blamed for successfully developing students' reasoning without giving them the proper experience or context in which to use it correctly. When one considers the early Enlightenment philosophers in Germany, the name of Christian Thomasius (1655–1728) comes to mind as a philosopher who had already distinguished between university learning and learning derived from experience. In the *Einleitung zu der Vernunft-Lehre*, Thomasius distinguished carefully between learnedness that is gained from experience [*Gelahrheit*][23] and learnedness that is gained from concepts in the schools [*Gelehrtheit*].[24] Thomasius criticized *Gelehrtheit* because there were often no practical applications for the subtle distinctions advanced in the schools. The court philosophy he proposed instead was a kind of practical philosophy directed toward the world and not toward the school.[25] In other words, he dedicated himself to developing a popular philosophy in much the same way as Kant. In chapter 6, I will argue that Kant's distinction between cosmopolitan philosophy and scholastic philosophy mirrors this distinction from Thomasius.

Kant sees the teacher's task in this that she/he should be concerned about "forming first the informed person, then the judicious and finally the scholarly person in their students."[26] The goal is not just to make students skillful in scholastic methods, but also to guide them so that they "become more skillful and more prudent for life."[27] Kant's emphasis on developing judgment in his students is the key to understanding what Kant intended with his lectures on anthropology.

By this point, Kant has been teaching barely ten years, but his experience with students has developed and he sees the failings in the academic system. The students are mostly taught thoughts but not to think. This is especially dangerous or useless for those who will go back into the world, since their knowledge will prove useless, if they have not learned to apply it. To remedy this situation he suggests that students, "should not learn *thoughts*, but rather to *think*; they should not be *carried*, but *guided*, if it is desirable that they should be skillful in the future at thinking for themselves."[28] Thinking for oneself is one of the great impulses of the early German Enlightenment of Thomasius and his students.

In this passage in the *Nachricht*, "skillful" means the ability to apply the knowledge one acquires. Kant is not referring simply to the skill in applying the knowledge for academic contexts, but also to the ability to apply it "prudently" [*klug*]. For the first time, an essential element of his later thinking about pragmatic anthropology enters the picture, and this not just in the context of physical geography but also in relation to all academic lectures which he held.[29] One of the main goals for Kant's lectures on anthropology was to teach his students prudence and wisdom, both of which required broad historical knowledge of human nature. Prudence and wisdom cannot be taught, however, in the same way that one informs another person of facts.

The problem of inexperienced young students requires a teaching style that guides students to "philosophize," rather than informing them of the history of "philosophy." Even at this point Kant expresses a theme that he will often refer to in his reflections and even in the first Critique. Philosophy and the historical sciences require a type of knowledge of the world that is at the same time knowledge of one's own nature. In contrast to the mathematical sciences, the historical sciences are dependent on "one's own experience or on foreign testimony."[30] Knowledge of the world has to play an important role for all the historical sciences and not just anthropology. Here philosophy is also counted as a historical science, which can either be memorized or really learned in that one can then philosophize.

Already in the 1760s, Kant was interested in anthropology, though he did not have a lecture course about that yet. He dealt with the theme, nevertheless, in his other courses. He considered anthropology not only in his lectures on metaphysics, but also in his lectures on ethics and physical geography. Even in the ethics at this period, he was not concerned with bare formalism, but also with "the realities of the human nature which it purports to guide."[31]

Kant states explicitly, in this announcement to his lectures, that he is interested in human nature since "in the doctrine of virtue I always consider historically and philosophically what *happens* before I point out what *ought to happen*."[32] This method is the method of pragmatic anthropology, since it teaches first what has happened in providence or nature, and then what human beings can conclude about their place in the universe based on this knowledge. The point that Kant makes here had already been made by a Thomasius student, Christian August Crusius (1712–1775), whose *Anweisung vernünftig zu leben* (1744), was written in the Thomasius initiated tradition of a theory of prudence [*Klugheitslehre*]. Crusius writes in the first chapter, "one must first recognize how the will is constituted and works before one can adequately explain how it should be."[33] Kant does not acknowledge Crusius as an influence, but he knows Crusius well and mentions him forty-three times in his various works, especially in his early works. Interestingly, Kant calls him the "well-known" Crusius.[34]

In the introduction to the physical geography lecture itself, we see that Kant was not only interested in the extraordinary and peculiar aspects of the Earth, but also in the relationship of the whole Earth to human beings. He claims he wants to make the first part of the physical geography, which concerns the peculiar aspects of the Earth, shorter in order to make room for the other parts, which concern the Earth's relationship to the human species:

> Since then I have gradually expanded this sketch, and now I plan to broaden out in that I abridge those sections [some] more which concern the physical peculiarities of the Earth, in order to gain time for lectures about the other parts of [physical geography] which are even more generally useful. This discipline will be a *physical, moral* and *political* geography, wherein first the peculiarities of *nature* in her three kingdoms will be pointed out, but with the selection of those among the uncountable others, which [arouse] universal intellectual curiosity [*Wißbegierde*] through the charm of their rarity, or also through the influence which they have on governments by means of commerce and trade. . . . The *second* section considers *human beings* on the whole earth, according to the manifold of their natural characteristics and the differences among them, what is moral about them; . . . a very important consideration. . . .[35]

More and more Kant concentrated on the anthropological aspects of physical geography and consequently his theory of providence developed at the same time, because it is what defines the relationship of the human being to the whole of nature. Kant's theory of the human being is developing here from a purely cosmological being to a pragmatic-moral being, who lives on the Earth and has a relationship to the events of nature.

Finally, in the section on the physical geography in the *Nachricht*, he explains again that he saw at the beginning of his teaching years

> a great neglect among young people who study, consists primarily in that they learn early to reason speciously [*vernünfteln*], without possessing sufficient historical knowledge, which could take the place of experience [lack thereof].[36]

Thus, Kant decided to make the history of the present condition of the Earth or geography, in the broadest sense, into a pleasant and understandable study of the Earth, which would serve to prepare his students for practical and prudential reason.

One of the major impulses, which inspired Kant in the development of his pragmatic point of view, came from the concern for his students' maturity. He saw clearly their need for a more historical and worldly perspective. He could not give them the wisdom that only age could bring, but he tried to give them the expanded historical horizon that would make them more adept at using their knowledge in the world and more competent to make sound judgments about themselves and their world.

THE DEBATE CONCERNING THE ORIGIN OF KANT'S ANTHROPOLOGY LECTURES

With "Von den verschiedenen Racen der Menschen," we have reached the end of our history of the origin of the anthropology lectures. This essay served as an introduction to and announcement of his lectures on physical geography and anthropology for 1775. Although the anthropology lectures had already begun a few years earlier, this is the first official announcement that we have. That Kant chose to talk about race anthropology as an introduction to both lectures shows the intimate relationship between physical geography and anthropology. The anthropology begins where physical geography ends; the different climates and environments, explored in physical geography, explain the different kinds of human beings in the world, but the inner germs and natural predispositions, explored in anthropology, explain why the human being can adapt itself to the different climates and environments.

In this essay, Kant propounds not only a Darwinian-like thesis that the species adjusts itself to fit the environment in which it lives, but he goes one step further and asserts that the human being can adjust to any different environment, because it has many different germs in it that can be unfolded out of it. There is a twofold thesis here: (1) the human being can adjust itself to almost any climate is an indication that human beings were meant to exist in all climates and environments, (2) this ability to accommodate indicates that there are all different types of germs in the human being planted by providence, which providence intends to unfold in human history. The human being

> was destined for all climates and for every soil condition; conse-quently, various germs and natural predispositions must lie ready in him to be on occasion [*gelegentlich*] either unfolded [*ausgewickelt*] or restrained [*zurückgehalten*], so that he would become adapted to his place in the world and over the course of generations would appear to be as if native to and made for that place. And with these notions, we would like to go through the whole human species in the whole wide world and adduce purposive causes of its variations therein, in cases where the natural causes [*naturlichen Ursachen*] are not well recognizable, and, contrast, adduce natural causes where we do not perceive the purposes [*Zwecke*]. Here I only note that *air* and *sun* appear to be those causes which deeply influence the generative power and produce a lasting develop-ment of the germs and predispositions, i.e., are able to establish [*gründen*] a race;[37]

In the *Racen*, Kant introduces for the first time the distinction between germs [*Keime*] and natural predispositions [*natürliche Anlage*]:

> The grounds of a determined unfolding [*Auswicklung*] which are lying in the nature of an organic body (plants or animals) are called *germs* [*Keime*], if this unfolding concerns particular parts; if, however, it concerns only the size or the relation of the parts to one another, then I call them *natural predispositions* [*natürliche Anlagen*].[38]

These are the clues Kant uses to read the purposive intent of nature for the species. He differentiates between germs and predispositions, and this is important for the later development of his anthropological teleology, which is concerned with the development of the natural predispositions. The very fact that Kant's anthropology is teleological in nature indicates, however, that the origin of the ideas in his lectures and the book is from some other source than the psychology section of his metaphysics lectures. The teleological nature of physical geography lectures and the purposiveness Kant seeks in natural environments as they affect human beings casts more light on the origin of the ideas of anthropology, than does the rise of anthropology out of the psychology section of his metaphysics lectures as several interpreters maintain. In the previous section, we have only dealt with the rise of the anthropology lectures. We have not yet addressed the origin of the ideas. In this section, I will lay out the debate as it has developed in the secondary literature. Then I will address a promising new line of interpretation.

In German secondary literature, there is a great debate about the origin of Kant's lectures on anthropology. There are two opposing arguments, (1) the anthropology lectures have their origin in the empirical psychology section of Kant's metaphysics lectures; or (2) that the lectures arose out of Kant's works in cosmological-geographical works and lectures.[39] While Erich Adickes, Norbert Hinske, Paul Menzer, Emit Arnoldt, and Reinhard Brandt argue the former position, Wilhelm Dilthey, Benno Erdmann, and G. Gerland maintain the latter position.[40] G. Gerland refers to the *Entwurf* as proof that Kant's interests in geography and different parts of the world developed into his interest in race anthropology and his interest in the different developments of the essentially same humanity.[41] Race anthropology is a fundamental part of anthropology. Kant's *Racen* is the key connection between physical geography and anthropology. The concern for outer differences that the races present is a characteristic of anthropology and not of psychology.

The origin of Kant's *Anthropology* was initially debated between Wilhelm Dilthey and Erich Adickes as they discussed the placement of the *Anthropology* in *Kants gesammelte Schriften*.[42] In the seven letters they exchanged, both editors wanted to place the *Anthropology* based on their understanding of its systematic position in Kant's works. Dilthey argued that the anthropology lectures arose out of Kant's work in cosmology and physical geography, and he concluded that the *Anthropology* should be printed with Kant's *Physical Geography*. Adickes responded that the anthropology lectures arose out of the empirical psychology section of Kant's metaphysics lectures.

Despite Dilthey's success in convincing Adickes, the *Anthropology* and the *Physical Geography* were printed in separate volumes. The debate about the origin of the anthropology lectures, nonetheless, extends further in Benno Erdmann, Emil Arnoldt, Norbert Hinske, and currently Reinhard Brandt.[43] Erdmann argues the origin of the lectures from the physical geography lectures. Arnoldt, Hinske, and Brandt maintain the connection between Kant's anthropology lectures and the *psychologia empirica* of the Wolffian Alexander G. Baumgarten (1714–1762), whose text Kant used for his metaphysics and anthropology lectures. Hinske's position is based on the argument that Kant was already lecturing on anthropology in the metaphysics lectures in the place of empirical psychology. This is certainly true. With Hinske we can conclude that Kant's anthropology lectures began already in the metaphysics lectures and then they became a self-sufficient course of lectures. But that only, at most, supports the idea that Kant's metaphysics lectures gave rise to his anthropology lectures, it does not support the idea that the anthropology lectures originated in the metaphysics lectures. Kant was lecturing on physical geography along with the metaphysics lectures. The increasingly human-centered geography lectures could just as well have influenced Kant's development toward anthropology. Further, the experiential and enlightenment content of the *Anthropology* so far exceeds what was contained in Baumgarten's *psychologia empirica* that it is evident that some other strand of tradition was influencing Kant than just the Wolff school. I have already pointed out several key ideas, which Kant shares in common with the Thomasius school who saw themselves in conflict with the Wolff school.

Currently Reinhard Brandt appears to be following the arguments of the Arnoldt and Hinske tradition of interpretation on the origin of the anthropology lectures. In the first section of his introduction to Kant's *Lectures on Anthropology*, volume 25 in Kant's gesammelte Schriften, entitled "The Origin of the Pragmatic Anthropology Lecture" Brandt appeals first to the letter Kant wrote to Marcus Herz (1773) in which Kant explained his plan to develop an anthropology completely unlike that of Ernst Platner's *Anthropologie für Ärzte und Weltweise* (1772). Brandt then dismisses what Kant has to say in that letter because he claims Kant actually intended a speculative empirical psychology that corresponds to Baumgarten's *metaphysica* in his first lecture (Collins 1772–73, vol. 25). He proceeds then to argue that for Kant, the empirical psychology was freed from metaphysics and in doing so became its own lecture series. Brandt presents the origin of the anthropology lecture as developing out of the empirical psychology of Baumgarten's *metaphysica*. Brandt also extensively quotes Christian Wolff's (1679–1754) *Ausführliche Nachricht von seinen eigenen Schriften*, in order to establish a correspondence between Baumgarten (Wolff's student) and Kant.[44] It is true that both Wolff and Kant have put the empirical psychology before the other parts of the metaphysic lectures for much the same reasons, as Brandt maintains, but that only says that Wolff influenced Kant's metaphysics lectures; it does not establish that Wolff influenced his anthropology lectures. Brandt concludes his section on the origin of the anthropology lectures with a refutation of Benno Erdmann's position that the anthropology lectures arose out of the physical geography lectures. He believes that the lectures arose out of a dismembering of the empirical psychology from the metaphysics lectures: "there was never [as Brandt claims] a discussion of a parallel origin out of the physical geography."[45] In contrast, I have attempted to show that Kant not only associated physical geography with his anthropology lectures, but that he also progressively included anthropological considerations in his geography lectures. It appears more credible to believe the anthropology originated in the physical geography lectures than that it originated out of the empirical psychology section of Kant's metaphysic lectures. However, I am willing to concede that when Kant banned empirical psychology from his metaphysics lecture it did give him an opportunity to deal with that same material, which was anthropological, in a separate course, which he then called "anthropology" rather than empirical psychology.

Anthropology, for Kant, is more than empirical psychology.[46] This next section will try to point out some of the concepts at stake in Kant's understanding of anthropology and the possible sources that define the origin of the content of the anthropology lectures. These concepts and sources make it clear that Baumgarten's *psychologia empirica* gave at most the form of the lectures, but not the content, since it is clear that in the first half of his lecture, which we know from the students' notes, he did borrow the faculty psychology of Baumgarten that dealt with cognition and appetitive powers.

Kant does not explicitly identify the philosophical influences that prepared him for the new discipline of anthropology. Besides Baumgarten's *metaphysica* (1739), which Kant used as a textbook for the lectures, Kant claims that his "auxiliary means of building up anthropology, though they are not among its sources," include novels, world history, plays, and biographies, and these latter means could account for the variety of particular observations on human behavior and actions. These secondary sources do not, however, account for some of the most interesting philosophical concepts one finds in the *Anthropology*. The way that Kant uses and defines such concepts as "pragmatic," "wisdom," "thinking for oneself," "prudence," "thinking soundly," "prejudice," and "reflective judgment," though unique in some ways to Kant, are not sui generis, but have a historical precedence that can be traced to other philosophical thinkers in the seventeenth and eighteenth centuries like the Thomasius school.[47] The Thomasius school developed what was originally called "court philosophy," but which later became a *Klugheitslehre* emphasizing prudence and ethics.[48]

Further, if race anthropology developed out of Kant's physical geography lectures then there is also good reason to believe that pragmatic anthropology also developed out of the physical geography lectures. The final causality of the natural predispositions (animal, technical, pragmatic, and moral) plays an essential role in both race anthropology and pragmatic anthropology. Kant established his position on race that all human beings share the same essential humanity in so far all human beings share the same natural predispositions or germs in their generative power and differ in race only in so far as these germs have developed differently due to natural environmental causes. In other words, races developed because of natural causes that affected not the generative power of reproduction but only the capacity for preservation. Human beings have various capacities for preservation because of the same seeds and predispositions they share in common and their differences arise only due to different environmental influences requiring differing strategies for survival. The teleological perspective is clear in that it is providence that has outfitted human beings with germs and natural predispositions.

In *Von den verschiedenen Racen der Menschen*, Kant announces that physical geography is a pre-exercise in cosmopolitan knowledge, and this is "that which serves to give a pragmatic [character] to all otherwise achieved sciences and skills, through which they are not merely useful for the university, but also for life."[49] The "pragmatic" character of anthropology means that it helps students find their way in life, on the stage of their destiny [*Bestimmung*]. At this point (1775), both physical geography and anthropology belong explicitly to knowledge of the world. They are not simply scholastic studies, but are meant to open the world to students. The world, then, cannot mean simply the physical world, but the world of society and what that means for all human beings.

One of the first interpreters to defend the thesis that the anthropology lectures arose out of the physical geography lectures is Benno Erdmann (1882). Erdmann argued that even the physical geography lectures were motivated by Kant's interest in anthropology, and not so much an interest in physical geography itself as a scholastic discipline.[50] Indeed, as early as 1757 in the *Entwurf*, Kant declares his interest in displaying "the inclinations of human beings as they grow out of the particular region in which they live; the variety of their prejudices and types of thinking, in so far as all of this can serve to make human beings more intimately acquainted with themselves."[51] His interest in human beings is already an interest in anthropology. Further, the point of the view of the traveler is taken by Kant and that is already the sign that he is aiming at cosmological philosophy [*Weltkenntnis*] and not merely science or speculative philosophy.

DID KANT INTEND HIS ANTHROPOLOGY LECTURES TO BE EMPIRICAL PSYCHOLOGY?

Kant's *Anthropology* has frequently been identified with empirical psychology, and therefore the unique character of pragmatic anthropology has not been given sufficient attention. J. H. von Kirchmann (1869) introduced his *Erläuterungen zu Kants Anthropologie*, with this announcement:

> In that Kant excludes physiology [from anthropology], this leaves only psychology, and this alone is not that which forms the object of his work either. With "pragmatic" Kant only wants to indicate that he is excluding the hypothesis, which transcends observation, about the essence of the soul and its elements, and will primarily deal with what is empirical. Since empirical [realities] are partially

dependent on the will, it is possible for human beings to have an formative and bettering effect on them.[52]

Although part of the character of "pragmatic" is recognized in that it is meant to deal with the will, and thus belongs to practical philosophy, Kirchmann still associates the *Anthropology* primarily with empirical psychology and does not recognize the critical framework, namely, teleological judgment, which is also necessary for organizing empirical observations.

Takiyettin Mengüsoglu gives a more decisive argument for associating Kant's anthropology with empirical psychology, in that its base seems to be faculty psychology:

> Because this writing is in the contemporary sense a practical psychology, which treats of human capabilities—divided into lower and higher faculties of cognition—and the character of people, and thus the problem of human psychology according to the then prevalent faculty psychology.[53]

In other words, according to Mengüsoglu, Kant's anthropology is not much more than a faculty psychology, in which the three most important faculties, the cognitive, the appetitive, and the feeling of pleasure and displeasure are analyzed in the Didactic of the *Anthropology*.[54] This argument gains credence through Kant's repeated use of the theory of faculties in many of his writings. It is possible, on the other hand, to see the use of such terms as "the powers of the soul" as tools, which form merely the schema or framework for the application of his critical thought.

If Mengüsoglu's argument were extended to Kant's other works, then it would be a basis for criticizing Kant's critical philosophy as well, since Kant also analyzes the faculties of pure reason, understanding, and judgment. Kant admitted that there were necessary concepts in his critical philosophy, which are simply taken over from psychology. He assumed that these concepts were already understood, and he could use them without critically discussing them.[55] As Friedrich Paulsen sees it, some framework is necessary for the development of the critical system:

> The soul has the form and the division of the faculties first into the faculty of knowledge and the faculty of desire, then further into a higher and lower, or mental and sensuous faculty of knowledge and desire. He adopted this scheme and laid it at the basis of his investigations.[56]

In other words, Kant used the scheme of faculty psychology proposed by Baumgarten, Wolff, and Aristotle only as a framework. We have no basis for claiming from this that it also had an essential influence on the content of the

Anthropology any more than we can claim that it had an essential influence on the content of his critical philosophy.[57]

The main reason the *Anthropology* has this scheme at its base is because Kant almost always used Baumgarten's *psychologia empirica* as the textbook for his lectures.[58] Baumgarten, who was Christian Wolff's student, appropriated from him this doctrine of the "faculties of the soul." Baumgarten distinguished between the *facultas cognoscendi* and a *facultas appentendi*. The third faculty of feeling which Kant includes in the *Anthropology* was probably first introduced by J. G. Sulzer who distinguished between feeling, willing, and thinking in his treatise for the Berlin Academy (1751).[59] Norbert Hinske uses this relation to Baumgarten as one of his main arguments for the development of Kant's anthropology out of empirical psychology. Hinske's third thesis about Kant's *Anthropology* reads: "The *Anthropology* is on the whole the philosophy of a discipline in a subordinate position," just like Baumgarten's *empirica psychologia*, which is not concerned with the "nature of human beings," but rather with mere observation.[60] With this association of anthropology with empirical psychology, Kant's *Anthropology* can then be dismissed as secondary to critical philosophy, and as not answering in any serious way the question it seems to pose for itself: "What is the human being?" Pragmatic anthropology does answer this question however; it does deal with the *Bestimmung* of human beings, in so far as Kant articulates his theory of the four natural predispositions.

We know, further, that the Baumgarten *metaphysica* was used not only for Kant's lectures on anthropology, but also for his lectures on metaphysics, the *philosophia practica universalis et Ethica* lectures, and his geography lectures.[61] In the case of the physical geography, however, he used Baumgarten at the request of his students, because they found it more fundamental, though also difficult.[62] In F. C. Starke's *Menschenkunde*, we read that Kant used Baumgarten's metaphysical psychology "since there is no other book about anthropology." He takes it only as a guiding thread since it is "rich in material, but very short in follow-through."[63] Vladimir Satura does not believe the influence from Baumgarten was great. According to him, Kant used Baumgarten only formally as format for the lectures on anthropology, because Baumgarten lacked richness in observations. He took only those themes from Baumgarten

> which interested him, and these form only a stopping point, to which he attached the rich material he collected from other and broader literature or from his own observations and considerations. Baumgarten's empirical psychology is . . . in positive empirical content poor, there was not much left to take from it besides the scheme.[64]

Aloys Neukirchen also thinks that in a "comparison of the pragmatic anthropology, for example, with the empirical psychology of Baumgarten one recognizes without effort how little support he gets with regard to content."[65]

There is no question that Kant used Baumgarten as he lectured. It was required by the Königsberg University that he supply a textbook, but this is no proof that the whole content of Kant's *Anthropology* was influenced by the content of Baumgarten's *metaphysica*, any more than there is solid proof that it decisively formed his lectures on ethics. He still brought to his lectures his wealth of learning and observations, from the multitude of books he read, as well as from his critical powers of reason.

In the *Nachricht* (1765–66), Kant reports that he will begin his metaphysic lectures with empirical psychology, "which is actually a metaphysical science of the experience of human beings."[66] Then in 1773, Kant wrote in his letter to Herz that the empirical psychology contains less since he started lecturing on anthropology.[67] Paul Menzer takes this as proof that Kant simply brought the overflowing materials from psychology over to his anthropology lectures and this decisively formed the character of pragmatic anthropology. With this

> the character of anthropology as an empirical and pragmatic science is finally established, the announcement of the lecture from 1775 also needs the latter expression. The next sequel to the new lecture is [accomplished] in relieving the metaphysics course [of psychology]. . . . Baumgarten's order is retained, and dealt with according to a general division of the mental faculties.[68]

From this Menzer concludes that "the *Anthropology* arose out of the basis of empirical psychology."[69] In essence this is also a claim that the *Anthropology* is nothing other than psychology. To check this claim it is necessary to see what Kant says about psychology and anthropology in relation to one another.

First of all, Kant distinguishes between rational psychology and empirical psychology. Rational psychology has as its object the "logical ego," which is the subject of apperception. It does not consider the soul through experience, but "rather through *principia* of pure reason."[70] Or as Kant says in his metaphysics lecture, it is the knowledge of objects of the inner sense, "so far as they are derived from pure reason."[71] If it were possible to derive knowledge from inner sense, one could conclude that there is good reason for believing that rational psychology belongs to critical philosophy, or at least that it has a chance of becoming a science in a genuine sense. However, since the "I" or ego is empty, we cannot derive knowledge from inner sense, and this method cannot provide the basis for a science.[72]

Later, in the *Critique of Judgment*, Kant asserts that there is a psychology which as "mere anthropology of the internal sense, i.e., is the knowledge of our thinking self in life," but even this is empty as theoretical cognition. The most that rational psychology can claim for itself is still based on "a single inference of moral teleology,"[73] and therefore it cannot be a genuine science.

Empirical psychology, on the other hand, is knowledge of objects of the inner sense, so far as they are strained from experience. In the precritical period, psychology belonged to metaphysics; after the critical epoch it became separated from rational psychology. In the *Critique of Pure Reason*, Kant predicts that psychology will find a place within a complete anthropology.[74] Empirical psychology, however, cannot qualify as a genuine science because it lacks a pure a priori basis. If rational psychology had qualified, then we would also have a genuine science of empirical psychology, just as we have a genuine science of empirical physics based on a rational physics. Therefore, empirical psychology's observations are interesting, but we can give them no form, which has a genuine scientific base. There is no critically justified method with which to measure which observations are more important than others.

Kant's *Pragmatic Anthropology*, on the other hand, does not concern itself with "what nature makes out of the human being," but "what the human being, as a freely acting being makes, or can and should make of itself."[75] Kant does refer to anthropology as a science, though it has difficulty in becoming so.[76] It is empirical, teleological, and ethical and must therefore have an empirical methodology as well as a rational methodology. Anthropology is empirical in so far as its method is based on observations, teleological in that the maxims of teleology are presupposed and used reflectively, and ethical and rational in so far as those observations and reflections are subordinated to the ethical final ends of human existence.

The method of observation, which is appropriate to a pragmatic anthropology, however, cannot be equated with psychology's methods of introspection or descriptive physiology. In the *Anthropology*, Kant warns that introspection of inner states are not only misleading but also dangerous and can lead to insanity.[77] Observation is indeed important to the methodology of pragmatic anthropology, but it is not observation of inner life alone, but also of the outer expressions of inner life. The Didactic of the *Anthropology* recognizes both the inner self and the exterior self, while the Characteristic concerns discerning the inner from the exterior.[78] It is oriented to the world, society and the behavior of human beings, not to inner states and physiological characteristics.

In the *Anthropology*, Kant makes it clear that anthropology cannot be identified either with rational psychology or empirical psychology. Where psychology is concerned with the inner sense, "in anthropology we abstract from the question of whether the human being has a soul (in the sense of separate incorporeal substance" which is *psychological*.[79] In contrast to rational psychology, which deals with soul as noumenal, and not as an object of experience, in anthropology, "appearances united according to laws of understanding are experiences, and in discussing how we represent things, we do not raise the question of what they are like apart from their relation to the senses (and so in themselves)."[80] Anthropology is concerned with "experiences" and objects of experience.

In a reflection on anthropology from 1780s, Kant stresses that

> (g Pragmatic anthropology should not be psychology: in order to research, whether the human being has a soul or what originates in the thinking and feeling principle in us (not in the body), also not the physiology of the doctor: in order to explain the memory from the brain, but knowledge of human beings.)[81]

Not only are the methods of psychology and anthropology different, but the ends of the particular scientific procedures are quite different. Where psychology aims at explaining phenomena, anthropology's goal is knowledge of the world. Knowledge of the world must be distinguished from any type of explanation. Knowledge of the world is based on the function of judgment, that is, reflective judgment, whereas explanation is based on the concepts of the understanding, and their schematism through determinative judgment.

The pragmatic anthropologist, according to Kant, seeks to observe the phenomena to find or reflect upon the rules of understanding in them. This is what makes phenomena experience, and not mere occurrence. Anthropology's method requires reflection in addition to observation: ("s Observation and reflection; the latter: in order to find the rules.)"[82] Therefore, that observation is the method of anthropology, just as it is for psychology, does not allow us to conclude that anthropology is nothing more than psychology, or that every observation is of equal worth.[83] Pragmatic means, in the first instance, knowledge, which is useful for the world. Kant did not want to write a physiology nor an anthropology like Ernst Platner's which was merely scholastic. In his letter to Herz, he explained that his plan was quite different.[84] Kant speaks of pragmatic anthropology as knowing human beings and what can be made of them, and "for [this] a higher standpoint [*höher Standpunkt*] of anthropological observation is required."[85]

The *higher standpoint* of anthropological observation that is contrasted with introspection is achieved through cultural sources. As he says in the *Menschenkunde*, "we have to, therefore, observe human beings"[86] in all that they do. This can be done by traveling or reading travelogues. Social intercourse "with many circumstances and with educated human beings is a very fruitful source of anthropology."[87] These sources are not always certain sources of knowledge, though, since in all human action, incentives are always present and these cannot be seen when they are in play. Therefore, secondary sources of human behavior such as history and biographies can also be helpful. History and biographies cannot serve as first-degree sources since they always presuppose an anthropology for their principles of interpretation.[88]

Pragmatic anthropology as we have already seen, does not have the same pretensions to science as empirical or rational psychology do. It is not a science that seeks to explain, but rather to judge. The observations only have value in that they are interesting and lead to knowledge of human beings and the world. This is the popular and ethical character of the *Anthropology*. Kant wrote to Herz that he was always observing in order to make it interesting for his students:

> I stick so unrelentingly to observations of [our] ordinary life, that my listeners never have dry, but rather an entertaining occupation, through the opportunity, which they have for constantly comparing their usual experience with my remarks.[89]

For anthropology, not every fact is important, but rather those facts that bring one to reflect on one's own experience and further one's ability to judge soundly.

Not only from the *Nachricht*, but also from his *Lectures on Education* and from his letter to Herz (1773) do we come to know a Kant who was not just interested in instructing his students in theoretical knowledge, but also in guiding them in historical and worldly interests, so that they could find their place in the world. As early as 1765, he saw his task as that of teaching them to philosophize and to think through the problems for themselves: "In short, he [the student] should not learn *thoughts*, but rather to *think*; they should not be *carried*, but *guided*, if it is desirable that they should be skillful in the future at thinking for themselves."[90] The teacher should not just teach scholastic or speculative knowledge, since this would mean that the teacher carries the student, but rather the teacher should lead the student to make judgments in relation to the problems of philosophy, the problems of life, and learn to carry that over to the world. Clearly the intent of the anthropology lectures was not to develop cognition as it was to develop judgment. In the next chapter, we will see what Kant means by prudent judgment and how this *Klugheitslehre* informs the idea of a pragmatic, not a speculative, anthropology.

CHAPTER TWO

The Character and Content
of the Anthropology

In his letter to Marcus Herz (1773), Kant claims he is working on a "doctrine of observation" for his students, which teaches them how to exercise their skills in prudence and wisdom.[1] The meaning of one sense of prudence [*Klugheit*] will become clearer in chapter 4, but for initial purposes it does not only mean cleverness in using other people, but also in being useful for the world, being useful as a citizen of the world. Kant saw it as his task to give direction and purpose to the development of the talents and skills of his students, so that they would see their use for the world,[2] and thus take their places as citizens of the world.

Having prudence means being able to use one's skills effectively with respect to other human beings. The development of skills should be followed by, or even coincide with, the development of prudence since prudence makes the skill useful for the world. Without prudence, the final stage of education cannot be reached. Moral character as the final stage of the development of the natural predispositions requires the development of prudent, socialized, civilized, and refined behavior in society, for in this way human beings find themselves subjected to laws and rules that human beings themselves have made universally valid.

The educational development of the natural predispositions should always follow the stages of knowledge which are developed in "(*a*) scholastic ability, (*b*) [skillfulness] in practical matters to act with good sense, (*c*) the training of moral character."[3] Prudence, the middle stage, is necessary to reaching the last stage of moral character, and Kant's lectures on pragmatic anthropology were meant to deal with this middle stage, as well as with the last stage of moral wisdom.

Kant was very much aware of the importance and difficulty of education. As he concludes in his lecture on *Education*: "Hence the greatest and most difficult problem to which human beings can devote themselves is the problem of education."[4] Education is important because "human beings can only become human beings by education,"[5] and because "with education is involved the great secret of the perfection of human nature."[6] Kant foresaw the continual improvement of human society as well as the development of "the human beings' natural predispositions in their due proportion and in relation to their end," as the tasks of education. The development of the natural predispositions and the continual improvement of human society are the ways in which human beings contribute to "advance the whole human race toward its destiny [*Bestimmung*]."[7]

The secret of education lies not only in developing talents, and knowledge, but also in leading the student to know how to use them as a citizen of the world.[8] Kant was aware of the difficulty of arousing the moral feeling in students, which would lead them to use "the many excellences of reason" morally.[9] "*Weltkenntnis*" or "cosmopolitan knowledge" was meant to prepare his students for steering themselves safely within society, which would be a necessary stage in the development of morality, not just in the individual, but also in the species.

THE MEANING OF PRAGMATIC ANTHROPOLOGY

There are several senses of pragmatic that Kant uses. The first sense concerns differentiating pragmatic anthropology from physiological anthropology and speculative anthropology. The second sense of pragmatic has to do with the pragmatic predisposition. This latter account concerns the development of prudence in the individual and the development of a constitution and positive law for the species. Sometimes these two concepts are intermingled, but they can also be clearly differentiated. To begin with the first sense of pragmatic we need to return to Kant's initial intentions for the course of lectures.

From his letter to Herz, we know that Kant resisted the temptation in the period of Enlightenment to develop an anthropology influenced by Newtonian science or Leibnizian monadology, which is precisely what Ernst Platner did, in his *Anthropologie für Ärzte und Weltweise*.[10] Kant tells Herz this is exactly what he wants to avoid. That is not the only kind of study that Kant wants to avoid. Kant did not want to presuppose the dualism of the soul and body and try to find someway to show their interaction. He recognized that dualism was no basis for a science of anthropology that he was attempting to build, because the interrelationship of the soul and the body was merely speculative. Yet, this science should not be a natural science that was based on physiological knowledge of human beings; it should only be pragmatic. As Kant prefaces his text: "A doctrine of knowledge of human beings, which is conceived systematically (anthropology), can adopt either a physiological or pragmatic point of view."[11] He has decided to develop an anthropology that is from a pragmatic point of view. Even a pragmatic point of view can be considered systematically and later we will see that he can legitimately claim this because he is using the critically grounded faculty of reflective teleological judgment.

Kant gives some examples to illustrate the difference between an anthropology from a pragmatic point of view, and an anthropology from a physiological point of view. An explanation of the law of association, for example, might be made from a physiological point of view (though Kant denies this is possible), or it may be made from a pragmatic point of view. An explanation of association from a physiological point of view would construct a hypothesis; a judgment from a pragmatic point of view would further our ability to practice the art of association.[12] It is the difference between knowing how something happens and knowing how to use it. Kant developed a discipline limited to those realities that we can have an effect on in our actions. There are a number of places in the *Anthropology* where Kant explicitly tells us what belongs to pragmatic anthropology and what does not.

Use of alcohol, for instance, influences our understanding and has an effect on our consciousness of life, hence it does belong to pragmatic anthropology.[13] It is important to cover mental illnesses in order to explain what one should not do, and that is at least indirectly pragmatic.[14] An account of the linguistic arts of rhetoric and poetry also belong to pragmatic anthropology because they are capable of producing "a frame of mind that arouses it immediately to activity."[15] Physiological differences between the sexes belongs partly to pragmatic anthropology, because these are indicative of the different purposes that nature has provided for in sexual differentiation.[16] Finally, it is important to pragmatic anthropology to give an account of the differences of nationalities and races because then it is "possible to judge what each can expect from the other and how each could use the other to its advantage."[17]

Even though a physiological description of the differences of the sexes would not lend itself to furthering our ability to change those differences, yet it does give us an account of the purposes of nature to which we can conform our behavior. Kant gives an account of the physiological differences between the sexes, and draws the inference from there that nature has different purposes for males and females. Women are more oriented toward preservation of the species and toward the civilization of the species, whereas men are more oriented toward the propagation of the species.[18] If this is so, it may be that we are going against our own natural tendencies when we pursue purposes contrary to nature's ends. So the description of the differences between the sexes is pragmatic, because we can change how we respond to things we cannot change.

All of these examples are also examples of the use of teleological judgment. Descriptions that admit of teleological characterization are included in pragmatic anthropology because this is what allows us to see the intersection of nature and the free will.[19] As Kant claims right in the beginning of the *Anthropology*, "the most important object in the world to which he can apply them [knowledge and skill] is the human being, because human beings are their own final end."[20] With this statement we are already alerted to the critical framework in which Kant will be viewing human beings. Kant will be using the critically grounded faculty of teleological judgment to view human nature in terms of "what human beings as free agents make, or can and should make of themselves."[21] Organized nature, as Kant describes it in the Critique of Teleological Judgment, is organic nature. Organic nature is constituted by parts, which are reciprocally means and ends for each other. That is the concept of intrinsic purposiveness in the Critique of Teleological Judgment. In chapter 5, I will show that this pragmatic approach is dependent on reflective teleological judgment and is critically grounded, but let me here focus on some of the instances in which Kant clearly uses the teleological language of internal purposiveness. He understands human realities and faculties in terms of means and ends. He judges the appropriate ends of our faculties and determines whether a particular action is an appropriate means to that end.

In the Didactic of the *Anthropology*, Kant explicitly uses teleological language to understand human realities. Kant warns us that we should be cautious about the affects of shame and rage when understood pragmatically and teleologically, because they make us "less capable of realizing their end."[22] If someone insults us, the emotions of rage and shame will interfere with our self-defense, and we will look bad to others. Emotions are extremely complex and it is unclear to empirical observation alone what the purpose of affects are. However, in a lecture note, Kant claims that the natural end of affects is happiness. Affects that are too strong can also cripple our prudence [*Klugheit*], which regulates our appearance in society, and as a result they frustrate the end of happiness:

> Prudence [*Klugheit*] is the capability of choosing the best means to happiness. Happiness consists however in the fulfillment of all inclinations. In order to be able to choose well, one must be free. Prudence however is frustrated by everything that makes us blind, and precisely for that reason also by affects.[23]

It is thus important to recognize where affects belong in the whole system of our ends in order to know how properly and pragmatically to relate to them in oneself. Affects orient us in relation to other human beings, and it is our relation to others and to our own happiness, which is at stake in our pragmatic predisposition.

Kant is even clearer about desire [*Begierde*]. Desire seems to have several different proper ends, one of which is the desire for honor. That end can be frustrated by pride because it is a "miscarried desire for honor which thwarts its own end."[24] The desire for honor belongs to our social or pragmatic predisposition, because it contributes to our ability to use other human beings for our own ends. If we are respected by others, they will not try to frustrate our ends, and are more likely to cooperate in furthering our ends.

Kant rejected the theoretical and physiological approach to understanding human beings and insisted on a pragmatic point of view that would indicate what human beings *should* make of themselves given what nature had made of them. He claims that an anthropology, which wants to be cosmopolitan knowledge of human beings has not succeeded, if it is merely an extended knowledge of the things of the world. He maintains in a reflection on anthropology that he is doing neither psychology nor physiology:

> The pragmatic anthropology should not be psychology: in order to research whether the human being has a soul . . . also not the physiology of the doctor: in order to explain the memory from the brain, but knowledge of human beings.[25]

The discipline must become knowledge of human beings as cosmopolitan citizens [*Weltbürger*], that is, knowledge of the human species in its destiny, in order to be recognized as pragmatic anthropology.[26] He is able to understand the human being not only from a point of view of the individual, but also the relation of the individual to the whole species because he uses teleological judgment systematically reasoning first from intrinsic purposiveness to extrinsic purposiveness and through this to relate the individual to the whole human species. In chapter 3, I will show that human beings necessarily have to be understood in relation to the community of human beings. The individual human being is fundamentally communal. To understand human destiny we have to use teleological judgment.

There is another concept of purposiveness in the Critique of Teleological Judgment, and that is of external purposiveness, where organic beings and inorganic beings serve as purposes for other organic beings. Pragmatic anthropology also deals with the possibility of using other persons for our own ends. This is the second sense of pragmatic for Kant. It concerns the pragmatic predisposition, which employs the skill of prudence to be able to use other people for our own ends. In this sense it is teaching prudence, and prudence is defined as the skill of "using other men for his purposes."[27] We can use others for our own purposes when we recognize from the exterior behavior what the interior of the person is like. If we see that a person is embondaged by a passion, then we know that we cannot use them without appealing to that passion. The ambitious man, for example, "wants others to love him, needs to have pleasant social relationships with them."[28] Knowing this about the ambitious man makes it easier to use him.

Some cautious word is called for, however, to make it clear that when Kant speaks of using other people he is not talking about taking advantage of them, or treating them in any way that they could not consent to. The ambitious man consents to being loved and perhaps even flattered. On the contrary, the one who does not gain informed consent is called the "cunning" [*Arglist*] person. This person takes advantage of others in the pursuit of his own ends and is clearly not acting consistently with moral maxims.[29] The person who gives the semblance of moral goodness, is also using others "to make them love or admire him," yet his actions can be construed to be consistent with morality, in that taste has the tendency to promote morality externally.[30] Prudence, the power of using others for one's own ends, is not necessarily immoral. Everything depends on whether others consent to this use.

Kant's distinction between prudence [*Klugheit*] and cunning [*Arglist*] can be understood in the following way. Cunning, "the head for intrigue, is often considered a great but misused understanding; but it is only the kind of thinking [*Denkungsart*] of very narrow-minded human beings, and very different from prudence [*Klugheit*], which it appears to be."[31] In outward appearances it is almost impossible to distinguish between someone who is merely cleverly trying to get you to buy something, a watch, and the one who is cunningly trying to get you to buy a watch which is worthless. The politeness and rhetorical skills are almost identical. It is only when you use the watch over a period of time that you can test the truth of the salesperson's words. If she was cunning, it may break down in a couple of days. Both salespeople succeed in selling the watch, so the question is whether the ends of both have now been served. Kant believes the ends of the clever salesperson have been served, but not the ends of the cunning salesperson: "Trusting people can only be deceived once, which is then very disadvantageous to the cunning person's own end."[32] It is the deception involved that differentiates cleverness and cunning.[33] The clever salesperson serves her own purposes and the buyer's; the cunning person only her own shortsighted end. In other words, her advantage is only short-term—no one will believe her again. The cunning person is not only immoral, but also imprudent.

Although on the face of it, it sounds as if Kant is being inconsistent with his moral philosophy when he advocates prudence and pragmatic reason as that which teaches us how best to use other people for our own purposes, it really is not.[34] First of all, he is suggesting exactly what Jesus proposed to his disciples before sending them forth in the world. Kant was also concerned about his students entering the world unprepared for cunning people who would use them as mere means. So he proposed that in "intercourse with human beings . . . [as it is in the Gospel]: clever like snakes, without being false like pigeons."[35] Young people are more vulnerable to cunning people, than those with more experience. Kant wants them to be clever or discerning enough to recognize [*erkennen*] the difference between cleverness and cunning, so that they will not become victims.[36]

Cleverness, however, does not capture the full significance of *Klugheit* for Kant. One can be clever, but not prudent and discerning. This is the meaning of the distinction between *Weltklugheit* and *Privatklugheit*.[37] If one has worldly prudence, one can have an influence on others and use them for one's own purposes, but if one has private prudence, one knows how to unify all these uses and ends to one's own lasting advantage. There is no lasting advantage in being clever if it leads other human beings in society to frustrate and resist our ends, or if we do not know how to secure our lasting advantage.[38] Knowing our secure lasting advantage through prudence is already cosmopolitan knowledge, not psychology: "The first education [*Bildung*] is for skill, the 2nd for prudence [*Klugheit*], i.e., judgment, in order to apply skill to the human being. Scholastic knowledge and cosmopolitan knowledge . . . the latter is pragmatic anthropology."[39] Although some have been dismayed that Kant believes it takes a whole lifetime to achieve, he does maintain that "the correct way of thinking [*rechte Denkungsart*] forms at last around age forty (also prudence, i.e., the ability to distinguish true interest from appearance) (to estimate the worth of things)."[40] All of this is evidently teleological in that we are attempting to construe the appropriate means to our ends. Prudence knows how to gain the cooperation of others for her own ends.

The *Anthropology* is not just about prudence, it is also about wisdom and morality. As Kant told Herz, his intention was to "make a pre-exercise of skill, prudence and even wisdom for academic students out of this very pleasant method of observation, which next to the physical geography is different from all other lectures and can be called knowledge of the world."[41] Moral character is acquired through the application of moral principles systematically and wisely throughout one's life, and it is the ability to estimate the relative values of things with respect to the final end of humanity. Having moral character is not just acting on moral principles but also making ourselves useful to society and useful to the furtherance of human destiny.

The fact that Kant is interested in morality in the *Anthropology* is further evidence that Kant is not doing an empirical psychology. Some examples will show that morality is on Kant's mind. Taste, Kant says, has the tendency of promoting morality at least externally.[42] Rhetoric and poetry stimulate the spirit and arouse the human being to a kind of activity, which is necessary for the human being to become moral.[43] Dispositions to joy, friendliness, and sociability promote benevolence, which is a moral duty.[44] Luxury, on the other hand, interferes with the progress toward morality, because it causes one to desire mimetically more than everyone can have.

He is also concerned about moral character. Not only does he start the book claiming we are going to determine what a human being "should" make of oneself, but he even dedicates a whole section to character as a "human being's way of thinking."[45] Human beings with character act on principles and are not involved in furthering the ends of bad people,[46] and that means we have to be able to distinguish bad characters [*schlechtdenkende Menschen*] from good characters on the basis of outer behaviors, signs, or effects. Yet distinguishing a clever person from a cunning person, when we most need to do so, that is, before we become deceived is extremely difficult. The cunning person is persuasive precisely because he appears to be a prudent person. He wears the mask of a trustworthy person. What is required, then, for us to be discerning, is a sophisticated power of observation that allows us to read the signs the other is giving us, without allowing them to see that we are observing them. To be able to do this sometimes experience is required:

> We must observe . . . human beings, so that we do not give the appearance of an observer, and we must dissemble. One must act, as though one is speaking without circumspection, and yet at the same time pay attention well to what others say. Yet it is always still difficult to get to know human beings, while one observes their actions, because this requires an educated and keen observer.[47]

The development of character also requires that we think for ourselves, which is the first maxim of wisdom, and not imitate others, because when we are faced with others in the world, there is no time to consult the ancient texts. The variations of human deception are extensive if not infinite, and only one who can recognize the inner way of thinking from these outer variations will be able to know whether to frustrate or further the ends of another. "Thinking for oneself" is not primarily opposed to superstition, but to imitation or parroting, and it does not mean privileging technical or instrumental reason, to creative reason.[48] Thus, Kant does not fall under the Enlightenment critique of Theodor W. Adorno and Max Horkheimer.[49] Kant is critical of those who allow themselves to be managed mechanically by authorities, and permit themselves perpetual imitative tutelage out of fear.[50] Clearly such considerations do not belong to empirical psychology, but rather to pragmatic anthropology.

The enduring significance of Kant's *Anthropology* lies in its figurative typic, which allows the inexperienced to distinguish between types of people according to the character or type of thinking [*Denkungsart*] they have. We have to discern imitations from the true thing. Although we know only how a person appears to us, we have to be able to reflect back to the coherent way of thinking, whether egoist or pluralist, cunning or prudent, that makes these appearances possible. Each distinction leads us to concern ourselves with the ends that people pursue. The egoist makes the world be the means to her own ends; whereas as the pluralist makes herself into the means to the world's ends. She is a citizen of the world. All of this makes sense from a teleological point of view. We are constantly presented with Kant's use of teleological judgment. And as Kant says himself, anthropology is not just observation, but observation and reflection and that reflection concerns the ends of the various faculties and capacities humans have.

In his teaching, we see that the Kant of the *Anthropology*, was concerned about the development of pragmatic reason and wisdom, and not just theoretical reason in his students. He originally thought he could best accomplish this through his lectures on physical geography. Later, he realized that knowledge of relations between people was also necessary to the development of pragmatic reason, and added his lecture on anthropology to the disciplines whose purpose it was to impart "cosmopolitan knowledge."

Theoretical philosophy makes one skilled, but not prudent or discerning, and Kant believed that we can indeed begin in the university to expand a student's horizon in order to prepare them for the world and morality. Therefore, anthropology needed to be:

> Popular (pragmatic), insofar as it is useful for being able to make a good application of what is known. One does not always become prudent because of experience and injury . . . all practical teaching is: (1) technical, teaching about art and skill, or (2) pragmatic, teaching about prudence, in order to use human beings for my purposes. e.g. the watchmaker, who can not do the latter, unskilled, but otherwise is skilled technically, cannot make a living.[51]

Earning a living is one end of pragmatic reason, but certainly not the highest end. Taste, sociability, politeness, and civilized behaviors are also ends of the pragmatic predisposition, and these prove significant to the development of morality. Kant argues, for example, that alcohol in excess can dull the sensibilities and interfere with sociability,[52] but it can also, in moderation, promote lively conversation, sociability, and candor, which is a moral quality.[53] Thus, alcohol, whose first effect and end is related to the body, can also be related to the pragmatic and moral predispositions.

TELEOLOGICAL CLUES IN THE CHARACTERISTIC OF KANT'S ANTHROPOLOGY

Above all, pragmatic anthropology is concerned with the ideals of human existence, not just with its realities. It has an internal teleological directedness, which is interested in that which cultivates, civilizes, and makes human beings more moral:

> The sum total of what pragmatic anthropology has to say about human destiny and the character of their development is this: they are destined by their reason to live in a society with others and in it to cultivate themselves, to civilize themselves, and to make themselves moral by the arts and sciences.[54]

The main characteristic of pragmatic anthropology that sets it apart from any other empirical science, in general, is its teleological nature. It is not just concerned with what human beings are, but what they should make of themselves. This teleological directedness toward the goal of perfection is the guiding thread throughout the *Anthropology*: a limit to the observations, a rule to experiences, and a basis for Kant's suggestions or guidance of behavior.

Pragmatic anthropology deals with the natural destiny of human beings, that is, with the natural determinations of their being, as well as with their moral destiny. Pragmatic anthropology mediates between the natural and moral determinations of human beings. In order to know what can be made of human beings it is important to know first of all what they are in their natural determination. In a reflection, Kant writes,

> (g Knowledge of human beings as knowledge of the world has the idea in its basis, that we can best use nature for our purposes, [that we] when we know how to use human beings for these purposes.— For this we must also know ourselves. The latter has merely the purpose of civilizing, but also moralizing).[55]

Empirical psychology cannot really supply us with the natural determination of human beings, because it cannot bring any order into its own observations. It lacks an a priori science that would supply the rational elements needed to form a consistent and complete picture of human nature. Pragmatic anthropology takes two a priori sciences as its presuppositions: first, it requires a teleological theory of the development of the natural predispositions of the human being, and second it requires a critical theory of morality, whereby the human being is seen as free to form its own character. Both of these presupposed theories require as guidance an ideal of humanity.

The fundamental idea of Kant's anthropology is that it is about knowledge of the world, which originally was thought to be comprised of knowledge of nature and knowledge of human beings. This definition was made explicit for the first time in Kant's *Entwurf* for his lectures on physical geography and anthropology. There he speaks of "a twofold field," of which students need "a preliminary synopsis" in order to be able to "order all their future experiences according to rules."[56] This twofold field was originally conceived of as knowledge of nature and of human beings, but later in his *Reflexionen zur Anthropologie*, which were notes he used for his lectures, he often refers to them both as simply knowledge of human beings: "Knowledge of the world. Nature and human being. Everything refers to human beings . . . knowledge of the world is knowledge of human beings."[57]

What Kant meant by knowledge of human beings was worked out in his anthropology lectures. We see, however, from the very beginning (1773), that he meant knowledge of human beings to include the nature of human beings. Knowledge of nature did not simply mean, for Kant, what it means today, that is, physical and chemical knowledge of the laws of nature; rather it meant the relationship between the Earth, the cosmos, and human beings. For Kant there was an intimate relationship between the way the Earth was formed, geographically, and the way the human beings developed themselves, their talents, their histories, and their governments. An earthquake, for instance, is not just a natural disaster, it is a sign about providence or nature's intentions with respect to the human species.

Kant's certainty that the human being cannot be understood apart from nature stayed with him his whole life, despite his theory of morality, which claims the independence of the will from the determinations of nature. The human being, for all that, is still a finite, sensuous and imperfect being. For that reason, even if the will acts freely, it does so within a being that is nevertheless determined in its drives, inclinations, talents, and desires by nature.

The elements of Kant's theory of the nature of human beings can already be found in his early writings, and these are the very same teleological elements that he defended critically in the Critique of Teleological Judgment, developed further in his lectures on anthropology, and finally published in the *Anthropology* itself. Of course, one can say that in his early writings, the teleological perspective on nature and human nature was uncritical. Put in another way, it simply had not been critically founded yet.

This teleological view of nature and human nature is essential to Kant's sense of pragmatic, and essential to knowledge of the world. There can be no systematic interpretation of pragmatic that does not also take account of the four elements of his teleological theory. These four elements account for the "idea" of the pragmatic anthropology that was not supplied by empirical psychology, but rather by the cosmological writings and Kant's lectures on physical geography.

The following three passages from the *Anthropology* will be used to illustrate the four elements of Kant's teleological theory of human nature:

> The sum total of what pragmatic anthropology has to say about
> the human being's destiny and the character of their development

> is this: human beings are destined by their reason to live in a
> society with other human beings and in it to *cultivate* themselves,
> to *civilize* themselves, and to make themselves moral by the arts
> and sciences. No matter how strong their animal tendency to
> yield *passively* to the attractions of comfort and well-being, which
> they call happiness, they are still destined to make themselves
> worthy of humanity by *actively* struggling with the obstacles that
> cling to them because of the crudity of their nature. Human beings
> must, therefore, be *educated* to the good.[58]

and

> It is *only from Providence* that human beings anticipate the educa-
> tion of the human race, taking the species as a whole—that is,
> *collectively* (*universorum*) and not in terms of all its individual
> members (*singulorum*), where the multitude does not form a system
> but only an aggregate gathered together. Only from Providence
> do they expect their species to tend toward the civil constitution
> it envisages.[59]

and

> The character of the species . . . is this, that taken collectively (the
> human race as one whole), it is a multitude of persons, existing
> successively and side by side, who cannot do without associating
> peacefully and yet cannot avoid constantly offending one another.[60]

The first element of this theory is that nature is guided by a providential
plan. It is only "from providence that human beings anticipate the education of the human race." Nature is not a collocation of atoms in the void or
a system of laws, but a highly organized system. Nature is so ordered that it
has a foreseeable conclusion. This is more than just the development of the
particular individuals into their "nature" in the Aristotelian sense. The cause
of the development of civilization in human beings is more than just the
internal directedness of human nature. Human nature is set up in such a way
that human beings will tend to choose to become civilized. Civilization is not
causally inevitable in the sense of genetic inevitability, but it is inevitable in
the sense that we can anticipate that human beings will choose it rather than
suffer the pain of being torn by conflicting inclinations and conflicting egos.

Nature's plan cannot in any way be compared with the plan of single
human beings, or even groups of human beings, since nature's plan is not
like a blue print, it is not like a design. Human beings still have free will to
respond to nature's organization. The best that human beings can do is to
be aware of nature's plan, and attempt to live their lives in a way that is not
contrary to it. In a reflection written between 1785–1788, Kant writes:

> Pragmatic history of the human species from the predispositions
> of their nature. The natural destiny [*Bestimmung*] of human beings
> to their fullest purposes (not of the humanity in the individual,
> but in the species). This history teaches at the same time, how we
> should work on ourselves in accordance with the most complete
> purposes of nature.[61]

The knowledge of how to work on ourselves "in accordance with nature" is
what Kant calls "wisdom." He often refers to the wisdom of nature, since
nature's plan is that human beings develop "wisdom."[62] This ultimate means
to the final ends of nature is something that human beings can achieve only
through education. If nature could realize its plan without free will then it
would not need to educate human beings. But since human beings do have a
free will, nature can only achieve its purposes by means of education. This
education is not one of teaching doctrine. Rather it is an education through
experience. This experience is the experience of the dynamic of unsociable-
sociability, which will be defined below. Out of this experience human beings
freely choose to submit themselves to civil laws and develop civil constitutions.

The second element of Kant's teleological theory of human nature is that
nature has planted natural predispositions in human beings that it intends to
care for and develop in a purposive way. This element is meant when Kant
claims that the human being is in need of education. It is also meant when
Kant claims that the human being is not the rational animal [*animal rationale*],
but rather the animal capable of becoming rational [*animal rationabilis*].[63] This
distinction is crucial. Kant does not agree with the Aristotelian formulation
of the identity of humanity. Human beings are characterized as having the
potential for becoming rational, and the focus on the potential rather than
the actual orients the observer of human nature to attend to the possibilities
of individuals rather than to the behavior that falls short of truly rational
action. Such a perspective also requires that the observer attend to a discern-
ment of the ends and means that are used to achieve a specific end. The
rationality of human action resides in the relationship between the ends and
the means. Human beings have four natural predispositions: animality, technical, pragmatic, and moral. Each one of these predispositions has a kind of end
that is to be accomplished by specified means. Preservation and propagation
are the ends of animality and discipline is the means to achievement of these
ends. The technical predisposition aims at culture and does so through the
development of skills. Happiness is the purpose of the pragmatic predisposition
and this is accomplished by virtue of the development of prudence and civilization. The moral predisposition aims at the development of character and
does so through the acquisition of wisdom. This will be developed further in
chapters 3 and 4.

These natural predispositions are not just for the sake of individuals, but are also for the capacity of the human species for culture, civilization, and even morality itself. Nature, or providence [*Vorsehung*] as Kant often refers to her, intends for these natural predispositions to develop in such a way that one stage of development builds on another. The moralization of the human species cannot be achieved until human beings have achieved civilization and luxury.[64] Civilization cannot be achieved until human beings have begun to form some sort of culture. Culture depends on the disciplined development of individual talents in the arts and sciences. In other words, animality needs to be disciplined in order to develop the technical predisposition to culture, the antagonism that arises in culture, as people compete, leads to the development of civilized behavior, and this type of culture furthers the capacity for operating on laws that are universally valid for all human beings.

The third teleological element of pragmatic anthropology is that the plan of nature, which is the development of all the predispositions in human beings in a purposive way, can never be achieved fully in the individual alone but only in the species. Unlike all other animals, who achieve their fullest determination in reproducing themselves and in each individual being, the human being reaches its fullest determination and perfection only in the species. Reason cannot achieve its fullest expression in any one individual; rather, the individual is always a member of society, and the society is always a step toward perfection, but never perfection itself. Therefore, no individual could possibly reach its own perfection. Nature's purpose is far too complex for any one human being.[65]

The fourth teleological element is Kant's doctrine of unsociable-sociability. In the *Anthropology*, like in the *Idea of a Universal Natural History with a Cosmopolitan Intent* and in the Critique of Teleological Judgment, Kant presents his position that the human species has the character of needing to be sociable with one another, while preserving the tendency toward unsociability. These two conflicting tendencies compel human beings to submit to the "compulsion under laws," which would regulate the nature of sociability and hinder the tendencies toward unsociability. Kant explains the progress of civilization in this way. To resolve the conflicting inclinations human beings submit to civil laws which are valid for everyone.

With the exception of the doctrine of unsociable-sociability all of these elements can be found in Kant's early cosmological writings, and in his writings on physical geography. This thesis would not be contended among defenders of the theory that the anthropology lectures developed out of the empirical psychology. Menzer believes in the empirical origin of the anthropology, but does not see the concurrent development of Kant's theory of history and his anthropology. He shows the origin of Kant's theory of history by means of these very same anthropological elements in Kant's early writings on cosmology. If Kant's theory of cosmology is the origin of Kant's theory of history, then it is also the origin of his theory of anthropology. Weyand shows how the teleological principles of the *Critique of Judgment* developed out of Kant's early writings on cosmology. He argues that these principles are the foundations of Kant's theory of history.[66] These principles are also the foundations of Kant's theory of human nature.

No one has yet acknowledged the relationship between Kant's *Anthropology* and his theory of history.[67] They are both "cosmopolitan" and their intention is not scholastic, but they are both for the purpose of developing "citizens of the world" through pragmatic knowledge of the world: "The historical type of teaching (ˢ of history) is pragmatic, if it has another intention than merely the scholastic one, [that is, it] is not merely for the academic world, but also for the world of ethics."[68] Pragmatic history borrows from pragmatic anthropology: "Pragmatic anthropology. Prudence is directed to the community, in which we stand with human beings. All other pragmatic sciences borrow from it. Pragmatic history."[69] Therefore, it is impossible to show the development of Kant's theory of history without giving at the same time an account of the origin of Kant's pragmatic anthropology. It is the development of Kant's thinking about teleological judgment that constitutes the history of the development of both pragmatic anthropology and Kant's philosophy of history.

CHAPTER THREE

Kant's Theory of Human Nature

Kant's systematic theory of human nature is slowly beginning to crystallize as scholars contribute pieces of the puzzle. In 1966, Norbert Hinske argued, based on earlier scholarship, that Kant's anthropology is empirical in nature.[1] In 1975, Gerhard Funke emphasized the concept of freedom in Kant's theory of human nature.[2] That introduces the nonempirical nature of Kant's theory.[3] In contrast to other theories of human nature, Kant makes freedom play a central role. In his 1974 piece, "Kants Stichwort für unsere Aufgabe: Disziplinieren, Kultivieren, Zivilisieren, Moralisieren," Funke articulates Kant's goals for education of the human being.[4] In 1981, Monika Firla pointed out Kant's belief in the four natural predispositions: the animal, technical, pragmatic, and moral.[5] Funke's account of the four educational goals for human beings makes sense because human beings have these four natural predispositions. In addition to these elements of Kant's theory of human nature, one has to also take account of Kant's concept of unsociable-sociability, which Allen W. Wood does in his paper "Unsociable Sociability: The Anthropological Basis of Kantian Ethics."[6] In this chapter, I will pull together these pieces of Kant's theory of human nature and add the additional point that Kant believed that human nature is fundamentally communal rather than individualistic. We can educate the individual, but it is always within the community of the human species. In harmony with Funke, who rightfully emphasizes Kant's point that we can plan the education of the individual, I am going to show the points where Kant argues that nature also has a plan for the development of human predispositions up to but not including the moral predisposition. Like Funke, I want to emphasize that Kant's theory of human nature presupposes his belief in freedom, but I want to show specifically how that freedom is preserved in Kant's theory of human nature.

Many theories of human nature locate a natural aspect of human beings as the primary determinant of human nature and then the theory runs into trouble when it tries to understand human motivation for altruistic or moral action. Evolutionary psychology for instance believes the natural end of survival is the real end of human life, but as a result they have difficulty explaining altruism. Kant's theory puts moral directives right square in the beginning of the theory and there is no need to explain moral motivation as an afterthought. The human being can be understood as having four natural predispositions: the predisposition to animality, the technical predisposition, the pragmatic predisposition, and the moral predisposition. The very nature of human beings includes the capacity for moral deliberation.

Yet, Kant makes an intriguing claim in his *Anthropology from a Pragmatic Point of View* and also in his lectures on anthropology, that only animals achieve their full destiny and that individual human beings do not.[7] This thesis makes sense only when the central role that Kant's doctrine of unsociable-sociability plays in his theory of human nature is grasped. Kant articulates the concept of unsociable-sociability in the *Anthropology* as "the characteristic of his species is this: that nature implanted in it the seeds of discord, and willed that man's own reason bring concord."[8] The realization of each one of the pre-dispositions depends on the individual's relationship to the whole of humanity and the impulse to move from animality to humanity. Unsociable-sociability functions to progress the human being and the species toward that goal.

A complete account of Kant's theory of human nature must include not only an understanding of the function of the predispositions in the individual, but also how the dynamic of unsociable-sociability functions in progressing not only the development of the individual, but also the development of the human species in the direction of becoming more moral, but not including the moral predisposition. There is a fundamental tension in human beings that impels them to develop from mere animality to a rational being even while they have a duty to do so. Kant writes in the *Metaphysics of Morals* that a human being has a "duty to raise himself from the crude state of his nature, from his animality (*quoad actum*), more and more toward humanity, by which he alone is capable of setting himself ends."[9]

Yet, this duty is not something one has to accomplish through the mere will alone. Nature without and nature within help one to develop toward humanity. The character of the species, according to Kant, is that its "natural destiny consists in continual progress toward the better."[10] Kant says that it is the natural character of the species that is in continual progress and that means that nature is working in that direction, not just the will. In another place in the *Anthropology from a Pragmatic Point of View*, Kant claims that "it is only from Providence that man anticipates the education of the human race, taking the species as a whole. . . . Only from Providence does he expect his species to tend toward the civil constitution it envisages."[11] Providence is the concept Kant uses to characterize our reflection "on nature's purposiveness in the flow of world events," and he regards it to be "the underlying wisdom of a higher cause that directs the human race toward its objective goal."[12] Kant does not seem to believe that by the will alone that the human species will develop all of its predispositions. Indeed, in the *Grounding*, Kant says humans have a duty to develop their talents, but he says nothing about the duty to develop the predispositions. As we will see, the predispositions relate the individual human being to the entire species, and that is not something the individual has control over and so it is impossible to demand that the individual develop all her predispositions. This point can be maintained in spite of Kant's assertion that "providence has willed, that man shall bring forth for himself the good that lies hidden in his nature . . . thy happiness and unhappiness depends upon thyself alone."[13] This passage refers to the type of providence that implanted what "lies hidden," and this can be understood as the four natural predispositions. In addition, nature provides talents and "natural gifts" but these are not inevitably developed the way animal talents are developed. This passage must be understood as saying that nature has not provided instincts for the development of the natural predispositions and hence wills that human beings develop them through their own willing, which they can only do by acting on maxims. Yet, although nature has not implanted instincts, she has arranged human nature in such a way that human beings will respond to internal conflicts by willing and thus contribute to the development of the predispositions.

The developmental perspective implicit in the above is articulated in Kant's distinction between definitions of the human being. To Kant, the human being is not "the rational animal" as Aristotle claims, but rather "the animal capable of becoming rational."[14] The human being can become rational and that means it must develop its predispositions beyond animality. That Kant thinks this takes time is evident in *Anthropology* when he suggests that a person reaches his full use of reason as far as skill is concerned "around the age of twenty," as far as prudence is concerned "around forty," and as far as wisdom is concerned, "around sixty."[15] Reason is actualized over time and the development of the technical predisposition precedes the pragmatic and the moral predispositions.[16]

It turns out that the key to understanding how one can have a duty to develop into humanity when indeed they can only expect it partially from nature and it takes a long time, lies in the fact that in order for human beings to actualize their nature as reason, they have to make use of maxims. These maxims are not just moral maxims but everyday ones as well. The structure of maxims is teleological, namely, they relate ends to means. They make use of ends suggested by reason and means provided by nature. They mediate the natural destiny of human beings with their destiny as rational beings. This key helps us unlock the mystery of how a purely natural being becomes a rational being.

This chapter will primarily focus on a clarification of Kant's claim that individual animals reach their destiny, but in the human species only the species at most reaches its destiny.[17] I will argue why this is really a theory of human nature that presents the human being as an intrinsically communal being, rather than an isolated individual. And it will show that humans are capable of freedom in spite of the doctrine of unsociable-sociability.

To begin with, Kant compares human beings to animals. Even though in several places he claims we cannot compare human beings to animals, he does often differentiate human beings from animals, because Kant believes fundamentally that human beings are unique as a species.[18] It is important to understand first what specifically makes human beings unique. Kant has many views on animals, most of which, are much more positive than what one usually finds in the history of philosophy. For instance, in the *Critique of Judgment*, Kant proposes that animal behavior by analogy with human behavior shows that animals are not machines, as Descartes thought, but rather that they also operate on "presentations."[19] I take this to mean that Kant believes animals have consciousness even as human beings do. In the *Lectures on Ethics*, Kant surmises that cruelty toward animals would lead to cruelty toward human animals precisely because humans are analogous to animals.[20] We have, hence, indirect duties to animals. Yet, Kant also makes it clear there that animals are not ends-in-themselves as human beings are. They lack self-consciousness and hence are means to human ends. Human beings, in contrast, are final ends because, as Kant writes in the *Critique of Judgment*, they are the only beings that can conceive of purposes and set purposes of their own choice.[21] Human beings are the final purpose of creation because "only in man, and even in him as moral subject, do we find unconditioned legislation regarding purposes."[22] It is this very capacity for setting purposes and final purposes and using nature as a means for those purposes that sets human beings apart from animals.[23] Humans set ends and achieve those ends through maxims, which ultimately must be evaluated by the moral law. As Kant writes in the Critique of Teleological Judgment, human beings are the final purpose of nature, only on the condition that he has "the understanding and the will to give both nature and himself reference to a purpose that can be independent of nature, self-sufficient, and a final purpose."[24] This final purpose is the capacity human beings have for giving themselves the moral law. The moral law governs maxims. Hence, it is the capacity to act on maxims evaluated by the moral law that gives human beings their unique capacity and also their freedom from natural laws.[25]

In the *Education*, Kant claims that animals do not require nurture or education, because nature's plan for them is "to use their powers as soon as they are possessed of them, according to a regular plan—that is, in a way not harmful to them."[26] Most likely Kant means they do not need to be instructed, since certainly animal babies do need to be shown what to do. Nonetheless, this indicates the most important distinction between animals and human beings. Human beings have to be educated or instructed in order to achieve their nature. Maxims are taught to children as they are being educated. Maxims are suggested and also imposed on children. The ends of human nature are achieved through the use of maxims. And it is through maxims that human beings achieve freedom. Unlike animals, which are guided by instincts as natural laws, humans have the capacity for acting on their "conception of law."[27] This is why Kant repeatedly says in his lectures on anthropology that the human being is in need of a "Herr" (lord or master).[28] Humans have to be educated to operate on maxims and the conceptions of laws. These laws must be taught. Kant identifies the means to the education of the human species as "1. public education. 2. Public law giving. 3. Religion."[29]

The freedom to act on the conception of law applies not just to maxims of morality, but also to maxims whose end is to develop the natural predispositions. In the *Critique of Pure Reason*, Kant argues that the practical is what is possible through freedom.[30] In his Education, Kant defines practical education as aimed toward developing (1) skills, (2) good sense, and (3) the training of moral character.[31] Practical education, which is aimed at freedom, includes the development of the technical predisposition, the pragmatic predisposition as well as the moral predisposition. In what follows, I will lay out the connection between them more closely, but let it suffice here to say that skill is the means to development of the ends of the technical predisposition, pragmatic skill (or good sense or prudence) is the means to the ends of the pragmatic predisposition, and the training of character through wisdom is the means to the ends of the moral predisposition.

Human beings accomplish the coordination of means and ends through the use of maxims. That Kant believes maxims can run the gambit of human experience and not just moral experience is evident in his account of the hypothetical imperative. The purpose of the hypothetical imperative is to impose on human beings that they link not just any means to an end, but that they link the necessary means to their ends. Since the hypothetical imperative encompasses both technical and pragmatic ends, it is referring to the necessary means to achieve both arbitrary ends (technical) and essential ends (pragmatic).[32] Hence, maxims coordinate the means to arbitrary ends, essential ends like happiness, and necessary ends like human beings.

Kant claims that the human being is "capable of perfecting himself according to the ends that he himself adopts."[33] The kind of ends that human beings can adopt can be categorized in four areas: (*a*) animal ends, (*b*) technical ends, (*c*) pragmatic ends, and (*d*) moral ends. In the *Education*, Kant lays out the four goals of education, (1) discipline, (2) culture, (3) prudence, and (4) morality.[34] These correspond to the four natural predispositions: the predisposition to animality, the technical, pragmatic, and moral predispositions. It is by virtue of the latter three ends that human beings are distinctively human and develop their freedom. Kant claims that practical education, which teaches one to live as a free being consists in (1) the development of ability, (2) instruction in prudence, and (3) in the training of moral character.[35]

In order to realize these three ends, we have to use our reason, which means operating on maxims. This seems straightforward and appears to pose no difficulties until we attend to the fact that human beings have conflicting ends, conflicting inclinations, and conflicting maxims. In addition, these maxims must be learned from other people and even if they are imposed, human beings are still free to reject them.

In the *Anthropology*, as Kant is laying out his understanding of the pragmatic predisposition, he claims that "when any other animal [species] is left to its own devices, each individual attains its complete destiny, but in man's case only the species, at most, achieves it."[36] From there he argues that it is through the progress of innumerable generations that the human species works its way up to its destiny. After Kant lays out the three natural predispositions, the technical, pragmatic, and moral, he then concludes that the sum total of what anthropology teaches is that human beings are meant to be cultivated, civilized, and made moral by the arts and sciences. Then he argues that human beings must be educated to the good by "men who are themselves still involved in the crudity of nature and are supposed to bring about what they themselves are in need of."[37] This statement is reminiscent of what Kant often says in his lectures on anthropology, namely, that human beings, unlike animals, are in need of a "Herr" (lord or master), but here it is clear that the Herr is also in need of a Herr. At this point, Kant says, "this explains why man is constantly deviating from his destiny and always returning to it.—Let us cite the difficulties in the solution of this problem and the obstacles to solving it."[38] With this statement Kant begins to lay out in sections A, B, and C, the difficulties in achieving the ends of the natural predispositions in the individual (KGS, VII: 325–27).[39] It is in these passages that I believe Kant is explaining why the human species at most realizes the natural predispositions and not the individual.[40] "Difficulties" are causing human beings to deviate from their destiny and these are the difficulties the individual experiences. Although Kant does not say this explicitly in the *Anthropology*, reference to his lectures on anthropology establishes this connection.

Already in the Friedländer anthropology lecture (1777–78), Kant addresses the question of the character of human beings in general [*Vom Charackter der Menschheit überhaupt*] and says, "the human being has two destinies, one with respect to humanity, and one with respect to animality."[41] He goes on to say that the two destinies are at variance with one another because "we do not achieve the perfection of humanity in the destiny of animality, and when we want to achieve the perfection of humanity, we must do violence to the destiny of animality." To clarify, Kant introduces the example of the sixteen-year-old youth who in a state of nature could not only conceive and procreate, but also preserve his progeny. Yet, that same youth is in no position in civil society to preserve his progeny without first developing skills and having experience, and this delays the fulfillment of his animal inclinations. In order to perfect his humanity, he must do violence to his animality.

Then in 1781–82 in the *Menschenkunde*, Kant first expresses the thesis that "in animal species every individual attains its destiny, in contrast, in the human species a single human being can never reach its destiny, but only the whole human species."[42] He goes on to explain that human beings are made for society and that "all work for one, and one works for all" whereas an animal can seek it's food without help from another. Shortly thereafter, Kant brings up the example of the youth again, only he is now fifteen-years-old. Again, he is presented as being able to propagate his species, but not able to preserve his family.[43] In this lecture, the close proximity of this thesis with this example shows that the example is meant to illustrate the thesis. Later, we will see that this same example occurs in the *Anthropology*.

In 1784–85, according to Mrongovius, Kant again asserts the thesis that every individual in an animal species achieves it destiny, but the human species requires generation after generation to reach its destiny.[44] Once again, following this statement, Kant refers to the sixteen-year-old who can conceive his species, but cannot preserve his species.[45] At this point Kant goes on to assert that the "impulse to culture has no relation to the length of life."[46] Directly following that Kant claims that all human beings are equal by nature, but that through culture, civilization, and moralization, inequality is introduced. Kant proceeds at this point once again to address the conflict between the two destinies of human beings.[47]

In sections A, B, and C of the *Anthropology* (KGS, Anth, VII: 325–27), we have exactly these same three points made: (A) youth are not able to preserve the children they can conceive; (B) scientific knowledge as a form of culture is "completely out of proportion to a man's life span"; and (C) "Our species seems to fare no better in achieving its destiny with respect to happiness" because of the inequalities introduced by culture, civilization, and moralization.[48] These three problems correspond partially to the three predispositions Kant just introduced. The first problem in A is the problem the human being faces in not being able to completely fulfill its animal predisposition. The second problem in B is the issue that arises for the fulfillment of the technical predisposition. The third problem in C arises because of the human beings' pragmatic predisposition, which orients us to happiness and equality with other human beings.

Further on in the *Anthropology* Kant again asserts his thesis that animals attain their destiny by the wisdom of nature, but human beings only as a species.[49] This is followed by the claim that human beings should develop good out of evil, namely, that as "culture advances they feel ever more keenly the injuries their egoism inflicts on one another" and out of this evil they will develop the good of submitting to "a discipline (or civil constraint)."[50] This is another formulation of the principle of unsociability-sociability, because out of unsociable tendencies of egoism, they realize only submitting to a civil constitution can preserve sociability. This passage shows the importance of the doctrine of unsociable-sociability for the thesis that humans attain their destiny only in the species.

Now I will present the arguments in sections A, B, and C while elucidating them with reference to other passages in Kant's other writings. The major difficulty in realizing the natural predispositions is that human beings have to be educated to their nature. The ends of animality as procreation and preservation, to begin with, cannot be achieved without learning and following the maxims suggested by civil society. In section A, Kant uses the example of a young man in civil society who must develop his technical skills "learn a trade" and pragmatic skills "acquire clientele" before he will be able to support his wife and his children.[51] He needs the community of human beings to teach him the technical skills he needs and also the pragmatic skills of selling, persuading, pleasing, and convincing other people that his product is a good one. If he learns and exercises these maxims, he will achieve his animal ends to some extent. However, his participation in civil society does interfere with the direct achievement of his animal ends.

In another section of the *Anthropology*, Kant mentions the savage who does not want to submit to other people's maxims and leaves civil society. That is certainly a possibility, but it doesn't change Kant's assessment. The savage still operates on his own freely chosen maxims, and must develop maxims to survive and thrive.[52] If we take Henry David Thoreau as an example of someone who does not want to submit to the maxims of civil society, we still see that he does submit to the maxims he learned in civil society that taught him how to build a cabin, keep accounting records, and maintain a garden. This desire to leave civil society illustrates the central dynamic of the animal inclinations to sex and sociability, on the one hand, and to freedom on the other hand. The savage wants to operate on his own maxims. Every person who enters civil society has this inclination to freedom, which Kant calls the "sensuous idea of outer freedom."[53] People want to operate on their own freely chosen maxims, yet entering civil society means operating on

maxims suggested or imposed by other people. In order to fulfill the one inclination to sociability (participation in society), one is not able to completely
fulfill the inclination to freedom (being the master of one's own maxims).
This is the dynamic of unsociable-sociability operating on the predisposition
to animality. These conflicting inclinations impel one to discipline one's
inclinations and to develop one's skills and that is true of the savage as well
as the person who enters civil society. Discipline is the means to the achievement of the ends of the predisposition to animality. Discipline frees the will
from the unruliness of impulses and "prevents a human being from being
turned aside from his appointed end."[54] It "subjects the human being to the
laws of humanity and begins to let him feel the force of laws."[55]

The animal inclinations to both sex and freedom are difficult to
achieve completely in the individual because both are fulfilled through maxims
that are taught by other people.[56] The inclination to sex must be postponed
until the right skills have been achieved so that one can not only procreate,
but also preserve the progeny. The inclination to freedom can never be completely fulfilled if one lives in civil society because that means operating on
maxims imposed or suggested by others. Yet, civilized people find ways of exer-
cising freedom operating within these maxims, and indeed we have the moral
requirement to operate only on those maxims we could will to be universal.
This implies that we are free to reject maxims that cannot be universalized, and
it also implies that we reside in a community of other people because we are
willing that all people could operate on that maxim. The human individual
does not perfectly develop the animal predisposition because of the conflicts
between the inclinations to freedom and sexuality or sociability.

In section B, Kant discusses an issue relevant to the technical predisposition. The technical predisposition is already evident in the human hand,
according to Kant, because it can be manipulated for any ends whatsoever.
The technical predisposition means that human beings can develop skills.
Skill is "dexterity in achieving whatever ends one has chosen."[57] The ends of
the technical predisposition are arbitrary. There are no grounds within the
technical predisposition itself for preferring one end over the other, for
instance, preferring to become a philosopher rather than an engineer. Yet,
nature does provide some guidance for preferring some skills to other skills,
namely, because she has provided each human being with talents. In a reflection from his anthropology lectures, Kant explains, "talent, gift of nature:
concerns cognition, determines the market price, is capable of cultivation."[58]
Kant's position is that we have a moral obligation to develop our talents into
skills. A talent becomes a skill when it submits to some end and is a profi-
ciency in achieving that end. The end is arbitrary because it is not survival
specific. Human beings have freedom already in the technical predisposition

because there is a wide range of choice of ends unconstrained by the ends of the animal predisposition. That Kant believes we are free in the culture of skill can be seen already in the hypothetical imperative, which rules over skill and enjoins one to take the necessary means for achieving a specific end. But because the categorical imperative rules over the hypothetical imperative, one has grounds for evaluating the means to one's ends and if the only means for achieving the end are immoral then the end must also be abandoned. If we were not free, we could not abandon the end.

In section B of the *Anthropology*, Kant lays out the difficulties in achieving the technical predisposition fully. The technical predisposition is at most fulfilled in the species because skilled individuals progress a science only in the time they are living, and when they die, the knowledge dies with them. Younger scholars must learn what older scholars already have known, and this pattern is repeated each generation, with the new generation learning anew in order to keep the science progressing.[59] It is then only in the whole species that the fulfillment of the technical predisposition is realized. Again we see that the full completion of the technical predisposition does not occur without a community of human beings. Science itself extends far beyond the range of the skills of an individual scientist. In a reflection, Kant clarifies that "science does not belong to the determination of the individual human being, but to the human species."[60] Not only can individuals actualize skills because they have reason, but also as a member of the entire human species individuals have the opportunity of participating in culture (science) as a phenomenon that relates individuals to the past, present, and future generations of human beings.

Unsociable-sociability functions in the technical predisposition as well and causes individuals and the species to develop the pragmatic predisposition in order to resolve the conflicts. Culture and the development of skill bring out competition between human beings as well as eliciting feelings of envy and jealousy.[61] This competition makes for a disharmonious social situation as well as antagonism (unsociable). Human beings, however, long for peace and harmony (sociable), and so they have to learn to be civilized in their relationships with one another. Although Kant occasionally calls civilization "culture," he tends to distinguish the two: culture causes rivalry,[62] civilization brings about harmony. Culture, and its consequence of rivalry and antagonism, is the spur to the development of the pragmatic predisposition, and civilization is the species' end in this predisposition.

In section C, Kant lays out the difficulties in achieving our pragmatic predisposition. The pragmatic predisposition is aimed at developing the skills of sociability for the sake of happiness in the individual. Again we will see that this end is not completely fulfilled in the individual and that the most we can hope for is that the species will become more civilized. In the *Anthropology*, Kant defines the pragmatic predisposition as "man's predisposition to become civilized by culture, especially the cultivation of social qualities, and his natural tendency in social relations to leave the crude state of mere private force and to become well-bred."[63] The skill that one must achieve in order to fulfill these ends is prudence. Prudence is "skill in the choice of means to one's own greatest well being."[64] Kant defines prudence in many places including the *Anthropology* and his treatise on *Education*. In the *Anthropology*, prudence is "using other men for his purposes."[65] Kant refines this in the *Education*, but it amounts to the same definition: prudence [*Weltklugheit*] "consists in the art of turning our skill to account; that is, of using our fellow-human beings for our own ends."[66] That Kant does not mean by this something immoral is clear in his further elaborations of prudence. The purpose of prudence is that the person "may conduct himself in society, that it may be liked and that it may gain influence. For this a kind of culture is necessary which we call "refinement" [*Civilisierung*]. The latter requires manners, courtesy, and a kind of prudence which will enable them to use all human beings for their own ends."[67] Prudence means being able to use others with their consent[68] and without coercion, otherwise, one would only meet with resistance and the end of this predisposition, namely, happiness, would not be achieved in any degree.

In section C of the *Anthropology*, Kant articulates the reason why the end of happiness is difficult to achieve in the individual and why we can really only hope for civilization of the species, which is the end of the pragmatic predisposition for the species. He refers to Jean-Jacques Rousseau's argument that once human beings leave the state of nature and become enculturated, they lose any possibility of happiness. Kant gives three reasons why: (1) human forces become weakened in a state of culture; (2) inequality and mutual oppression result; (3) unnatural moral education is imposed.[69] Kant does not elaborate in this passage on these three. However, in the *Religion* and in the Critique of Teleological Judgment, Kant does flesh out the second reason. The sum of what we can conclude from those passages is that equality among human beings is essential to happiness, but the fact is that everyone strives to gain superiority over the next person in order that they do not gain "hated superiority" over oneself.[70] Even the attainment of this superiority does not ensure happiness since then one becomes subject to insatiable inclinations. The strife, greed, envy, and jealousy that results insures that no one is happy until they submit to the universally valid laws of a civil constitution and learn to discipline their inclinations. Hence, it is only through civilization that the species fulfills the pragmatic predisposition. This again forms the community that a human being needs in order to fulfill at least partially the ends of the pragmatic predisposition. Kant argues this explicitly in an anthropological reflection: "The human being has the distinctive drive that seeks to establish himself as an equal, because his well being does not depend on himself, but on the help of other human beings."[71] Happiness, as the end of the pragmatic predisposition for the individual, cannot be completely achieved by the individual alone. It depends on the possibility of equality with other human beings and that is insured only by the civil constitution (which includes positive laws). Submitting to the civil constitution is submitting to laws that are universally valid laws, laws that preserve equality among human beings. So we see also that the dynamic of unsociable-sociability impels human beings to submit to universally valid laws. This prepares one for the requirements of the moral predisposition, but the development of the moral predisposition does not arise out of the principle of unsociable-sociability. Nature cannot compel one to act on the conception of law. Nature cannot give rise to moral freedom.

From an anthropological point of view, it is unusual to talk about the predisposition to morality since it is not a natural ability in the strict sense. Yet, Kant calls it a natural predisposition for personality in the *Religion*, and it is the predisposition for the motivating force of the will.[72] However, there are results of the natural predisposition that present a law likeness and that is character. Character is defined in the *Critique of Practical Reason* as "a consistent practical habit of mind according to unchangeable maxims."[73] In the *Education* where Kant writes explicitly "morality is a matter of character," he claims that our ultimate aim is the formation of character which "consists in the firm purpose to accomplish something, and then also in the actual accomplishing of it."[74] Elsewhere in the *Education*, he defines character as the "readiness to act in accordance with 'maxims.'"[75] Kant doesn't specify here whether character can be either good or evil, but in the *Anthropology* he talks about character as good, when we say that a person "has character" since then we are "paying him a great tribute."[76] Indeed, when he writes that character has "intrinsic worth and is exalted beyond any price" he must surely be meaning a good character.[77] Kant wants to differentiate in the *Anthropology* between the kind of character by means of which we know what to expect from a person, and character as such. The former is what Kant means when he talks about the character of the sexes, the nations, and the character of the species. The latter is moral character, which is dependent on the type of maxims one adheres to. It is important to notice though that Kant calls character a kind of "way of thinking" [*Denkungsart*].[78] In a reflection to anthropology he writes that "Character, Denkungsart: refers to the will, gives inner worth, is capable of moralization."[79] There is a cognitive aspect to realization of morality as character, and Kant calls this cognitive aspect "wisdom."

Like the other three predispositions, the moral predisposition does appear to have an end, character, and also the means to achieving it. Kant appears to believe that wisdom is the means toward achieving character as prudence is the means to achieving happiness. In the *Verkündigung des nahen Abschlusses eines Tractats zum ewigen Frieden in der Philosophie*, Kant writes to a young man who wants to study critical philosophy. He explains that wisdom is "for human beings nothing other than the inner principle of the will to follow moral laws."[80] If a person achieves wisdom, then they will acquire character. There are other passages, which also indicate that Kant thinks developing the moral predisposition is also developing wisdom. In a reflection on anthropology from the 1780s, Kant says the human being "is cultivated (through school) (Skill), civilized (norms) moralized (virtue). (Skill-prudent-wise)."[81] The cultivation-civilization-moralization triad corresponds to the skill-prudent-wise triad, which means that the actualization of morality requires the skill of wisdom. In a reflection to moral philosophy, Kant writes, "the skill, which has purely good ends, is wisdom." He goes on from this definition to then lay out an account of four practical sciences that resembles almost perfectly the account Kant has in the *Education* of the four goals of education:

Practical sciences:

1. Skill (the end is arbitrary) (imperatively problematic)
2. Prudence (imperatively categorical)
3. Morality (imperatively apodictic)
4. Wisdom (wisdom is a morality, which is supported through prudence (administratively).[82]

Finally, in Mrongovius (1784–85) Kant says that pragmatic anthropology covers skill, prudence, and ethics "which is taken up with all the purposes of human beings and through which one becomes wise."[83]

As I have argued, skill is the means toward development of the technical predisposition, prudence is the means toward the development of the pragmatic predisposition and this leaves morality and wisdom as the means toward the development of the moral predisposition. In the *Education*, Kant associates wisdom clearly with morality, although it is one that is also associated with prudence. This makes sense since all the stages of skill must be achieved in order to achieve the final stage of moralization. As Kant maintained in the *Anthropology*, the development of wisdom comes after the development of prudence.[84] Another way to put this is that a certain kind of prudence is necessary in order to develop character since character is the ability to actualize one's maxims in a consistent way, and this has to be done in the face of many counterinfluences besides the natural inclinations. One also has to find and hold on to moral maxims while other people are and are not acting on moral maxims. The difficulty in achieving the ends of the moral predisposition lies in the fact, according to Kant, that human beings have to be educated to the good by those who are themselves not free from the innate propensity to evil.[85] We know from the *Religion*, that this propensity to evil is the tendency we have to make exceptions for ourselves. The maxims that one learns from other people may also include maxims that permit one to make an exception for oneself from the universally valid moral laws.

This is why Kant emphasizes, in the *Anthropology*, the importance of thinking for oneself. Acquiring wisdom requires that one act on maxims that promote the likelihood of moral maxims being acted upon. Kant gives us the three maxims for attaining wisdom in the *Anthropology*: "(1) to think for ourselves, (2) to think ourselves into the place of others (when communicating with them), (3) always to think consistently with ourselves."[86] Obviously, these maxims are important to actualizing morality in the individual since they refer to our ability to evaluate what others say and do and what we say and do. While the second maxim reminds us of the need to take other people into consideration, the first and third maxims tells us that morality requires judgment. We not only need to judge whether a particular maxim conforms to the moral law and hence is universally valid, but we also need to evaluate the appropriate means for actualizing our maxims. It is one thing to evaluate a maxim to know whether it conforms to benevolence, it is quite another thing to judge exactly which actions would actualize benevolence. Testing the maxim against the categorical imperative suffices for the former, but not for the latter. Nor can we rely on imitating others to know which actions actualize benevolence and truth. We have to think for ourselves.

I believe we can sum up what wisdom means for Kant. It means recognizing our common destiny and recognizing that as individuals we do not achieve perfection, but achieve our destiny in common with the whole human species. We are destined to become cultivated and civilized, but not yet moralized through our very nature. Each and every individual must undertake the last step of moralization. Moralization does not appear to be something nature can bring about.

Kant believes that the human species is capable of moralization, even as the individual is capable of developing character. Unsociable-sociability has been seen to be the driving force of the development of the first three predispositions, but it does not appear to be the force behind the development of the moral predisposition. Progress in the species is noted in the technical predisposition as culture. Progress in the pragmatic predisposition means civilization. Yet if Kant asserts that human beings are becoming more moral through unsociable-sociability, then he might be overstepping his own critical positions. In the Critique of Teleological Judgment, Kant differentiates between the final purpose of creation and the ultimate purpose of nature, and claims that the final purpose cannot be sought in nature, but only in human beings as moral subjects. The ultimate purpose of nature is what nature can do to prepare human beings for their final destiny.[87] The principle of unsociable-sociability is the mechanism of nature to accomplish that end. Kant's anthropological writings acknowledge the principle of unsociable-sociability, but it does not appear to apply beyond the predisposition to animality, the technical predisposition, and the pragmatic predisposition. And hence, we can conclude that unsociable-sociability does not lead to progress in moralization.

First of all Kant tells us that being a person of principles, having character, is possible even for the person of the most ordinary human reason. Kant writes in the *Anthropology*,

> and since having a character is both the minimum that can be required of a reasonable man and the maximum of inner worth (of human dignity), to be a man of principles (to have determinate character) must be possible for the most ordinary human reason and yet, according to its dignity, surpass the greatest talent.[88]

It would appear that even in primitive states, human beings were capable of acting on the conception of the moral law, being capable of formulating maxims and operating on maxims that had universal applicability, and being able to recognize that humans are ends in themselves. None of these actions of reason appear to depend on empirical conditions.

If we pay careful attention to the times Kant uses the principle of unsociable-sociability, it is always civilization that is the final end aimed at in the resolution of the conflict between unsociable tendencies and sociable tendencies. In the *Anthropology*, right after Kant lays out sections A, B, and C, he comments, "a civil constitution artificially raises to its highest power the human species' good predisposition to the final end of its destiny."[89] The civil constitution resolves the unsociable reality that results from "man's self will [that] is always ready to break forth in hostility toward his neighbors, and always presses him to claim unconditional freedom, not merely independence of others but even mastery of other beings that are his equal by nature."[90] Egoism pushes one to claim superiority over others, but submitting to the universally valid laws of the civil constitution preserves equality. Kant then goes on to make the decisive distinction that nature moves human beings in that direction, from culture to morality, but reason prescribes the opposite direction from morality to culture: "this is because nature within man tries to lead him from culture to morality and not (as reason prescribes) from the morality and its law, as a starting point, to a culture designed to conform to morality."[91] There is no question that the ultimate end of nature and unsociability in human beings is to make human beings conform to universally valid laws, but these are laws of coercion, not laws that one willingly submits to out of respect for the law and respect for the human being. The very fact that Kant distinguishes the movements indicates that he thinks morality has a different source than nature. Nature only "tries" to bring one to morality, but it does not accomplish it. It prepares the way, but is not the event.

In a passage that follows the above material, Kant again refers to the movement of nature when he writes, "as culture advances they feel ever more keenly the injuries that their egoism inflicts on one another; and since they see no other remedy for it than to subject the private interest (of the individual) to the public interest (of all united), they submit, though reluctantly, to a discipline (of civil constraint)."[92] Although the mechanism of unsociable-sociability is a "feeling of injury inflicted," and perhaps can be called "empathy," and is not motivated by fear, it still results in the submission to civil constraint, not to morality. This is the great impulse of civilization: a feeling for the hurt that egoism causes, and submitting to civil constraint as a result of it. Nature and unsociability, then, results in the progress of the natural predispositions up to the moral predisposition, but does not include the moral predisposition. As Kant writes in Pillau (1777–78), the ultimate end of human nature is the civil constitution, which unites human beings to a whole.[93]

Human nature is made up of four natural predispositions, and each of these predispositions relates us to the community of the human species. Achieving this perspective is the fundamental task for human beings. Kant begins the *Anthropology* with an account of the types and forms of egoism. Egoism is where all human beings begin by regarding themselves as the whole world. The task is to become a pluralist and regard oneself as a citizen of the world.[94] One is a citizen of the world if one realizes his or her participation in the ends of the human species, rather than viewing the whole world as serving the achievement of the ends for the individual. As Kant writes in the *Doctrine of Virtue*: "Human beings have a duty to themselves to be useful members of the world, since this also belongs to the worth of humanity in their own person, which they ought not to degrade."[95] We have a duty to be useful members of the world. That means actualizing the maxims that we share in common and that relate us to the communal goals of the natural predispositions, science, arts, and civilization.

Having argued this, however, I do want to point out that Kant believes it is still important to maintain a certain sense of individuality which is necessary so that one can judge for oneself and evaluate one's maxims according to the moral law. He writes of the education of personal character that it is of a "free being, who is able to maintain itself, and to take its proper place in society, keeping at the same time a proper sense of individuality."[96] The maxims of the first three predispositions need to be evaluated against the moral law. It is not enough that human beings learn to pursue any ends whatsoever; they must also learn to follow good ends and evaluate whether or not to pursue the ends suggested by the first three predispositions. This is the activity of the individual. Ultimately, the individual must decide for herself whether the ends are good ends, and whether appropriate means exist to achieve those ends.

CHAPTER FOUR

Kant's Theory of Human Nature as Natural Predispositions

We recognize the human being for the first time in its natural specificity when we reflectively judge it as a natural purpose in terms of its predispositions. In the *Anthropology* and in the *Religion within the Limits of Reason Alone*, we have two different accounts of what Kant considers to be the predispositions of human beings. In the *Anthropology*, Kant lists the predispositions as the technical, the pragmatic, and the moral. In contrast to all other living beings on the Earth,

> human beings by their *technical* predisposition [*Anlage*] for manipulating things (a mechanical predisposition joined with consciousness), by their *pragmatic* predisposition (for using other human beings skillfully for their purposes), and by the *moral* predisposition in their being (to treat themselves and others according to the principle of freedom under laws).[1]

In the *Religion*, the three predispositions named are the predispositions to animality, humanity, and personality:

(1) The predisposition to the *animality* of the human being, as a *living being*;

(2) To the *humanity* in him, as a living and at the same time *rational* being;

(3) To his *personality*, as a rational and at the same time a *responsible* being.[2]

The *Anthropology* fails to mention the predisposition to animality, while Kant does not discuss the technical predisposition in the *Religion*. One could argue that there is a conflicting account or inconsistency between the two books, but I believe Kant gives enough of an explanation within the two passages to warrant the claim that there is no inconsistency. The purpose of the account in the *Anthropology* is to lay out what distinguishes human beings from all other living beings on the Earth. Human beings share animality with animals and thus there is no reason to mention it here. The purpose of the discussion about the natural predispositions in the *Religion* is to uncover the source of evil in human beings, and there animality does and should be treated since there are thousands of years of philosophies that have found the culprit for

sin to lie in a human being's flesh and animal desires. But the technical predisposition is not likely to cause evil and so Kant does not address it.

Still we have the problem that Kant calls our third predisposition
"humanity" in the *Religion* and the "pragmatic predisposition" in the *Anthropology*. We can identify the pragmatic predisposition with the predisposition to
humanity because of Kant's similar descriptions about what this predisposition
entails. Both accounts consistently present the end of this predisposition as
happiness. In the *Religion*, it is by virtue of this predisposition that we compare
ourselves to others and judge ourselves happy or unhappy.[3] In the *Anthropology*,
the pragmatic predisposition is defined as the "predisposition to become civilized
by culture"[4] and, as Kant discusses the obstacles to attaining the destiny of this
predisposition, he argues that "our species seems to fare no better in achieving
its destiny with respect to happiness."[5] Happiness is the end of this predisposition for the individual. For the species, it is civilization that functions as the end
of the pragmatic predisposition. In the next sections, I am going to illuminate
the predispositions and show their relevance to the *Anthropology*.

THE PREDISPOSITION TO ANIMALITY

In the *Religion*, the natural ends of the predisposition to animality are said to
be, "*first*, for self-preservation; *second*, for the propagation of the species,
through the sexual drive, and for the preservation of the offspring thereby
begotten through breeding; *third*, for community with other human beings,
i.e., the social drive."[6] Kant often talks of the impulse or inclination toward
self-preservation and propagation of the species within the *Anthropology*,
especially in the section on the Character of the Sexes.[7] The social impulse is
referred to periodically throughout the *Anthropology*.

In many areas of the *Anthropology*, Kant does deal explicitly with human
animality. Some feelings and affects, for example, have to be acknowledged as
important to the predisposition to animality, since they can be 'threatening to
life': "Exuberant *joy* (that is tempered by no apprehension about sorrow) and
overwhelming sadness (that is alleviated by no hope)—that is, *grief*—are
affects that threaten life."[8] Some affects, like weeping and laughter, promote
health and, therefore, also self-preservation.[9]

Insofar as these affects promote or threaten health, they belong to the
account of the predisposition to animality. When they are experienced in a
social situation, they belong to the social predisposition to humanity. For
instance, laughter and weeping can also be interpreted socially, as well as
physically: "laughter is *masculine*; weeping, on the other hand, is *feminine* (in
men it is effeminate)."[10]

Kant refers often to the "vital force" in human beings. Monotony makes our sensations grow weak for instance, whereas working, conversing and entertaining ourselves "strengthens the mind."[11] Drunkenness produces the illusion that our vital force is being increased.[12] The state of health is constituted by "slight inhibitions" alternated with "slight advancements" of the vital force.[13] Kant notes that "laughter, the exhaling of air by fits and starts (convulsively, so to speak) strengthens our feeling of the vital force by its salutary movement of the diaphragm."[14] Laughter also helps in digesting food by moving the diaphragm and intestines.[15] Competition with others protects the "vital force from lassitude" and keeps it alert.[16] Nature also stimulates the vital force through illusion, namely, where we mistake our subjective grounds of action for something objective.[17]

In the Didactic of the *Anthropology*, Kant suggests that human beings have two natural *"inclinations to freedom* and to *sex.*"[18] Providence has implanted "various *inclinations* that, as natural animal needs, are indispensable to living nature (even man's nature)."[19] The inclination to freedom, to start with, introduces something new in the discourse about human animality. One might think that Kant would address freedom under the moral predisposition, which he does in the *Groundwork*. The inclination to sex clearly falls under the predisposition to animality as Kant defines it in the *Religion*, however, the inclination to freedom may be treated in the account of the predisposition to animality in so far as it refers to the inclination to "sensuous outer freedom." Freedom for the moral predisposition means inner freedom, not outer freedom. Moral freedom is freedom *from* natural law and freedom *to* legislate one's own actions normatively; sensuous outer freedom refers to freedom *from* the rule of others, freedom from constraint, and freedom *to* make one's own actions the results of one's own maxims. A newborn cries, for example, because "he regards his inability to make use of his limbs as constraint and immediately announces his claim to freedom (an idea that no other animal has)."[20] Although animals don't share the idea of freedom, Kant still calls this a natural inclination to freedom, because it occurs as soon as a baby is born. Culture, or socialization, has no chance to have an input before the inclination to freedom arises. Of course, this is merely speculative, but it is a point to ponder. Why do human babies cry when first born when it could be detrimental to survival?

Kant appeals to other evidence as proof of the inclination to freedom. "The man whose happiness depends on another man's choice (no matter how benevolent the other might be) rightly considers himself unfortunate."[21] If one's options are not at one's disposal a person can lack sensuous outer freedom. If others determine what our options are, we are not free to go and do as our inclinations propose. The fact that this person considers himself unfortunate is dependent on the judgment that freedom consists in having external options at one's disposal. If human beings didn't have an inclination to freedom, then they would not resent someone else making decisions for them.

Kant also appeals to the example of the savage who wants to live as far away from others as possible, in order to enjoy his freedom from submission. Evidently, Kant believes that being in society with other people inevitably involves submitting to someone else's will. That is certainly true if society includes submission to civil constraint. The savage wants to be free of all civil constraint. The next example Kant uses is nomadic people who are "not bound by any land." The fact that they are haughty about their way of life is evidence that they consider their freedom from a piece of land to be far superior to those who are settled on land.[22] This is a type of environmental freedom. The final evidence Kant appeals to is people who are purely hunters and who "ennobled themselves by this feeling of freedom."[23] They, too, are not subjected to a particular piece of land but wander, as they will, in search of prey.

Kant calls all these types of freedom that people desire the "mere sensuous idea of outer freedom."[24] The freedom these examples are referring to is freedom from external constraint, freedom to be the source of one's own decisions, and freedom from environmental constraints. In each case, freedom is freedom from some external source of determination, and is not the same as freedom under moral laws that one gives oneself, a freedom that implies one assents to those moral laws. It is simple to conceive of one still having moral freedom in spite of external constraints. Moral freedom is not a type of freedom that can be taken away; external freedom can be.

The distinction Kant makes in the *Religion* between the *Willkür* and the *Wille* seems to make sense of the distinction between the inclination to sensuous outer freedom and the freedom one achieves in submitting oneself to universally valid laws of one's own assent. *Willkür*, or freedom of choice, appears to be a faculty all human beings have regardless of their submission to moral laws, while the inclination to freedom is also universally shared, even though having the freedom of choice and having an inclination to freedom does not guarantee outer freedom. However, no matter what external conditions are imposed upon one, a human being does have a true sense of freedom under universally valid laws. As Kant puts it in the *Groundwork*, "so the free will and the will subject to moral laws are one and the same."[25] This could mean that one has a free will only in so far as one is subject to moral laws, or it could mean one is free only in so far as one subjects oneself to the moral law. The first alternative means that all human beings are free since all human beings are subject to moral laws. Freedom means that human beings have an option between being motivated by natural inclinations (heteronomous) or being motivated by the moral law (autonomous). The fact that they can operate on a maxim that is consistent with the moral law means they can act differently than they in fact do and even if they choose to be motivated by natural inclinations, they could have acted differently and so are responsible for their actions.

The second alternative implies that only those human beings are free who submit to universally valid moral laws. Allowing oneself to be motivated only by natural inclinations or wants does not insure freedom even if one has options of which inclinations and wants to fulfill, because the origin of those wants and inclinations is not in freely chosen actions. Their origin derives from a heteronomous source and one is hence unfree when motivated by them. One is only truly free when one submits to universally valid laws that derive from one's own reason.

I would suggest that Kant means both of these possibilities. And that means that trying to fulfill the natural inclination to freedom through sensuous outer freedom alone will never give one true freedom. It also means that we are indeed responsible for our actions because we can act differently than we in fact do since we have the option of being motivated by the law itself. A human being can submit to civil laws and still be free in doing so. A man who submits to the civil requirements of marriage in fact does not lose true freedom, though he does indeed lose the outer freedom to give in to his inclinations.

Kant supports his position that we have an inclination to freedom by giving examples that are not really ordinary. Could he make his case with examples from citizens of a civil society? Indeed that is what he does later on in the book in the section "On the Character of the Sexes." A woman, Kant claims, wishes she were a man, so that she "could give her inclinations wider scope and freer play."[26] He adds, "No man would want to be a woman." Clearly in civil society, and this is the context of his assertions, since he is talking about the civil institution of marriage, a man does experience sensuous outer freedom in that he can (to a great extent) do as he is inclined to do (wants to do). Women didn't have that kind of freedom in Kant's time, except for the possibility of gallantry or coquetry where a "woman's desire to play with her charms on every well-bred man" is given expression.[27] "Woman lays claim to freedom over against man" by his leave.[28]

Still, Kant is not consistent on this point, because a few lines later, he says "it is by marriage that woman becomes free; man loses his freedom by it."[29] He means that a woman can give free reign to her coquetry only within the institution of marriage, and she also becomes free of the tutelage of her own father. A man, on the other hand, can give reign to his inclinations in a much more limited way. The woman reigns in the house. A woman should "reign" in a marriage and this means that "inclination reigns" while a husband governs through his understanding outside of the house. A woman presumably is allowed to give play to her inclinations only within the civil institution of marriage, but since man governs, he can easily "violate her right" and hence she "feels compelled to comply with his wishes," by being "obliging and attentive in her treatment of him."[30] If these claims by Kant are true then they certainly do support the claim that human beings have a natural inclination to freedom even in a situation of civil constraint.

Kant's purpose in giving examples of those people outside of or not yet in civil society is actually to establish more than that there is an inclination to freedom, rather that there is also a passion for freedom. A passion is not possible for animals, since it requires reason "which alone establishes the concept of freedom."[31] Only human beings have reason so only they have the possibility of freedom. It is interesting that each example of Kant gives is of a person having a passion for freedom outside of civil society. Could Kant mean that the very act of avoiding civil society is evidence of a passion for freedom that ultimately "misses his final end?"[32] Isn't it the case that for human beings to achieve wisdom, "which admits of no passions at all" one must enter civil society? One must recognize one's interdependence with other human beings? This is what must be concluded from what Kant has to say about the natural predispositions and why they are fulfilled in the species, but not in the individual human being. That fifteen-year-old boy, who can fulfill his sexual inclinations at fifteen, cannot meet the norms of civil society since he does not yet have a job and cannot support his progeny. Let us imagine a young man who does not want to marry and support his children; he is precisely the one who has a passion for freedom. He wants to satisfy his inclinations without taking into consideration the consequences to his progeny.

The other inclination Kant locates under animality is the inclination to sex. Interestingly, Kant does not at all address the inclination to sex following his introduction of it in the *Anthropology*.[33] The topic is touched on however throughout the book, and especially in the section entitled, "The Character of the Sexes." Animals can have a vehement inclination to sexual union but that does not count as passion. The reason why Kant says this is because that in order to have a passion one needs reason and that passions are "concerned directly with ends." Passions unlike inclinations "aspire to the idea of power combined with freedom by which alone ends in general can be attained. Possession of the means to what ever purposes we may choose certainly extends much further than inclination directed to one single inclination and its satisfaction."[34] Animals don't have reason nor ideas of power, which play a role in the establishing of ends. So animals will not have a passion for sexual union. That means alternatively that human beings have the predisposition to animality, they, too, have an inclination to sexual union, but that does not mean they have to have a sexual passion.

In contrast with the inclination to freedom, which seeks to avoid other human beings, the inclination to sex seeks to use another person as a means to one's own enjoyment. Sexual union, as Kant defines it in the *Metaphysics of Morals*, "(*commercium sexuale*) is the reciprocal use that one human being makes of the sexual organs and capacities of another."[35] Such a definition of sexual union already implies that, for human beings, the inclination to sexuality involves the use of reason because the language of ends is being employed. Kant goes on to say that one makes oneself a thing in giving one self up to the other for the purpose of sexual enjoyment.[36] In this sense, Kant means that our bodies and organs become a tool for the other person's ends. This type of talk already tells us that the inclination to sexuality is being taken up into a maxim and presupposes reason. The animal end of sexual union is not accomplished without reason in the human being. Now, one has a choice as to whether the ends of sexual union are defined merely by the inclination or whether they are determined by the principles of reason. Exclusive monogamous marriage is the only form that rescues sexual union from the abyss of exploitation, which in Kant's time always favored the man, and perhaps still does today in the double standard, in spite of the sexual revolution.

Kant holds that even in marriage sexual union reduces both people to means for the other's sexual enjoyment. But what makes the situation morally tolerable is the fact that it is their mutual use and that each makes a claim on the other.[37] Another way of putting this is that in becoming a means to her husband's enjoyment, he allows himself to become a means to her enjoyment, safe in the realization that "acquiring a member of a human being is at the same time acquiring the whole person, since a person is an absolute unity." This mutuality establishes "equality." This equality with another human being is essential to a human being's happiness, and the actualization of the ends of the pragmatic predisposition. When a marriage does not preserve equality, it then becomes a victim of unsociability. In fact, Kant believes that marriage has progressed toward monogamy under the impulse of unsociable-sociability.[38]

In Kant's time, a woman would lose her status if she engaged in a sexual union outside of marriage.[39] But men too were expected to "learn a trade and acquire clientele" before satisfying his sexual inclinations, because he had to "maintain his wife and children."[40] Both sexes were expected to wait until marriage to engage in sexual relations. Human beings are not like animals in this sense. Human beings ought not to fulfill their natural sexual inclinations apart from what reason prescribes as a legitimate context. Is this old-fashioned Victorian values or can Kant persuade us that even today during the sexual revolution that waiting until marriage (a legitimate contractual relationship) is put into place is essential to one's self-respect and respect for the other's humanity? If Kant is right that sexual relationships reduce the two people to means to the other's ends, some intervention from civil society is needed to restore the humanity to each person. In civil society, contractual relations preserve people from being mere means to one another's use. They insure that each person is truly informed and that each person has consented and if there is a failure on the part of the one, the other is compensated. Of course, there will always be exceptions since no one can ever be completely informed, but that is a problem endemic to human life and the risk of false information can only be minimized, not eliminated. Being married can not ensure that one will not become a mere means to another's ends, but it can give the injured party options one would not have had before.

Most of Kant's discussion of the marital life in the *Anthropology* is heavily influenced by the then current stage of marriage among the well to do in his time. But his use of teleology is evident throughout his discussion of marital relations. There is purposiveness latent in the physiological differences between males and females. And because women can achieve their goals (limited though they were in Kant's time) with less force and more grace, Kant holds that they are more artful.[41] The ends of nature are more important to understanding a woman's nature, than the kinds of actions (dominating and pleasing) that a woman engages in.[42] In other words, Kant is well aware that the way women were in his time was due to the situation of male privilege in which women had to define their role as rational beings. As he puts it, there have still been heroic women within their own households, who credibly "maintained a character in keeping within their vocation."[43]

The meaning of a woman's life is neither defined merely in terms of the kinds of actions women engage in, in response to men, nor in their condition of enjoying only the civil right of marriage, but women have the purpose of preserving the species, instilling the "refined feelings that belong to culture," and ruling men within marriage.[44] Kant does not claim that they have to do these things, but he does attribute a higher meaning to a woman's life than just what men arbitrarily want her to be. It is not the case that Kant just sees the purpose of women as having babies and preserving the human species. He believes that because women are weaker (in general) than men that they gain what they want only by developing refined and civilized means. These tactics become a part of civil society and lead to the refinement of civilization. As a result, brutal means become increasingly unacceptable in civil society. In fact, Kant believes that women have already refined marriage to the point where it has become monogamous.[45] For Kant, women are clearly capable of human action and the dignity of being fully human.

This is consistent with how Kant evaluates the meaning of human life in general. The meaning of human life is not just to develop skills, make a lot of money, get ahead in the world, be well liked, but also to develop character, and become worthy of happiness. The arbitrary ends that human beings pursue do not succeed in characterizing the final end of the species. The human being who realizes her talents and skills and places all ends under moral laws does suffice to identify the final purpose of human beings. What some people find problematic is Kant's insinuation that women can't develop character. Indeed, he says that the feminine principle "what the world says is true, and what it does is good" is a principle hard to unite with character. In other words, she is not a good critical thinker, and does not think for herself, which is the first principle of wisdom for developing character. But what Kant doesn't say is that all women have this principle, or even that all women should have this principle. He merely says it is a feminine principle, not a principle that all women have. It may well be that this is a principle that women have, as it says eleven lines later, because of "the relation in which she was placed."[46] Namely, the relation in which women have been placed is one in which she has limited rights and limited opportunities. In such a relation, she might have to adopt that kind of principle to survive. So there is no evidence that Kant thinks women are "naturally" incapable of having character. The socially constructed character of "feminine" may well entail certain maxims and principles that are not conducive to the development of character itself, but that doesn't mean that women are not capable of character.

In the *Religion*, Kant associates the social impulse, which desires community with other human beings, with the predisposition to animality. All social associations, such as society itself and the family, would, then, have to be reckoned to this predisposition. This raises some problems, since these associations also presuppose laws and therefore rationality as well. How can sociability, which requires reason, be dealt with adequately under the predisposition to animality, which requires no reason?[47]

We can resolve this seeming incompatibility if we remember that the social inclination is part of the predisposition to animality, only insofar as these societal associations preserve the individual, contribute to its social well-being, promote the preservation of the species, and promote outer freedom. Society and the institution of marriage will have to be considered as effects of the pragmatic predisposition as well, insofar as these institutions are based on laws, rules, or reason.

Insofar as sociability is for the sake of preserving, propagating, and well-being, then, it is appropriately discussed under this heading. In the *Anthropology*, Kant refers to the inclination to sociability in several different contexts. In the section, On the Character of the Sexes, Kant maintains that nature's foresight provided human beings "with social inclinations to stabilize their sexual union in a domestic union."[48] Nature intends with the inclination to sociability that human beings not only propagate themselves, but that they also preserve themselves. The domestic union is meant to preserve the individual and promote its well-being. Social inclinations, hence, serve the ends of the predisposition to animality.

Kant questions whether human beings are "by nature a sociable animal or a solitary one who shies away from his neighbors?" and comments that they are most probably the latter.[49] This raises the issue of whether the inclination to freedom or the inclination to sociability is stronger in the human being. Kant surmises that the inclination to freedom is stronger. It is the conflict between these two inclinations that makes for the instability of human nature in what some Kantians have called unsociable-sociability. Human beings, as we saw, do want outer freedom, but they also want relationships, and the push and pull of the differing inclinations leads ultimately to a refinement of civil society so that human beings can have freedom within a civil order.

The ends of the predisposition to animality are self-preservation, the preservation of the species, sociability, and "the preservation of the subject's ability to enjoy the pleasures of life, though still on the animal level only."[50] These ends are given by nature, but the means to these ends are to be accomplished by human beings through discipline. The human being is not equipped with instincts that fulfill the purposes of the predispositions automatically as is the case with animals, but rather human beings have to use their reason to work out a plan for themselves. Since human beings come into the world so helpless and undeveloped as babies, they have a tendency to act rashly, and can endanger themselves. They, therefore, need to discipline and restrain their animal impulses. Discipline changes "animal nature into human nature"[51] when it restrains the tendency to disobey rules which we developed in order to insure our self-preservation, social well-being, and preservation of the species.[52]

EVOLUTIONARY THEORY AND ANIMALITY

There are numerous attempts to define human nature, but one of the most current and also most provocative is the evolutionary theorist's attempt to define human nature and morality through evolutionary principles combined with a comparison of human and animal behavior. It is instructive to look at Kant's views on human animality in comparison to these attempts to define humanity. It is essential to the evolutionary position to maintain that there is a continuity between human and animal behavior because human beings evolved from animals. In fact, human behavior is understood on the basis of "survival of the fittest" and how a behavior is adaptive to the environment. Even human moral behavior is scrutinized for its adaptivity. Because it was observed that there is altruism in human behavior and that does not appear on the face of it to be adaptive and survival of the fittest oriented, it caused animal behaviorists to look more closely at animal behavior and discover "reciprocal altruism" and "kin selection" there. This, then, is used to explain human moral behavior.

Kin selection takes the basic drive to pass on one's genes and extends it to those related to oneself genetically, such as nieces and nephews. One will behave altruistically toward those who possess one's genetic potential. This still means that the final goal of human life is to pass on one's genes. Kant would certainly object to that characterization of human nature. This is not where the dignity of human life exists. Evolutionary theorists also theorize that human behavior and animal behavior exhibit "reciprocal altruism," and they believe that this explains why some animals will make sacrifices for others. If animals exhibit it, then it explains why humans exhibit reciprocal altruism. In fact, they go further and assert that all moral behavior at the most is or should be reciprocally altruistic. However, this too would not be acceptable to Kant. His position in ethics is that our moral actions are duty based, and not based on consequences and certainly not based on prudence. He would grant that there is prudent action (reciprocal altruism) in human relations, but prudence does not define morality. For Kant, what differentiates human action from animal behavior is that human beings are capable of acting on the conception of a law, namely, the moral law. That moral law commands even when the consequences are not good, and even when it would be imprudent. Animal behavior exhibits prudence at most, but not true morality. What humans have in morality separates them strictly from animals. They have the possibility of dignity that animals do not. They also have the possibility of losing dignity and orderliness in ways animals cannot.

It is unlikely though that evolutionary theorists, or evolutionary psychologists will admit that there might be human actions or behaviors which radically depart from the ultimate principle that whatever "should be" must be subjected to what will "aid and promote-and not hinder-the evolutionary process."[53] Such a principle would permit using some people to promote other people and would run contrary to Kant's moral law. So how does Kant construe human nature in a way that it does not run contrary to the moral law? Obviously, he cannot claim that human beings are just like animals if in the end we are going to be able to claim that human beings are ends in themselves, and not to be used as mere means to nature's ends, even to the preservation of the human species. He may claim that human beings are subject to nature's providence and laws, but he cannot claim that they are in the long run merely subject to nature's ends.

Kant's unique contribution to the philosophy of human nature lies in granting that part of human reality is animal, and subject to nature's providence and laws, but an even greater part is determined by the faculty of reason and that is where human nature departs from animal nature. Human dignity lies in its capacity for reason and specifically in its capacity to submit itself to universally valid moral laws.

The way that Kant characterizes human nature is in terms of the four natural predispositions [*Naturanlagen*]. He grants that humans are predisposed toward animality, but he also maintains that human beings are predisposed to use their reason and that in strikingly specific ways, namely, toward technical, pragmatic, and moral ends. The very use of ends indicates that for humans reason is already involved with their animality. Where animals have only inclinations to pursue animal ends, human beings use their understanding to pursue their animal ends within the permissible bounds of reason. Human beings are not just interested in the propagation of the human species, but they also must concern themselves with the education of the young. A human being may well choose to not propagate the species and still achieve a fulfilling life. It is not propagation that insures that a human being achieves her final end, but rather in education. As Kant puts it: "A human being can become fully human only through education. He is nothing but what education makes of him."[54] This is a completely contrasting theory of human nature to what evolutionary theories of human nature maintain.

A contemporary Kantian may well have no problem with the idea that human beings evolved from animals, but she would have problems with comparing human beings to animals where this means one understands human behavior based on animal behavior as evolutionary ethicists do. Even if human beings evolved, they now have reason, which must be understood in terms of its own lawfulness. We might put it this way, given neuroscience: the neo-cortex so radically differentiates humans from animals that the distinction is now enough to give rise to a completely new ability with its own rules. Kant held that human beings have a capacity for ideas, and, as he puts it in the *Groundwork*, a capacity for acting on the conception of a law. In the Critique of Teleological Judgment, Kant asserts that human beings are capable of setting ends and taking the appropriate means to achieve those ends. And ultimately they have the capacity to subject themselves to a moral law that derived from their own reason. These ways of formulating reason and what reason is capable of, clearly sets humans apart from animals. Human beings have a dignity that animals do not. Kant's position is clearly a challenge to evolutionary ethicists. The next three predispositions show how reason informs human nature.

THE TECHNICAL PREDISPOSITION

In the technical predisposition, reason is already present. As Kant puts it, even the human hand indicates that human beings are "fit for manipulating things not in one particular way but in anyway whatsoever, and so for using reason."[55] In this description, we have an insipient account of Kant's views on the technical predisposition, which is also the predisposition for skill.[56] Nature has not implanted instincts in human beings in the way it has for animals.[57] Where animals have instincts, human beings must learn to develop the skills they need. Skillfulness [*Geschichtlichkeit*] is not survival specific, but gives human beings the capacity for relating to any ends whatsoever. Skill also presupposes instruction and following rules rather than impulses. The development of skill results in culture, but this continues to be dependent on the discipline of animal impulses.

Animals require no nurture, Kant claims, because nature's plan for them is "to use their powers as soon as they are possessed of them, according to a regular plan—that is, in a way not harmful to them."[58] Human beings do not have instincts to guide them in safety, for instance: human infants cry at birth and this is a behavior, which would immediately endanger most other animal species. Human beings, thus, need to restrain their animal impulses and this occurs through nurture and discipline, which precedes the development of skill and culture. As Kant puts it in the *Education*, "education includes *nurture* of the child and, as it grows, its formation [*Bildung*]. The latter is firstly negative, consisting of discipline . . . secondly, *positive*, consisting of instruction and guidance, and this belongs to culture [*Cultur*]."[59]

Skill is not just the ability to manipulate things physically, but presupposes knowledge of the object. Skill "consists in knowledge and ability [*Können*]."[60] From the pragmatic point of view, skill arises through the development of the natural talents and gifts of nature, and for Kant this development is only possible through knowledge: "Talent, gifts of nature: refers to knowledge."[61] Skill, in contrast to discipline, is not intended to cancel a mode of action already present, but is rather the acquisition of a positive or new talent through knowledge. Discipline also requires knowledge of rules, but its function is primarily negative, not positive.[62]

The development of skills, nevertheless, presupposes the discipline of animal impulses and hence presupposes the development of the predisposition to animality. In the *Education*, Kant lays out the four goals of education, (1) discipline, (2) skill, (3) prudence, and (4) morality.[63] These four ends are possible because we have four natural predispositions and the actualization of each end presupposes the actualization of the ends of the preceding predisposition. This also confirms, by the way, the position that Kant has four natural predispositions in mind in both the *Religion* and the *Anthropology*.

Skill, as the second goal of education, belongs, on the one hand, to the human being's natural perfection in contrast to its moral perfection, since it is the development of the human being's natural talents. Skill belongs to the human being's natural perfection, "insofar as it is capable of enhancement, and this can be of many kinds, such as skill in the arts and sciences, taste, bodily adroitness, and so forth."[64] The development of abilities is essential to skill. The abilities that a child develops must include reading and writing, which are essential to any further development of skill in a specialized area.[65] Abilities do not determine any end, but are adaptable to various ends. With the development of the abilities arises the possibility of the sciences and arts, which do have ends, though arbitrarily determined ends.

All sciences, Kant clarifies

> have a practical part consisting of problems saying that some end is possible for us and of imperatives telling us how it may be attained. These can, therefore, be called in general imperatives of skill. Here there is no question whether the end is reasonable and good, but there is only a question as to what must be done to attain it.[66]

All sciences and arts are the effects of the cultivation of skill.[67] Since skill is what we develop in our institutions of learning, then all theoretical or scholastic knowledge belongs to the technical predisposition. This also includes philosophy in so far as it is theoretical and scholastic, and requires skill for its practice.[68]

Yet, the development of skill, which is included under practical education, in Kant's *Education*, aims also at the development of freedom, since it aims at the capacity for setting ends.[69] It is one way in which we can develop our aptitude for setting ends. Kant claims that practical education, "which has reference to freedom" consists "(1) in the scholastic-mechanical formation with reference to skill, which is thus didactic (Instructor), (2) in the pragmatic formation with reference to prudence (private tutor), (3) in the moral formation with reference to morality."[70] Although Kant includes the development of skill in practical education, it is also possible that skill is merely physical if it is merely based on exercises and discipline[71] and if the student merely follows the lead of another. For this reason, Kant sometimes argues that practical culture is only pragmatic and moral, whereas physical cultivation is about scholastic culture.[72] The reason for this is that "moral culture must be based on maxims, not on discipline. The latter "prevents bad habits, the former forms thinking [*Denkungsart*]."[73] Physical cultivation of skill, then, does not require maxims, but may mean only discipline of animal impulses, while following the rules that others devise. Skill that requires the use of maxims that one thinks out for oneself will belong to the practical cultivation of skill.

The development of skill aims at the development of freedom in so far as skill refers in general to the development of our ability to set and achieve any ends whatsoever. Skill is "dexterity in achieving whatever ends one has chosen."[74] It is the technical use of our reason.[75] In other words, skill contributes to the freedom we have to set arbitrary ends, ends dependent on free choice [*Willkür*]. Kant argues in the Critique of Teleological Judgment that the culture of skill is what nature can do to promote human reason. Nature purposes "man's aptitude in general for setting himself purposes, and for using nature (independently of [the element of] nature in man's determination of purposes) as a means [for achieving them] in conformity with the maxims of his free purposes generally."[76]

Skill is the presupposition for culture, because culture "consists chiefly in the exercise of the mental faculties,"[77] which depends on the cultivation of natural skill.[78] Culture produces in a rational being an aptitude for purposes in generally (hence [in a way that leaves] that being free)."[79] Skill is related to arbitrary purposes. Culture, then, as an effect or phenomenon, belongs to the development of the technical predisposition as its end. It is the end of the technical predisposition for the human species. It is the effect of the technical predisposition, and is therefore also a purpose of nature, since it is the end of this natural predisposition. As a purpose of nature, culture extends beyond particular skills and becomes a determination of human nature. As Kant maintains in the *Anthropology*, human destiny [*Bestimmung*] is to become cultivated, civilized, and moral.[80] Not only can individuals actualize skills because they have reason, but as a member of the entire human species individuals have the opportunity of participating in culture as a phenomenon that relates individuals to the past, present, and future generations of human beings.

Kant maintains the position in the *Anthropology*, that no individual human being can realize the full potential of the natural predispositions. Irrational animals do fulfill completely nature's purpose for them, "but with man, only the species achieves this."[81] The ends of the natural predispositions extend beyond what the individual alone can achieve and this is true of the technical predisposition as well. We have already shown that for the predisposition to animality, the ends of this predisposition are in conflict with the ends of a civil society, so that in the individual the natural purposes are not necessarily fulfilled, or at least challenged, since a young man must learn a skill and acquire a clientele before he can maintain his family in a civil society. The fulfillment of the technical predisposition is similarily challenged. Kant argues that the "drive to acquire scientific knowledge, as a form of culture that ennobles humanity, is completely out of proportion to a man's life span."[82]

Scholars make progress in their fields to the point where they can make an original contribution, but then die and the next scholar must learn anew what the other already knew before more progress can take place. Hence, no individual ever actualizes the technical predisposition perfectly. We can only hope for the perfect actualization in the entire human species.

THE PRAGMATIC PREDISPOSITION TO HUMANITY

The pragmatic predisposition, or the disposition to humanity, extends beyond immediate social relations between human beings, and it requires skills beyond technical or scholastic culture. Where the development of the predisposition to animality depended on discipline, and the development of the technical disposition depended on the culture of skill, the development of the pragmatic predisposition depends on the social civilization of human beings. The pragmatic disposition

> is the human being's predisposition to become civilized by culture, especially the cultivation of social qualities, their natural tendency in social relations to leave the crude state of mere private force and to become well-bred (if not yet moral) being destined for concord.[83]

A number of points here clarify what the pragmatic predisposition prepares human beings for. First, it is about the capacity for becoming civilized, and thus through culture, by which Kant means primarily the arts and sciences. Second, the development of this predisposition is about the cultivation and refinement of social qualities, like eloquence and politeness. Third, there is a natural tendency within us to want to use force to achieve our ends. This predisposition is a natural counter to that crude tendency. We are also inclined to submit to legal authority that mediates conflicting claims to freedom. We submit to a publicly enforced civil constitution because we are naturally inclined to harmony and agreement. Civilization, then, as the end of the pragmatic predisposition comes about in three different ways: (1) through the cultivation of the arts and the sciences, (2) through cultivation and refinement in social life, and (3) through the civil constitution. These three ends have in common that they are all achieved by nature by means of the dynamic of unsociable-sociability. In the following, I will show how Kant uses unsociable-sociability to exhibit how cultivation occurs in the species, in marriage, and in the civil constitution.

Kant's well-known concept of unsociable-sociability can be found in the *Anthropology*, although the formulation of it there needs some completion by reference to other texts. At the same time, Kant gives a unique twist to it that makes the *Anthropology* stand out as having a special formulation of unsociable-sociability. The basic idea of unsociable-sociability is captured well in the following passage:

> The characteristic of his species is this: that nature implanted in it the seeds of *discord*, and willed that man's own reason bring *concord*, or at least a constant approximation to it, out of this. In the *Idea*, this *concord* is the *end*; but in *actuality*, discord is the *means*, in nature's schema, of a supreme and, to us, inscrutible wisdom which uses cultural progress to realize man's perfection, even at the price of much enjoyment of life.[84]

Nature has implanted seeds of discord not in our natural animal inclinations, which are to sociability, preservation and propagation, but rather in our capacity for culture. Culture creates discord, as Kant argues in the Critique of Teleological Judgment, by creating a situation of inequality. The inequality arises out of the disparity in skills that culture promotes and furthers. These skills are possible partly because nature has implanted various talents, which then may be developed into skills. Skill is also possible in part because of reason's capacity for setting ends and arbitrary ones especially.

Culture and the development of skill bring out competition between human beings. This competition makes for a disharmonious social situation as well as antagonism. Human beings, however, long for peace and harmony, and so they have to learn to be civilized in their relationships with one another. Although Kant occasionally calls civilization 'culture', he tends to distinguish the two: culture causes rivalry,[85] civilization brings about harmony. Culture, and its consequence of rivalry and antagonism, is the spur to the development of the pragmatic predisposition, and civilization is the species' end in this predisposition.

In the Critique of Teleological Judgment, the origin of civilization under the banner of unsociable-sociability happens in this way. Two classes emerge in the inequality of the culture of skill and one class oppresses the other while the leisure that results in the higher class also gives rise to a type of oppression, namely, that of insatiability, an inner oppression.[86] Kant proposes that both classes experience an impairment to their freedom and hence submit themselves to the "lawful authority within a whole called civil society."[87] In order to resolve the mutually conflicting freedoms that arise out of the culture of skill, civilization is created through lawful order. Yet this lawful order remains threatened by "ambition, lust for power, and greed," in other words, unbridled human passions.[88] War is then inevitable. Yet even in war nature's purposes are fulfilled in that "war is one more incentive for us to develop to the utmost all the talents that serve culture."[89] Our natural technical predisposition is further developed in the species even though its development conflicts with permanent happiness. Like Jean-Jacques Rousseau, Kant thought that culture led to unhappiness; but unlike Rousseau, Kant did not blame civilization, but rather culture. Civilization, for Kant, is the cure to the conflicts of culture.

There are two ways in which Kant considers civilization to be the cure for the conflicts of culture. We find both answers in the Critique of Teleological Judgment. The first solution is the establishment of a civil constitution because this mediates the conflicts of outer freedom. Yet, Kant maintains that even under a civil constitution, passions and animal tendencies continue to manifest themselves and threaten to dissolve the constitution and its effectiveness. The culture of skill then which gives rise to the civil constitution is not sufficient to prepare human beings for their complete destiny, which also includes their moral destiny. This is why Kant appeals to a second requirement for culture, namely, the culture of discipline. The culture of discipline of our animal inclinations to enjoyment leads us to becoming civilized [*gesittet*] in a second way. And this civilization combats the conflicts of inner freedom. This form of civilization, which is not based on external coercion, but rather on inner discipline combats the tendency to loss of freedom through passions. As was argued above, Kant considers the phenomenon of insatiable inclinations to be a hindrance to freedom.

Another way in which civilization arises is through marriage. I have already mentioned that Kant believes that marriage is evolving under the impulse of unsociability. Women have furthered the development of marriage by being the civilizing impulse in the marriage. Polygamy, for instance, was overcome when men found it too disconcerting to have many women fighting to be the primary woman in the marriage. Women, having less brute strength, use verbal means to effect their will. Marriage may well be progressing even now since women have all the civil rights that men have and bring these into the marriage with them. The clash of egos and the desire for power may well progress marriage to the stage where the partners are less interested in getting something out of the marriage, then they are fearful of inflicting harm on the other due to the conflict of egos.

Marriage is often considered an effect of the pragmatic predisposition, for instance, when it is described as the social relationship between men and women. When Kant asserts that "it is by marriage that woman becomes free: man loses his freedom by it,"[90] he cannot be referring to natural freedom, since this is not something one can gain or lose. The freedom he is referring to here must belong to the pragmatic predisposition or predisposition to humanity. Freedom here does not refer to self-preservation since marriage is obviously helpful for self-preservation: "love aims at the preservation of the individual."[91] Freedom means something more like *power to use other human beings for one's own ends*, which belongs to the pragmatic predisposition. Women gain power over men through marriage, because now they are free to be coquettes and flirt with other men besides their husbands,[92] whereas a man becomes restricted in what he can do when he is married.[93]

The development of skill can be done merely in relation to one's own natural abilities and in disciplining one's animal impulses to laziness. The development of the pragmatic predisposition, however, presupposes social relationships in which human beings compare themselves to one another, in which they judge each other, and in which they must get along with one another. The predisposition to humanity, in the *Religion*, is explained as the possibility of comparing oneself to others in terms of happiness. Only

> in comparison with others does one judge oneself happy or unhappy. Out of this self-love originates the inclination *to gain worth in the opinion of others*, originally, of course, merely *equal worth*; not allowing anyone superiority over oneself, bound up with the constant anxiety that others might be striving for ascendency.[94]

The pragmatic predisposition is developed in the socializing tendencies and inclinations, whereby human beings learn to live with each other in a competitive and unequal social hierarchy. Therefore, for the development of the pragmatic predisposition, prudence [*Klugheit*] is necessary. Prudence "refers to the community wherein we stand with human beings."[95] So where skill was necessary for the development of the technical predisposition, prudence is necessary for the development of the pragmatic predisposition. And where skill is the ability to use our talents for any ends whatsoever, prudence is the ability to use other human beings for our ends of happiness.[96] This does not refer to the immoral use of human beings as mere means, since prudence refers to our ability to be a part of social life and is necessary to social survival and happiness, as well as to our development of the moral predisposition.

All human beings are inherently interested in their own happiness, which is the end of the pragmatic predisposition. Nature gives us this universal end for the pragmatic predisposition, even though she does not seem to help us achieve the end. In contrast to the technical predisposition, nature does not supply us with the means (such as talents) to achieve the end of the pragmatic predisposition, but wants us to determine and develop the means of achieving whatever we decide happiness is. She only supplies feelings which help us judge whether we are happy or not.

Nature does, however, supply the negative conditions from which we will then want to develop the means for achieving our happiness. Not only nature's destructive operations, plagues, hunger, and perils deny the human being immediate access to happiness, but also the inconsistency of our own natural predispositions, as well as the inequality that arises as a result of the development of the natural talents through culture.[97] We are thus driven to the development of prudence which then helps us to achieve at least some degree of happiness. Prudence "is the readiness in the use of means to the universal end of man, namely happiness."[98] Since this happiness is intimately and unavoidably tied up with the opinion of others, we need prudence to know how to get along in society, and how to measure ourselves by the opinion of others. Prudence includes within its range both social taste and tact, which help one to acquire worth in the opinion of others.

Since the pragmatic predisposition is oriented toward happiness, it is also concerned with what makes for happiness. According to Kant, "determination of the end of happiness, and what it consists of, is the first task of prudence, and the means to it the second."[99] What happiness is, however, is impossible to determine for the individual since it is always tied up with the opinion of others, and with the degree of luxury achieved in any particular era. The comfort one requires for individual happiness, and which luxury affords, must always be limited by taste and sociability in order not to offend others and lose worth in their opinion.[100] For this reason, the individual never achieves fully its end of happiness, and the pragmatic predisposition is not fulfilled in its destiny for the individual.

The pragmatic predisposition is the possibility of developing prudence, which Kant in numerous places defines as the ability to use others as means to one's own ends.[101] Of course, he doesn't mean "use others without their consent." Kant clearly distinguishes between the cunning person [*Arglist*] and the prudent person [*Klugheit*].[102] The cunning person uses others without their consent or informed consent, while the prudent person knows how to gain the cooperation of others in her endeavors. Since happiness is the end of the pragmatic predisposition, prudence is the means to happiness. Lasting happiness cannot be achieved through cunning. Kant claims the cunning person will be found out and no one will believe them again. The prudent person would, however, gain the cooperation of others in a way that they would not later regret. As Kant, however, makes clear in his moral writings, prudence must be subordinated to the moral law, if there is a conflict. The person who subordinates her prudent interests to the moral law, would in no way be able to use others without their consent or treat them in a way that did not respect them as ends in themselves.

THE MORAL PREDISPOSITION

There are more difficulties tied up with the moral predisposition or the predisposition to personality, in terms of labeling it a predisposition. On the one hand it "is the susceptibility to respect for the moral law as *of itself a sufficient incentive to the power of choice*."[103] On the other hand, it cannot legitimately be called a predisposition to personality or morality since the idea of the moral law and respect for the moral law is "personality itself."

The problem lies in the fact that the moral law is present in human beings from birth and does not need to be developed out of them. We already see this in children who feel some injustice has been done to them. They do not have to learn what justice is, before they have an idea of it. And we do not learn that we have a free will. As a predisposition, however, we mean that it is possible to develop the qualities in the process of education. The idea of morality and knowledge that we have a free will cannot be passed on through education; it is innate, and valid for all human beings. In the *Anthropology*, Kant explains that

> Man is a being who has the power of practical reason and is conscious that his choice is free (a person); and in his consciousness of freedom and in his feeling (which is called moral feeling) that justice or injustice is done to him or, by him, to others, he sees himself as subject to a law of duty, no matter how obscure his ideas about it may be.[104]

The problem of whether human beings have a natural moral predisposition resolves itself when we see a human being as both a moral being and as a natural being. It is as a natural being that the human being has need of education and development of the moral predisposition. As natural beings we develop a character during our lives, and this character reflects the development of the moral predisposition. That the human being can acquire a character is an effect that presupposes a cause, which we can only call the predisposition to morality. The good character,

> as in general every character of the free power of choice, is something that can only be acquired; yet, for its possibility there must be present in our nature a predisposition onto which nothing evil can be grafted.[105]

Over time the free will acquires a character whether good or bad. It is the very nature of the free will that it can acquire either a good or bad character. Nature does not determine whether it is a good or bad character. Since, however, the moral predisposition is a natural predisposition, nature does have an intention with respect to it, and it must therefore have a natural end, which would bring it in relationship to the other three predispositions, since within an organized being nothing is in vain, and "*everything is a purpose and reciprocally also a means.*"[106]

The question naturally arises here whether the end that nature intends for this predisposition is a good character, or a bad character. Kant deals with this question not only in the *Anthropology*, but also in the *Religion*, when he discusses the predisposition to morality. It is the question whether human beings as a species are innately good or evil, or whether they are equally susceptible to both, according to their education. From extensive experience, we know that the individual is capable of both evil and good. If we are to attribute this to nature, however, we would have to claim, then, that the whole human species' character, that is, its natural destiny, is to be ambivalent and is to be both good and evil. Unfortunately, Kant has sometimes been interpreted to have characterized the human species as ambivalent in its very nature, that is, as being capable of both evil and good.[107]

This is a mistaken terminological characterization of Kant's position. If the human being is, in its very natural destiny, capable of both evil and good equally, then, there is no basis for claiming that good is better than evil, except perhaps on pragmatic grounds, and there is no basis for claiming that the human being should develop a good character. If the human being is by nature ambivalent, there would be no teleological process in which this ambivalence could or should be overcome. Kant would have no basis for claiming that the human species' character consists in its continual progress toward the better.

In fact, he does affirm the eventual progress of the human species. Asserting this belief would be inconsistent with a conviction of the inherent ambivalence of human nature. Kant articulates his faith in the inherent goodness of human nature in both the *Religion* and the *Anthropology*. The goodness does not refer to the nature of the individual, but to the nature of the human species. The character or nature of the human species can only be good, because they have the capability of practical reason and a free will:

> For human beings are the beings who have the power of practical reason and are conscious that their choice is free (a person); and in their consciousness of freedom and in their feeling (which is called moral feeling) that justice or injustice is done to them or, by them to others, they see themselves as subject to a law of duty, no matter how obscure their ideas about it may be. This is in itself the intelligible character of humanity as such, and insofar as they have it human beings are good in their inborn predispositions (good by nature).[108]

Human beings are good by nature, and nature intends that the end of the moral predisposition be a good character. To claim that the human being is "ambivalent" by nature would be to claim that nature intends the human being to develop both evil and good equally. The distinction in Kant that these writers fail to see is that human beings have only a tendency or propensity [Hang] to "actively desire what is unlawful even though they know that it is unlawful."[109]

In other words, as far as we can gather from experience human beings only have a tendency to evil in their sensible character. A tendency, however, cannot possibly have the same status as a natural predisposition. We cannot place a "tendency" on the same level with a predisposition and then claim that the human being has an "ambivalent" character in that it is good by nature, but has a tendency to evil. This would amount to the claim that the tendency should never be eradicated, since it belongs inherently to human nature.

Instead, Kant is very careful in his terminology. The nature of human beings refers to the natural destiny of human beings, and this is always toward the good. All the predispositions are *"to the good* (they demand compliance with it),"[110] and the development of them can only lead to goodness. Nature herself intends that the good be developed out of the human being through education:

> Good education is precisely that from which everything good in the world originates. The germs which lie hidden in the human being need only be more and more developed; for the rudiments of evil are not to be found in the natural predispositions of human beings. Evil is only the result of nature not being brought under rules. In human beings there are only germs of good.[111]

It is the individual human being with a free will, who does not bring itself under rules and laws, which is responsible for the evil in the world. The most that we can say from experience is that there is evil in the world, and that human beings are responsible for it. There is no ground, however, for claiming that evil is original and not to be extirpated. We do not have a natural predisposition to evil, we only have a tendency to evil. The natural predispositions, on the contrary, are original, because "they belong to the possibility of human nature. The human being can indeed use the first two inappropriately, but they cannot eradicate either of the two."[112]

The natural predispositions are necessarily involved in the possibility of human beings, for it is impossible for human beings to exist without them. Evil, on the other hand, can be extirpated and is, therefore, only a contingent tendency.

The natural end of the predisposition to morality is then the development of a good character. Nature intends this by giving us the predisposition to morality. Like all other predispositions, it does not develop by itself, but must be developed and drawn out of the human being by education. We cannot educate the human being to have a free will, since this it has by nature, but we can educate the human being to use its free will to develop a good character. For the development of good character nature has also prepared the way, through the natural talents, temperament, and dispositions. In a reflection from the 1780s, Kant clarifies the relationship between what nature provides and what human beings have to accomplish:

> Talent, natural gifts: refers to knowledge, determines the price of the market, is capable of being cultivated. Temperament. Disposition: refers to feeling, provides the price of affection, is capable of being civilized (polished). Character, way of thinking: refers to the will, gives inner worth, is capable of moralizing.[113]

Nature supplies natural talents, temperament, and dispositions, the development of which are all necessary to the development of the moral predisposition, but has left it to human beings to develop them through education. Character, since it refers to the will, cannot be developed by itself, without its relationship to the other three predispositions. It is our capability of setting ends taken purely intellectually, and is therefore a way of thinking. Character manifests itself in the way that we relate to the other three predispositions, and in the way in which we have developed them. Character arises in how we relate morally to our natural destiny. Good character forms from a lawful development of the three other predispositions, bad character in a lawless development of the predispositions.

Like all other predispositions, it is necessary to develop the means toward the natural end of the moral predisposition which is good character. Where the means toward the development of the predisposition to animality are discipline, the means toward the technical predisposition skill, and toward humanity prudence, the means toward the development of good character and the moral predisposition lies in the acquiring of wisdom. Wisdom is not knowledge in the strict sense, since it *relates all knowledge to essential ends*, but since it is a way of thinking it has affinity to knowledge. Wisdom is also not prudence, but bears an affinity to prudence since it concerns the way in which one makes use of the other predispositions for the sake of life. Where prudence brings the predisposition to animality and the technical predisposition in essential relationship to one another by relating social well-being to the skill that one has developed, wisdom brings even the pragmatic predisposition into relationship with the *final ends* of human life:

> Skill consists in knowledge and ability. Prudence in the way [in which one] brings skill to bear on the human being. Wisdom [consists] in the final purpose, to which all prudence in the end amounts.[114]

Wisdom functions as a limit to prudence, which would normally consider only the advantage of any action for the sake of the individual. Wisdom relates the individual not just to society as prudence does, but to the whole destiny of the human species. Where prudence leads us to seek our well-being within society, teaches us how to make money by prudent use of our skill, and how to achieve the good opinion of others by prudent and tasteful behavior, which are the means to our well-being in society, wisdom leads us to disdain pragmatic advantage which considers only the welfare of the individual in society: "Prudence: to make money. Wisdom: to disdain it (^{S} to rule oneself). Prudence: to attain to honor. Wisdom: to disdain it."[115] Kant writes that in the final period of life, after the development of skill and prudence, human beings use their reason only negatively "to see into the follies of the first two periods."[116]

Prudence leads one to seek happiness and this might be either through making money or through honor and recognition of one's worth in the eyes of others. Wisdom sees that happiness cannot be secured through money and honor. Kant believes that "our species seems to fare no better in achieving its destiny with respect to happiness, which man's nature constantly impels him to strive for, while reason imposes the limiting condition of worthiness to be happy."[117] Not only are natural predispositions conflicted,[118] but happiness, as Kant argues in the *Groundwork to the Metaphysics of Morals*, admits of no determinate object. Neither can happiness be secured through culture. Kant agrees with Rousseau that culture has contributed to the overall unhappiness of people.[119]

Wisdom, for Kant, knows the limits of skill and prudence, and in seeing the limits, it also knows the purposes skill and prudence serve. Skill serves to further the technical predisposition through culture, while prudence serves to further the pragmatic predisposition through civilization. Although skills may be achieved which contribute to the science, the skills die with the person, so there is no perfection of skill in the individual; there is only a contribution to culture. Happiness may well be unachievable, as an end for the pragmatic predisposition, but civilization, tact, congenial behavior may well be achievable for the pragmatic predisposition.

In the *Anthropology*, after he lays out the three predispositions (technical, pragmatic, and moral), Kant discusses the obstacles and difficulties involved in educating human beings to the good in paragraphs A, B, and C.[120] Wisdom consists in recognizing these difficulties and limitations and coming to realize that the fulfillment of the natural predispositions does not occur in the individual, but at most in the species.[121] The predisposition to animality is frustrated in the life of an individual as Kant puts it because "even if, as a citizen of the world, a young man is able soon enough to satisfy his own inclination and his wife's, it is only much later that, as a citizen of a state, he can maintain his wife and children."[122] As a natural being he is able to fulfill the end of propagation of the species, but he is not able to contribute to the preservation of the species without becoming a civilized being. Hence, the ends of the predisposition to animality are frustrated until the pragmatic predisposition is developed enough for him to participate in society as a worker.

The technical predisposition is at most fulfilled in the species, because skilled individuals progress a science only in the time they are living, and when they die, the knowledge dies with them. Younger scholars must learn what older scholars already have known, and this pattern is repeated each generation, with the new generation learning anew in order to keep the science progressing.[123] It is then only in the whole species that the fulfillment of the technical predisposition is realized. The pragmatic predisposition's natural end of happiness is also frustrated in the individual, since happiness, as has been pointed out, is impossible to achieve in the life of the individual. It is for that reason, that the most the individual can hope for is that they become more civilized in the development of a civil constitution. Yet even the civil constitution remains threatened by the predisposition to animality, which "manifests itself earlier and, at bottom, more powerfully than pure humanity."[124] Wisdom recognizes that none of the natural predispositions can be adequately fulfilled in the life of the individual, and for that reason, there can be only hope of progress over innumerable generations.

Finally, wisdom recognizes that the progress one hopes for cannot be "attained by the free accord of individuals," but by the wisdom of providence which brings about "a progressive organization of citizens of the Earth into and towards the species, as a system held together by cosmopolitan bonds."[125] Such wisdom is an "idea of his own reason."[126] In other words, the wisdom that one gains through the experience of having one's ends frustrated is the wisdom that comes from reason. It is the realization that pursuing natural ends, animal, technical, and pragmatic do not completely lead one to one's destiny, because there is still the moral predisposition which must be fulfilled in order for human beings to actualize their complete determination [*Bestimmung*].

EDUCATION AND THE PREDISPOSITIONS

As we saw in the first chapter, through his lectures on anthropology and physical geography, Kant was interested in the whole education of his students and not just in their technical competence in philosophy. He wanted them to be able to apply the skill and technical knowledge they learned at the university to their lives. For this a pragmatic knowledge of the world was necessary.

The *Pragmatic Anthropology* is not just concerned with the development of the pragmatic predisposition and therefore also prudence, but also with the development of the moral predisposition and wisdom. Only wisdom relates the individual to its whole destiny. This concern for the whole destiny and the complete development of the predispositions is shown systematically in Kant's *Lectures on Education*. There the human being is presented as that living being which has to be educated to its destiny. A discussion of the *Education* will help illuminate more clearly the educational intent in the *Pragmatic Anthropology*.

For Kant a true idea of education is that one in which the end is the development of all the natural predispositions of human beings.[127] The talents and abilities of human beings are like germs that need to be developed out of them: "It is for us to make these germs grow into humanity, by developing the natural predispositions in their due proportion, and to see that human beings reach their destiny."[128]

The overall end of education is not just that human beings develop their skills, talents, and abilities, but that they also develop their predispositions, and these in "due proportion". Only through this can human beings "grow into humanity," which is the development of the natural predispositions in their "due proportion." "Humanity" here cannot be referring to the development simply of the pragmatic predisposition, although Kant does use "humanity" with respect to this predisposition. Rather, "humanity" here refers to the ideal of humanity. What is important to realize is that the ideal of humanity is realized in the proportional development of the natural predispositions. The underdevelopment or overdevelopment of any one of the predispositions will result in falling short of the final end of education, which is the realization of the ideal of humanity.

In contrast to animals, human beings can only attain their destiny [*Bestimmung*] through education, which is the development of the predispositions. In order to attain this human beings not only have to strive for it, but they also need an idea of the purpose of their lives. Animals accomplish their destiny unconsciously, but human beings have to have a conception of their destiny.[129]

It would certainly be possible to develop a predisposition without some conception of the final end of all the predispositions taken together, but it would be impossible for the human species to reach its final destiny without a conception of the relationship between all the predispositions, and without then striving to develop all of them in "due proportion." Without an *ideal of humanity*, educators would have no measurement of the effectiveness or trueness of their educational schemes. The human being can be educated in many ways, but if it is to be true to the whole human destiny, then, according to Kant, the educator must have an ideal of humanity toward which the education is aimed.

The two elements which are necessary to this ideal are the "Idea of Humanity," and a conception of the whole natural destiny of human beings, which would be the four natural predispositions:

> One principle of education which those people especially who
> form educational schemes should keep before their eyes is this—
> children ought to be educated . . . in a manner which is adapted to
> the idea of humanity and the whole destiny of human beings.[130]

Education should be adapted to accommodate these two separate elements,
for these two elements taken together within a scheme of education give the
rule and the ideal end that can be ever more approximated.

Here Kant speaks of the "idea of humanity" but that this should not be
confused with the ideal of humanity is clear from a passage in the *Critique of
Pure Reason* where he distinguishes between an "idea of humanity" and the
"ideal of humanity":

> Without soaring so high, we are yet bound to confess that human
> reason contains not only ideas, but ideals also, which although
> they do not have, like the Platonic ideas, creative power, yet have
> *practical* power (as regulative principles), and form the basis of the
> possible perfection of certain *actions*. . . . As the idea gives the *rule*,
> so the ideal in such a case serves as the archetype for the complete
> determination of the copy; and we have no other standard for our
> actions than the conduct of this divine human being within us,
> with which we compare and judge ourselves, and so reform ourselves,
> although we can never attain to the perfection thereby prescribed.[131]

The idea of humanity gives the rule by which our actions should be
judged, as being either moral or immoral. The ideal of humanity, however,
serves as an archetype of perfection, like the ideal of a wise human being.
The ideal is something that we want to attain to, and gives us a source of
measurement for how far we are from that ideal, so that we can attempt to
improve ourselves or "reform ourselves". Though Kant sometimes speaks of
an idea as though it were an ideal,[132] he is mostly consistent in his use of
the idea of humanity in relationship to morality, as the rule for judging our
actions; it is not something one can "grow into," for it is rule, not an ideal.
An ideal is a regulative principle, and has, therefore, practical power for the
regulative judgment.

For any educational scheme the educator needs not only the idea of
humanity, but also a understanding of the whole destiny of human beings,
which is an understanding of the natural predispositions of the human
species. Without an understanding of the natural predispositions, the ideal of
humanity would be incomplete, for we would have no idea of how we could
improve ourselves in an attempt to attain this ideal.

Kant, thus, lays out the four ends of education, which are based on the
supposition of the four natural and original predispositions of human nature,
and which are based on the teleological presupposition that their natural

ends are good ends, and, therefore, worthy as ends for education. A true edu-cation should supply a human being with discipline, culture, prudence, and moral training,[133] all of which are the natural ends of the four predispositions: the predisposition to animality, the technical predisposition, the pragmatic predisposition, and the moral predisposition.

The first end of education is discipline, in which the influence of our animal nature is restrained "from getting the better of our humanity."[134] The influence of our animal nature is the tendency to act without rules. Discipline then is negative and checks wildness or unruliness. Nurture and caretaking also belong to discipline, as the child must learn to take care of his physical nature in a disciplined and lawful manner.[135] Whereas animals have instincts that preserve them in their physical nature, the human being has to learn to distinguish what preserves it in its physical nature from that which harms it.

The second end of education, which can only be built upon the first end, is culture. Culture and the development of abilities are accomplished through information and instruction to scholastic culture. The abilities that are developed can then be used for various ends. With reading and writing, for instance, one is prepared for many different occupations. This goal is a positive one since it deals with the passing on of information, and the creation of a skill that was not there before.

The third end of education, which depends on the accomplishment of the first two steps, is to supply the person with prudence, "so that it may be able to conduct itself in society, that it may be liked, and that it may gain influ-ence."[136] The skills one has developed are to be brought to bear in relationship to other people. Here it is no longer a question of competent use of skill, but of applying that skill in one's own best interests, in relationship to other people. We need refined manners and courtesy in order to use other human beings for our own ends. If we are not gentle and gracious, our desires will only meet with resistance. Outward decorum and civilized behavior win us the approval and honor of other people, which contributes to our happiness.

The final end of education is the "training of moral character." Where the development of our skills is important to being adaptable to any end what-soever, training is needed so that one will choose only good ends, "those which are necessarily approved by everyone, and which may at the same time be the aim of everyone."[137] The true difficulties of education arise here in that one must encourage and not discourage the development of the free use of reason in the child or the individual, while constraining the negative inclinations that would develop into passions if left undirected. One develops moral character by learning to rule the passions when one has them already. More important, however, is taking care that "our desires and inclinations do not become passions, by learning to go without those things that are denied to us."[138]

Kant distinguishes between the development of "physical culture" and of "practical culture" in the *Education*. Any one of the three top predispositions can be developed in the direction of physical culture or toward practical culture. The ends, however, for the two are different; physical culture aims at nature, whereas practical culture aims at morality and freedom.[139] The development of physical culture depends on discipline and is, therefore, passive for the child.[140] The development of moral culture requires the use of maxims, and an appeal to the child's reason.

Physical culture is necessary as the basis of moral culture, but moral culture is the final end of education. Moral character is the final end of education, and therefore all the other predispositions have to be developed with that in mind.[141] For the formation of skill, more is necessary than just instruction, for it requires as well a development of the ability to work thoroughly according to rules. The formation of prudence must also be regulated by rules and maxims. Decorum is an art guided by rules of prudence. Learning to hide one's own feelings, while reading the character of others, requires rules, which tell us how much we can show, and how much we should conceal.[142] Moral character, as a final end, can only be developed in the formation of the habitual use of rules and maxims with respect to all the predispositions, for only in this way is practical reason strengthened in its use.

In order to develop the predispositions with regard to the final end of education, it is necessary to have an idea of humanity as a law-giving being. In order to develop the predispositions in their "due proportion," it is necessary to have a conception of the whole destiny of human beings as a species. That is, one must have a conception of the whole complex of natural predispositions with regard to their ends. For a child, both physical and moral culture must be the ends of the whole process of education. The child must be subjected to discipline and also led to see the necessity of rules. For the students, who took part in Kant's lectures on anthropology, discipline and physical culture were not the goals. The purpose of his lectures, in terms of educating them to their whole destiny, had to do with practical culture, both pragmatic and moral.[143]

The *Pragmatic Anthropology* deals not only with the development of the predispositions in the individual, but also within the species. In the anthropology lectures, Kant wanted to show his students the plan of nature for the whole human species, and therefore their role in the whole destiny of the human species.[144] Kant's doctrine of human nature in the species is not meant to be a constitutive account of human nature, but belongs rather to a practical account whose end is the education of individual human beings to their practical destiny through the acquisition of pragmatic knowledge of the world and wisdom.

That Kant was interested in the practical education of individual human beings is clear from this passage in the *Anthropology*:

> As far as *skill* is concerned (dexterity in achieving whatever ends they have chosen), human beings reach the full of their reason around the age of twenty, in *prudence* (using other human beings for their purposes), around forty; and, finally, in wisdom, around sixty. In this final period, however, they use their reason in a primarily *negative* way, to see into all the follies of the first two periods.[145]

Kant saw the lack of wisdom and prudence in his students in that they tended to be egoistic cyclops with respect to their skills in academic subjects.[146] They were incapable of applying that knowledge to life, or to their social relationships. What they lacked was pragmatic knowledge of the world, that is, pragmatic knowledge of the world of social realities, where human beings mutually use each other. And they lacked wisdom into the final ends of human life. With our account of the four predispositions, we can now see that his students were developing their technical skills without consideration of how to apply them to human beings, and without consideration for the final end of human life.

For Kant, two elements were important to the formation of character and wisdom in his students. One, they needed to see the plan of nature working to develop humanity in the human species even apart from their active participation and agreement with that plan. This supplies the subjection to a kind of necessity, which is important for the development of character. Through this necessity they could see themselves as part of the human species all of whom, without exception, are subject to nature's plan.[147] When the inclination to freedom is not subjected to any necessity, it becomes purely egoistic, and a passion.[148] The human free will is subjected not only to the limitations of the natural predispositions, but also to the plan of nature for the development of the predispositions. This necessity is, however, not constitutive for the will and does not determine the will, but is rather regulative for the will and affects it only in the practical determination of good and bad ends. This necessity is projected from reason itself.[149]

On the other hand, since the good will is the final end of education, human beings have to learn rules and maxims in everything, especially with respect to the development of the four predispositions.[150] We have to develop the habit of acting according to rules in all our actions, but this we do only if we believe all people to be subjected to the same necessity with respect to the plan of nature. The *Anthropology* deals not only with the plan of nature, but also with the rules that are necessary for developing the predispositions toward the practical end of moral character and wisdom. It is then important to show how Kant justifies talk of the plan of nature, and why for teleological judgment the first three predispositions cannot be considered either the final end of education for the individual or the final end of education for the human species. The plan of nature and its accompanying necessity is critically justified in the Methodology section of Kant's Critique of Teleological Judgment.

The methodology of teleological judgment argues the relationship of all ends to final ends. This is essential to pragmatic anthropology since all the natural predispositions are to be developed toward morality. That one predisposition can take precedence over the other predispositions is not a doctrine which follows naturally from the argument Kant developed in the analytic of teleological judgment. Nature in its inner purposiveness does not require a final purpose apart from the living organism. It is only when we think through extrinsic purposiveness that we require a final end for the process of human development and education, and, therefore, one of the predispositions has to function as that end.

KANT'S THEORY OF EDUCATION AND BEHAVIORISM

It is clear that if Behaviorism aims at controlling behavior through external sources of reinforcement and punishment, it is a theory that runs contrary to Kant's theory of human nature and what he considers to be the appropriate method for educating human beings morally. Kant holds that self-consciousness differentiates human beings from animals and is hence the source of human dignity. Human beings have a free will and are not determined by sensuously determined inclinations. His pedagogy would require that one address the consciousness of the human being. Children should be educated to know the difference between right and wrong, rather than have their behavior modified by external sources of punishment or reward. On Kant's theory children should be taught to exercise their free will by giving them options to choose from while encouraging the choice of the right option. This education would precede the behavior and would hopefully lead to the behavior never occurring, whereas on Behaviorism, one has to wait until a behavior occurs before responding to it. Clearly, here, too, is where Kant's theory of human nature would come in conflict with other theories of human nature.

CHAPTER FIVE

The Critical Foundations of the Anthropology

TELEOLOGY AS A RESEARCH PROGRAM

The Critique of Teleological Judgment establishes that there are two fundamental research programs, which are grounded in two very different "maxims."
The first maxim establishes mechanistic science: "All production of material
things and their forms must be judged to be possible in terms of merely
mechanical laws." The second maxim establishes teleological judgment and
science: "Some products of material nature cannot be judged to be possible in
terms of merely mechanical laws. (Judging them requires a quite different
causal law—namely, that of final causes)."[1] The foundation of these research
programs lies in the kind of causality they assume as relevant. For Kant there
are two types of causality: efficient (*nexus effectivus*) and final (*nexus finalism*).[2]
Mechanistic science looks for efficient causes, whereas teleological science
looks for final causes. Mechanistic science makes determinate judgments,
whereas teleological science makes reflective judgments.[3] Determinative
judgments are constitutive of objects, but reflective judgments are contingent
"in terms of all concepts of the understanding" and regulative.[4] Both sciences
are necessary for making judgments about nature and investigating nature.[5]
Mechanistic science reveals nature in terms of necessary laws and teleological
judgment reveals nature in terms of its purposiveness in organisms. The
research program that employs teleological judgment also involves a priori
principles as guiding threads for the investigation of organic nature. Biology,
Genetics, and Neuroscience all undertake the understanding of living organisms and in order to do so must make use of certain metaphysical principles
even if they do so unconsciously.[6] The a priori teleological principles that
"nature does nothing in vain" or that "nature makes no leap in the diversity of
its forms" or that "nature is rich in species and yet parsimonious in genera,"[7]
are presupposed in many investigations we make in nature.[8] Kant assumes the
a priori principle that 'nature does nothing in vain' in his *Anthropology* when
he identifies the purposes of our powers and characteristics, assumes that
nature has ends for our powers, and when he argues that attributes we consider useless are actually useful for promoting natural and human ends. In this
he is investigating human nature with the maxim of teleological judgment.

When we assume the a priori principle that "nature does nothing in vain," we are encouraged to keep looking and investigating until we find a purpose for an organ, a gene, a neuron, a molecule, or some other element we find in a living being. Anthropology and paleontology also assume such a principle as they investigate the purposiveness of the organs and faculties of both the individual organism and also elements of society. Looking and observing in terms of purposes is a kind of reflective judgment that establishes a research program. Modern medical science would be impossible if it did not make some kind of judgment about the purposes of organs in human beings and in animals. It judges, for instance, that the eye's purpose is to see. When we medically treat the eye, it is the function of medicine to bring the eye back to its purposiveness, in other words, to heal it so that it can be purposive for seeing.⁹ The judgment that eyes are purposive for seeing is a judgment that functions as a normative rule for medicine. Modern medicine assumes that being healthy and capable is better than being sick and incapacitated. As Kant puts it in the First Introduction of the Critique of Judgment, "a teleological judgment compares [two] concept[s] of a natural product; it compares what [the product] is with what it is [meant] to be."¹⁰ Kant goes on to argue that this principle of "what it should be" is a priori and is not derived out of experience. It is a teleological judgment, not a mere empirical observation. Judgment presupposes that there are purposes for natural beings and their parts and those purposes are normative for evaluating the condition of the parts. This judgment cannot be proven from experience alone, though it could also not be made without experience. Kant explains that we experience directly the capacity of the eye that "our eyes allow us to see." We also "experience directly their outer and their inner structure, which contain the conditions that make it possible to use them in this way. So we experience directly the causality [our eyes involve] in terms of mechanical laws."¹¹ However, there are many different conditions an eye can be in, so which is the right condition? It is not even just the statistically right one. The "is-to-be" or the "meant to" contains necessity that a "being be built a certain way, namely, in terms of a concept which precedes [the action of] the causes that build this organ."¹²

That Kant is using this principle in his *Anthropology* is clear in that he assumes the purpose of the various cognitive faculties, the purpose of sexual differentiation, the purpose of various national differences, the purposiveness of the natural predispositions, and so forth. He says anthropology is not just mere observation, but it is also about rules. As Kant writes in a reflection from the 1770s, "the latter [i.e., pragmatic anthropology] examines what a human being is only far enough to draw out rules concerning what he can make of himself or how he can make use of others. [It is] not psychology, which is a scholastic discipline."[13] In another reflection, Kant writes "(§ Observation and reflection; the latter: in order to find the rules.)"[14] The Friedlander manuscript has it this way: "to observe the human being, and his behavior, to bring his phenomena under rules, is the purpose of anthropology."[15] The rules that I think Kant is talking about are the judgments of purposes of the various faculties and characteristics that human beings have in addition to the rules of prudence which concern how to use others. The normative conditions or perfections of the parts of human nature establish rules for evaluating the aspects of human nature. Hence, anthropology is not merely an empirical science as psychology is; it is rather based in the critically grounded faculty of reflective teleological judgment. That is why it is misleading of scholars to refer to Kant's work in anthropology as merely empirical.[16] It hides from us the normative character of the judgments that Kant is making throughout the *Anthropology*. Kant is indeed attempting to do "science" in the *Anthropology*, because he is engaged in a research program of investigating the human faculties and characteristics in terms of their purposiveness. Much of his discussions revolve around how certain uses of our faculties interfere with the proper purpose of them.

Yet, this science is not based in constitutive judgments and hence Kant remarks that it has a hard time becoming a science.[17] It is certainly debatable whether the purpose of the cognitive faculty is acquisition of knowledge or orientation to the world. It is certainly debatable whether imagination interferes with our cognitive faculty and in what ways it does. But that our cognitive faculties have purposes is presupposed by Kant and by anyone who engages in the research program of reflective teleological judgment. Yet these normative judgments of purpose are not merely hypothetical as psychological explanations are such that for "any three different bases explaining [a mental event] we can easily think up a fourth that is equally plausible."[18] Judgments of purpose have necessity and are not hypothetical. When we judge then that the eye is meant for seeing, it is based on direct experience and also on an idea of reason, since "when the special presentation of a whole precedes the possibility of the parts, then it is a mere idea; and when this idea is regarded as the basis of the causality, it is called a purpose."[19] Kant explains further what a natural purpose is: "for a thing to be a natural purpose, in the first place it is requisite that its parts (as regards their presence and their form) are only possible through reference to the whole. For the thing itself is a purpose, and so is comprehended under a concept or an idea."[20] This idea of purpose then is used to systematize and evaluate the parts of the being, whether that is the inner structure of a plant or animal or an organ. Kant calls it a "regulative concept for reflective judgment."[21] It serves as a guiding rule for our judgment. For example, Kant writes:

If we say that the crystal lens in the eye has light rays [the result] that the light rays emanating from one point will be reunited in one point on the retina of the eye, all we are saying is that our thought of the causality nature [exercised] in producing an eye includes the thought of the presentation of a purpose, because such an idea serves us as a principle by which we can guide our investigation of the eye as far as its lens is concerned, and also because thinking the presentation of a purpose here might [help] us devise means to further that effect [if the natural lens does not do so adequately].[22]

Unlike psychology as well, judgments of purpose allow us to judge in a systematic way instead of merely enumerating an aggregate of experience. Once we determine the final purpose of human life, we can create a system of purposes and that makes it easier to judge the particular purposes of our faculties and natural predispositions.[23] Kant makes this argument in the Critique of Teleological Judgment. The following section will articulate his position on teleological judgment and organisms.

THE CRITICAL FACULTY OF TELEOLOGICAL JUDGMENT

To begin with, Kant argues, we find organisms in nature that require a judgment in terms of purposes, namely, plants and animals.[24] The principle that defines an "organized product of nature is one in which everything is a purpose and reciprocally a means."[25] Kant applies the a priori principle [that nature does nothing in vain] to the organized being and asserts that "in such a product nothing is gratuitous, purposeless, or to be attributed to blind natural mechanism." Kant contrasts organic beings and things in order to bring out for our judgment the difference between final causality and efficient causality and how the uniqueness of organic beings requires a different principle of judgment. Things, whether objects of nature or objects of human design and art, do not have the kind of intrinsic purposiveness that organic beings have. Organic beings have parts that serve as means and ends to each other. The parts are also means to the whole being's ends. We require teleological judgment of purposiveness to properly make sense of and judge organic beings. Unlike organic beings, objects and works of human art do not have parts that are means and ends to each other. The organic being produces itself, maintains itself and reproduces itself.[26] If a part malfunctions other parts of the being make up for it. If a part of the watch malfunctions, it ceases to work. Its parts are efficient causes of the movement of other parts but they are not productive of other parts. The parts of the organic being produce other parts. Hence, the organic being can be judged in terms of purposiveness. It can also be judged mechanically in terms of efficient causes, but Kant claims that we cannot grasp the organic being systematically if we don't judge it in terms of purposes.[27]

Not only does the organic being admit of being judged purposively in terms of its inner parts, but it also admits of being judged purposively extrinsically. Kant clarifies that by "extrinsic purposiveness I mean a purposiveness where one thing of nature serves another as a means to a purpose."[28] Organic beings are beings for which other beings and things can be purposive. Organic beings use other things and beings as means to their own ends. As Kant writes, the sandy soil "enabled extensive spruce forests to establish themselves."[29] Hence, the soil is purposive for the trees. However, we would not judge the trees to be purposive for the soil. It is always in terms of organic beings that we speak of habitats, the organization in the ecosystem that is purposive for the organic being. The habitat exists for the sake of the organic being not in an absolute way, but in a contingent way, that makes sense when we look at the purposes of the organic being, namely, its survival. The habitat is not objectively purposive, but for our judgment it is subjectively purposive. Extrinsic purposiveness is about how organic beings serve as means to other organic beings and as ends for other things and beings. This kind of purposiveness is merely relative since there is no objective purposiveness in nature.[30] For instance, an ecosystem is purposive for human beings, but there is nothing about an ecosystem that requires a human being. Horses are purposive for human beings but there is nothing objectively about a horse that requires a human being. Nonetheless, it is obvious that we make judgments like the following: the grass is purposive for horses and a means to their preservation. It is not objectively the purpose of grass to serve as food for horses, but nonetheless, it can and does provide horses with sustenance. Organic beings are those beings for which other things can be purposive extrinsically.

Now since Kant has discovered systematic purposiveness within an organic being such that the parts of the being are purposive for the whole of the being, it stands to reason that within the extrinsic purposiveness of nature there is also a whole for the sake of which the parts of nature exist. If we find a system in organic beings, there might well be a system in the whole of nature. Kant raises the question in the "Idea for a Universal History with a Cosmopolitan Intent," whether it would be "truly rational to assume that nature is purposive in its parts but purposeless as a whole."[31] In several places in the Critique of Teleological Judgment, Kant argues: "this concept of a natural purpose leads us necessarily to the idea of all of nature as a system in terms of the rule of purposiveness."[32] He says the concept of final causes entitles us to go further and use our supersensible principle (nature does nothing in vain) to conceive of all of nature as purposive under the rule of purposes.[33] Still, that nature is a system of purposes may of course be wrong, but it is again a principle for investigation. We won't find a system in nature unless we look for one. However, we could go through all of nature and never find a being that is the final end of nature since that being is also a means to other beings' ends. Even the human being is a means for other organic beings' ends, namely, viruses and bacteria to be sure. Yet, Kant believes that there is something in a human being that is a final end for which nothing else would be a means and that is the human being under moral laws.[34] There is nothing in nature that requires human beings to be subject to moral laws. It is true that for some people ethics is perceived to be useful for human society and establishing social relations between people, but that is not how Kant characterizes morality. The moral law is not meant to fulfill natural inclinations, sometimes it requires us to act against what we perceive to be our happiness, and it might even lead some human beings to act contrary to social impulses and inclinations. So morality is good for nothing and is hence a final end, not a proximate end. It is that for which reason exists. We come to this conclusion not because we are human beings and we are partial to ourselves, but because it is the logical conclusion of our teleological principle that nature does nothing in vain. Kant makes the theoretical point that without "human beings [as under moral laws] the whole creation would be a mere wasteland, gratuitous, and without a final purpose."[35] This is not just an argument meant to appeal to our sympathies, but rather it is the strict consequence of the teleological principle that nature does nothing in vain. All nature would be in vain without human beings under moral laws, or some other final end.

What we gain from identifying a final end is the possibility of defining a system of nature. When we understand human nature in terms of its four natural predispositions, we now know that the moral predisposition is not just one of the four, it is the final end for which the others exist. We can also judge the purposiveness of the faculties and characteristics of people with regard to their role in the realization of the natural predispositions and especially in terms of the actualization of the moral predisposition. We can now perceive a chain of mutually subordinated purposes.[36] This is where the system of the *Anthropology* lies: in judgments regarding the purpose of our faculties from the perspective that the final end of human life is for human beings to realize their predisposition for morality. According to the student notes in the Parow manuscript, Kant says, "we thus ask only about how the human being uses his powers and faculties, to which final end he applies them."[37] Reason is the source of morality so it is no wonder that Kant spends a lot of time in the *Anthropology* insuring that reason remains healthy and effective in our lives. In what follows, I will point to passages and statements in the

Anthropology and in the lecture notes that will show that Kant is using teleological judgment and is at pains to show that reason has the capacity to be the source of morality in that it is free.

Reason is not only the source of morality, but it is also the source of ideas. Thus, ideas should also be under our control if reason is to be free. Ideas can be voluntary or involuntary. That ideas are voluntary is evident in our "ability to abstract from an idea . . . for it demonstrates a freedom of the power of judgment and autonomy of mind, by which the state of its ideas is under its control (*animus sui compos*)."[38] We can have our power of attention in our control and instead of attending to a wart on the face or a missing tooth, we can "direct our eyes" elsewhere. However, Kant warns against "spying out the involuntary course of our thoughts and feelings" in order to record our interior history.[39] The natural order of our cognitive powers, where principles of thinking come first, is preserved when we observe the acts of our representative power, but it is reversed when we "eavesdrop on ourselves when [acts] occur in our mind unbidden and spontaneously (as happens through the play of imagination when it invents images unintentionally)."[40] From these passages, it is obvious that the purpose of our cognitive powers, according to Kant, is to orient us toward the external world, not to the internal world of sense impressions and ideas that are involuntary. Mental health consists in conforming our understanding to the laws of experience, not inner but outer experience. On the other hand, mental illness consists in the "tendency to accept the play of ideas of inner sense as experiential knowledge, though it is only an invention" that we "purposively put into our minds."[41] In mental derangement "the patient's thoughts take an arbitrary course with its own (subjective) rule running counter to the (objective) rule that conforms with the laws of experience."[42] Our cognitive health depends on understanding the *purpose* of our cognitive power, which is to orient us toward the world, rather than toward our personal sense of reality. As Kant puts it, "the one universal characteristic of madness is loss of common sense (*sensus communis*) and substitution of logical private sense (*sensus privates*) for it."[43] In order for reason to be free and have control, our ideas have to be tested against other people's ideas.

That common sense is the mark of mentally healthy people might also be why it is a mark of moral people as well. Perhaps this is why Kant begins the *Anthropology* with an account of egoism and pluralism. Egoists do not rectify their thoughts with other human beings, but a healthy human being knows that we have to "attach our own understanding to the understanding of other men too, instead of isolating ourselves with our own understanding and still using our private ideas to judge publicly."[44] The pluralist in contrast sees herself as a member of the world, a member of the human species living out her reason in a common world on the basis of common sense and common understanding.

The reason Kant stresses the fact that human beings need to be in control of their powers and ideas is because this is the only way that the will can remain free. Kant writes that the human being's inner perfection (purpose)[45] "consists of having control over the exercise of all his powers, so that he can use them as he freely chooses" and "this requires that understanding rule."[46] This statement refers back to the initial statement of the *Anthropology*, which was that the book is about "what man as a free agent makes, or can and should make of himself."[47] A human being's perfection lies in practical reason, as Kant succinctly says at the end of the *Anthropology*: "The human being is a being who has the power of practical reason and is conscious that his choice is free (a person)."[48]

Since the purpose of the *Anthropology* is to develop prudence and wisdom, Kant does restrict what he has to say about subjects to what human beings can change and have an effect on. That is, he is concerned to articulate human nature in such a way that we learn what we have within our control and how we can maintain that state of freedom. That is why Kant spends a lot of time on sensibility, habits, imagination, pleasure and displeasure, affects, and passions. They are all realities that can interfere with the proper ends of our powers and can take freedom away. In the following, I will address each of these topics (along with taste) to show that Kant is constantly using teleological judgment (ends and purposes) in the work. This will be evident in the way he talks about purposes and ends, how the ultimate end is served by a person maintaining a sense of control through reason, and how these purposes can be defeated.

Sensibility

In spite of the fact that some people think the senses deceive us; Kant explains that it is not the fault of the senses. The senses rightfully submit to understanding and hence it is our understanding that causes us to judge incorrectly.[49] It is important for Kant to take this position because it puts the burden on the understanding to correct itself, whereas we cannot correct our senses. We do have understanding under our control, but not the senses. The *purpose* of the senses is to distinguish objects, but there are ways that the senses can be impeded. If we expose ourselves to strong sensations it "can impede the ends of the senses, namely, from arriving at a concept of the object."[50] Senses "teach less the more they feel themselves being affected."[51] So Kant warns young men to deny themselves "gratifications (of entertainment, revelry, love and so forth)" in order to preserve the enjoyment they can receive from their senses in the future.[52] It is important to have control over our senses and not only does it lead to later enjoyments, but the "consciousness of having control" is itself a type of enjoyment. Ultimately, having control over our powers of sensation will further the free will more than indulging them will. Sense powers can be "weakened, inhibited, or lost completely as in the states of drunkenness, sleep, fainting, apparent death (asphyxia) and real death."[53] In the drunken state of excess alcohol consumption, for instance, "we cannot order our sense representations by the laws of experience."[54] Ordering our sense representations under the understanding is essential to freedom. Keeping the senses purposive and lively requires forgoing strong sensations at first and letting them come in measured degrees.[55]

Habits

Habits are objectionable because they "deprive even good actions of their moral value because it detracts from our freedom of mind; moreover, it leads to thoughtless repetition of the same action."[56] Every new situation requires that we use our reason to deliberate and find the correct judgment or understanding of the situation. If we just use the same habits all the time, it will keep us from recognizing what reason is calling us to do.[57] A human being who is habitually distracted for instance is "useless to society, since he blindly follows his imagination in its free play, which is not ordered in any way by reason."[58] To live without habits means we have to use our reason, which is, of course, how we remain free.

Imagination

The *purpose* of the imagination is the "power of [producing] intuitions even when the object is not present."[59] There are techniques such as using intoxicants that can stimulate the imagination. However, imagination can invent "unbridled or lawless" fantasies. These make the human being its "mere plaything and the poor fellow has no control at all over the course of his ideas."[60] We do have within our power ways of curbing the imagination, however, and that includes among other things, "going to sleep early so that we get up early" so the night does not animate the imagination.[61] Creative imagination can also interfere with an important *purpose*, namely, that of memory. Kant writes that the "formal perfections of memory are the ability to commit a thing readily to memory, to call it to mind easily, and to retain it for a long time."[62] Memory can "reproduce our earlier ideas voluntarily, so that the mind is not a mere plaything of the imagination."[63] Kant warns us though that imagination can interfere with memory's purpose of calling to mind accurately what occurred. Imagination can also cause mental derangement, when a person takes "the ideas he has himself made up for perceptions."[64] Imagination must submit to both memory and the understanding in order to preserve freedom.

Pleasure and Displeasure

We might be tempted to think that pleasure and displeasure or pain are experiences that we merely suffer, but Kant believes that they are in part dependent upon our perceptions, something which we have in our control and can make choices concerning. Sensitivity is a choice because we can "grant or refuse permission for the state of pleasure or displeasure to enter our mind."[65] We can make pain bearable for instance "if we compare it with other pains we ourselves might have suffered. If someone has broken his leg, we can make his misfortune more bearable for him by pointing out that he could easily have broken his neck."[66] Our perceptions of the situation we are in can change how we relate to the pain. Our thoughts can sooth pain and disappointment by realizing wisely that "life as such, considered in terms of our enjoyment of it, which depends on fortuitous circumstances, has no intrinsic value at all, and that is has value only as regards the use to which we put it, the ends to which we direct it."[67] This is another way of saying that it is through our choices that we have dignity as human beings, and it is ultimately up to us to decide if we are going to brood over things we can't change or simply accept it and move on. Our interpretations of our situations are up to us and those interpretations give rise to our experience of pleasure and displeasure. Change can be very upsetting, but we are able to make light of it through our perceptions and this is something we have in our control even if we don't have the change within our control.[68] We also choose our enjoyments and hence have that within our control, just as the wealthy man chooses social enjoyments that involve restraint so that they are beneficial not only to himself, but also to others.[69]

Taste

The *purpose* of taste is to communicate "our feeling of pleasure or displeasure to others" and "feel satisfaction (*complacentia*) about it in common with others (socially)."[70] Taste is purposive ultimately for promoting morality even though only in an external way, because it arises out of the subject's giving a universal law that originates in reason. Being well-mannered, well-behaved, and polished "prepares him for [morality] by the effort he makes, in society, to please others (to make them love or admire him)."[71] Taste is the "tendency to put a value on even the semblance of moral goodness."[72] When we attempt to look like we are moral, it has the effect of preparing us for true moral goodness, which has to do with submitting to the moral law through reason. The person of taste cares about what others think of her and as a result is not an egoist and is half way to the point of testing her judgment against others and concerning herself with whether all people could will her maxims. As occasions for expressing taste, rhetoric and poetry are both means of stimulating the mind and arousing it to activity.[73] They are *purposive* in that way for our practical life of choosing, because they help us know "what can be made of" the human being.

Affects

Two possibilities for our appetitive power exclude the sovereignty of reason: affects and passions.[74] Affects make it impossible to use our reason because "we are taken unawares by feeling; so that the mind's self-control (*animus sui compos*) is suspended." Affects are rash and overwhelm us like water breaking through a dam.[75] Not all feelings are obviously affects. Affects are sudden and overwhelming and make it impossible to deliberate and choose. Affects like anger and shame, for example, make "us less capable of realizing their end."[76] Presumably anger would be the result of a perceived injustice done to one, and rectifying that injustice would be harder to do in a state of anger, because it would rapidly turn into a desire or passion for vengeance.[77] Shame would arise out of a social impropriety and would make it harder to correct the behavior and reinstate our social belonging, because one is overwhelmed with the emotion. Affects are *purposive* for exciting or slackening our vital force.[78] Not all affects frustrate their own ends. Sympathy, in contrast, is *purposive* (nature's wisdom) for "holding the reins *provisionally*, until reason has achieved necessary strength."[79]

Passions

Passions are different than affects because they are based on a maxim "of acting in accordance with an end prescribed . . . by the inclination."[80] They make a part of one's ends the whole of one's ends[81] and keep reason from "comparing [the end] with the totality of all our inclinations when we are making a choice."[82] Having a passion means one is enslaved by it, primarily because one does not want to be cured of it, and it shuns the rule of principles.[83] It takes what nature intended only as an inclination and makes it into the only end one wants. Passions come into conflict with the concept of freedom, because their ends are not given by reason, but rather by nature. All passions, whether natural or cultural, are "concerned directly with ends."[84] Wisdom, which is the "idea of the practical use of reason that conforms perfectly with the law," admits of no passions.[85] Human beings miss their final end when they are enslaved to passions. Passions are purely evil for Kant and nothing good can come out of them. On the other hand, when we engage in work that "methodically achieve[s] an important end we have chosen (*vitam extendere factis*)," this is the only sure way to happiness.[86] Not only are nature's ends important, but also our ends in the choices we make, but nature herself is always construed to be in favor of and helpful for our development of the ability to make choices. Kant disagrees with Rousseau because he held that "civilization is out of keeping with the ends of nature." Instead Kant holds that civilization "complies with" the ends of nature.[87] Nature did not will us to have passions.

Nature Does Nothing in Vain

The principle that nature does nothing in vain is also used by Kant to talk about nature's intent for human beings. Even natural characteristics that would seem to be in vain, like laziness, are purposive for Kant. According to Parow, Kant claims "in order to be able to determine the character of a human being, one must be acquainted with the ends set for him by his nature."[88] Kant often says that nature wisely implanted or arranged things . . . for instance nature implanted "the tendency to give ourselves over readily to illusion" in order to preserve virtue.[89] Or he will say that nature has moved us in a certain direction in order to accomplish her ends, for instance to fall in love with a dissimilar person.[90] Sometimes Kant says, "providence" instead of nature, and by that he means the arrangement and organization of nature.[91] Sometimes Kant talks of either natural gifts, or he claims that nature wants to stimulate the vital force.[92] Even what appears at the outset to be a natural tendency that is not good, Kant construes as beneficial, because of his commitment to the principle of "nature does nothing in vain." Laziness for instance is beneficial because we want to rest often and that keeps us from "indefatigable malice" which would create more evil in the world. Cowardice is also purposive because it keeps "militant blood-thirst" at bay. Even duplicity can benefit human beings since it preserves entire states that otherwise would be at war.[93] Nature's ends are always perceived to be good, by Kant. For instance, in the *Education*, he writes, "one does not find the grounds for evil in the natural predispositions of human beings. . . . In human beings there lies only germs for the Good."[94] It is the human free will that eventually messes things up.

There are, of course, more references to purposes and ends within the Characteristic of the *Anthropology*. The conjectural ends of nature for women are preservation of the species and cultivation of society and its refinement.[95] Kant argues this because nature made women weaker than men, but since she is just as able to get what she wants, it is evident that nature put more artfulness in women than in men.[96] Kant assumes the principle that nature "wants every creature to achieve its destiny through appropriate development of all the predispositions of its nature, so that the species, if not every individual, fulfills nature's purpose."[97]

Although the foregoing is really only a cursory glance at the *Anthropology*, it does serve to confirm that indeed teleological judgment is thoroughly used and presupposed in this book. The *Anthropology* is not merely empirical because it uses and presupposes teleological judgment, which Kant critically grounded in the Critique of Teleological Judgment. It presupposes and uses a priori principles that are not derived from experience but originate in our reason. Judgment is seeking to harmonize with reason in teleological judgment because it is attempting to evaluate human life and experience in a systematic way. This systematic attempt assumes the final end of morality and freedom for human beings and then evaluates empirical realities for their purposiveness in achieving and maintaining freedom and morality in human life. It also is able to characterize empirical realities that impede freedom and morality insofar as they disable reason.

That human beings have control over the faculties and powers is evidence for what Kant concludes about the human being in the Characteristic, namely, that human beings have a character that they give themselves, that human beings are the animal capable of rationality, and, through setting their own ends, they are able to perfect themselves and become the rational animal.[98] Human beings must set their own ends through reason to cultivate, civilize, and moralize themselves, but nature can't be such that this is impossible.[99] Human nature has to be defined in such a way that it is possible for them to will their own ends. That is why it makes sense that the Didactic precedes the Characteristic. We have to know what the human being is before we can know what can be made of the human being. Kant emphasizes the connection between practical philosophy and anthropology, in the Lectures on Ethics:

> Practical philosophy (that is, the science of how human beings ought to behave) and anthropology (that is, the science of human's actual behavior) are closely connected, and the former cannot subsist without the latter: for we cannot tell whether the subject to which our consideration applies is capable of what is demanded of them unless we have knowledge of that subject. It is true that we can pursue the study of practical philosophy without anthropology, that is, without the knowledge of the subject. But our philosophy is then merely speculative, and an idea. We therefore have to make at least some study of human beings.[100]

Kant is indeed talking about human nature and not just about human beings. His anthropology is about general knowledge of human nature as Friedlander expresses it, "anthropology is pragmatic knowledge of that which flows from [the human being's] nature, but it is not physical or geographic, since these are bound to time and place."[101]

There can be no doubt that Kant is formulating a theory of human nature when he lays out the four natural predispositions in the Characteristic. I have covered that already, but I would also like to point out the fact that they too are understood from a teleological point of view. In the Idea for a Universal

History with a Cosmopolitan Intent, Kant also uses teleological judgment and the first thesis is articulated as "all of a creature's natural predispositions [*Naturanlagen*] are destined to develop completely and in conformity with their ends."[102] The ends of our natural predispositions are not just determined by human willing, but actually in part by nature herself. Nature supplies helping tendencies such as drives, inclinations, natural talents, feelings and desires. We know through these helping tendencies that nature wills that we develop our natural predispositions. Kant calls "providence" the very way nature is organized for human beings. Providence is the teacher of the human race from whom we can expect the education of the whole human race toward the fulfillment of all its natural predispositions.[103]

In the Critique of Teleological Judgment, Kant differentiates between the last purpose [*letzter Zweck*] of nature and the final purpose [*Endzweck*] of nature. The last purpose is what nature in its organization is capable of bringing about in human nature, namely the human being's "aptitude in general for setting himself purposes, and using nature (independently of [the element of] nature in human determination of purposes) as a means [for achieving them] in conformity with the maxims of his free purposes generally."[104] The last purpose of nature is culture, the culture of skill, and hence the technical predisposition. Nature can do this because she implants natural talents in human beings and through this we know that nature wills that we develop this predisposition. These natural talents create inequality in human beings and hence we will tend to want to develop a civil constitution in which there will be equality. We know that nature also wills that we will because nature did not supply us with inclinations that naturally harmonize, but instead conflict with each other. In the *Critique of Judgment*, Kant argues "what is more, man's own absurd natural predispositions land him in further troubles that he thinks up himself, and [make him] put others of his own species in great misery through oppressive domination, barbaric wars, etc., and [so] man himself does all he can to work for the destruction of his own species."[105] The only way to mediate conflicting inclinations and predispositions is through choice and willing.[106] We have already seen this disharmony in the inclinations to freedom and to sex, and the consequent need to submit to the norms of civilization.

The concept of unsociable-sociability is such a conflict of competing inclinations, one sociable the other unsociable.[107] Nature has arranged human beings such that there will be conflicts in their natures. These conflicts propel human beings to resolve the problem. To resolve the conflict of wills and freedom in the technical predisposition they develop civil society. It is in the civil community and the refined society that the individual first becomes aware of laws that are valid for all human beings, because as Kant writes in another reflection from the 1780s, "not the human being, but the human race, lives in the civilized [situation]."[108] In his *Lectures on Ethics*, Kant compares the process of the discipline of civilization with trees in a forest.

> The trees in the forest discipline each other; they cannot obtain air for growth in the spaces between them, but only up above, and so they grow tall and straight; but a tree in the open is not restricted and so grows crooked, and it is then too late to train it. So it is with human beings. Trained early they grow up straight along with their fellows; but if they are pruned, they become crooked trees.[109]

In social life human beings discipline themselves, though they would not necessarily want it so. Like trees, they cannot remain small and unproductive, but must grow tall in order to reach the sun and air above. The requirements of social life together with other human beings challenge us to develop not only our talents, but also virtues, which are at least on the path to morality. In a reflection from the early 1780s we read,

> The destiny of human beings is not ever to be happy here, but rather to be incessantly driven through pain, in order to develop their talents. . . . Human beings are so arranged, that they should cultivate one another. For that reason, social events plague, the rivalry and gossip. For this nothing can contribute more than pain, which makes us need to leave our [present] situation.[110]

Therefore, it is only in a culture of training (discipline), in which nature is the teacher, constantly striving toward a purposive cultivation in which many evils and insatiable number of inclinations are poured out upon us, that we begin to sense our receptivity to a higher purpose than happiness and the satisfaction of all of our inclinations.[111] It is the culture of discipline in civilized society, in contrast to the culture of skill, which "prevents human beings from being turned aside by their animal impulses from humanity, their appointed end."[112]

Nature is not a cunning teacher who achieves what she wants from her students even without their approval and response, rather she provokes her students and challenges them to arise out of their laziness and to develop themselves in all their possibilities. Nature expedites the progress of human species in the development of their predispositions, from one stage to another, through arranging nature in such a way that they must and want to develop their predispositions.

Discipline is necessary to overcome the "despotism of desires," but individuals alone cannot accomplish it: "Now I cannot dispute the preponderance of evils that are poured out upon us by the refinement of our taste to the point of its idealization."[113] The individual alone cannot discipline herself sufficiently against the evils of culture, and thus we need nature for that. Even the good will is not strong enough. Nature cannot discipline human beings to their moral freedom, but she can arrange to make human beings so unhappy that they will agree to live under a lawful authority in a civil community in which the greatest possible development of natural skills can take place and in which the abuse of conflicting freedoms would be minimized. This is why Kant claims at the end of the *Anthropology*, "our volition is generally good; but we find it hard to accomplish what we will, because we cannot expect the end to be attained by the free accord of *individuals*, but only by a progressive organization of citizens of the Earth into and towards the species, as a system held together by cosmopolitan bonds."[114] This progressive organization is the result of human beings dealing with the conflict of unsociable-sociability that nature has already set as our destiny.[115] But since this destiny is not meant to be a final destiny, but a situation in which human beings are impelled to make decisions and choose, it still doesn't establish the final end for human beings. It is the last end of nature, but it is not the final end.[116] Ultimately, human beings have to choose their own final end.

The *Anthropology* is not a book of trivialities as Friedrich Schleiermacher held. It orients our understanding about human nature and realities such that we can achieve our final end. It teaches both prudence and wisdom and these are necessary steps to maintaining our freedom from inclinations and passions that blind us to our final end. It does contain theories that can compete against other theories. It was meant to be popular so Kant did not spend time delineating the framework, but the systematic framework is there. In the next chapter, I will show that Kant not only considered what he was doing was popular, but he also believed it was philosophy and a worthy philosophy at that.

CHAPTER SIX

Kant's Pragmatic Anthropology
as Popular Philosophy

After Kant stopped lecturing on anthropology in 1796, he received many requests that he publish his anthropology lecture, since it had been so popular.[1] As Johann HeinrichTieftrunk (1760–1837) wrote to Kant on November 5, 1797: "The public is hoping for an *Anthropology* from you. Will it soon be published?"[2] When the manuscript was ready to be printed, Johann Grich Biester (1749–1816) wrote to Kant: "Your *Anthropology* will be received by the reading world with the greatest joy."[3] Kant had every reason to believe that the *Anthropology from a Pragmatic Point of View* would be well received when it finally appeared in 1798, but one of the very first readers to critique Kant's book was Schleiermacher in the *Athenaeum*, a journal published by Schleiermacher and the Schlegel brothers from 1798–1800. Schleiermacher does not mince words as he calls the *Anthropology* "a collection of trivialities." He believed that the "striving for the popular [quality] has been the downfall of the systematic [quality] . . ."[4] Schleiermacher could not understand the juxtaposition of the Kant of the Critiques and the Kant of the *Pragmatic Anthropology*. For him the *Anthropology* was a radical denial of the content and spirit of critical philosophy.

Currently, Reinhard Brandt is maintaining that pragmatic anthropology does not contain a theory that militates against other theories because the book never generated any controversy between supporters and opponents.[5] He also seems to think that the pragmatic anthropology is not philosophy, although sometimes he qualifies this by saying that it is not philosophy in the sense of Kant's critical and transcendental philosophy.[6] His latest view appears to confirm this negative appraisal. In fact he asserts, "Pragmatic Anthropology, however, although conceived systemically and as a science (*Wissenschaft*), is not a philosophical system—it neither belongs to philosophy in a strict sense, nor is it articulated as a system based upon an idea of reason."[7] Such views can also be found in Jacob and Kain's book, *Essays on Kant's Anthropology*. In fact the editors write: ". . . one might refer to Kant's anthropology as a 'philosophical anthropology' were it not that such a phrase would strike Kant as an oxymoron, given his critical view that philosophy is entirely rational and a non-empirical enterprise, while anthropology is completely empirical."[8] Most interpreters of Kant's anthropology assume that indeed the anthropology is empirical and thoroughly so, and hence is not philosophy. Chapters 3 and 4, have refuted the idea that Kant's pragmatic anthropology contains no theory, for indeed it contains a well-conceived theory of human nature which, as I have argued, does contradict evolutionary theories of human nature and also Behaviorism's account of human nature. In chapter 5, I have refuted the idea that the *Anthropology* is merely empirical. In Brandt's second claim that the anthropology is not philosophy in the Kantian sense, one has to wonder why only critical and transcendental philosophy are allowed to count as philosophy in a Kantian fashion. On Kant's definition of critical philosophy, even Plato would not be teaching philosophy. One wonders whether this is too rigid a criterion of philosophy and one wonders if Kant, himself, would have denied pragmatic anthropology the status as philosophy. In his characterization of pragmatic anthropology and what it is not, Brandt appears to mimic Schleiermacher's reaction to the book.

Given this disparity in reaction to Kant's anthropology lectures and the book, two questions pose themselves: Did Kant believe that his anthropology had no systematic foundation? Did Kant himself believe that popular philosophy was not as worthy as critical philosophy? The answer to the first question is that his anthropology has a systematic foundation, but Kant did not see the reason for showing in detail the systematic foundations for pragmatic anthropology, because the intent of the course of lectures was popular, and this thoroughness would only have detracted from its popular appeal.[9] The critical lines in the *Anthropology* can be traced back to his theory of reflective teleological or purposive judgment, which I have shown in chapter 5. Pragmatic anthropology has to do with purposiveness toward oneself and toward others. The critical faculty that justifies the concepts of purposiveness is teleological judgment. This faculty is critically grounded, because it involves a priori principles that derive from reason and not experience. If my argument is good, and the anthropology does presuppose teleological judgment, then it is not a purely empirical work and can hence also be philosophy. Kant simply does not exhibit this framework because the work is popular. What I will address here is how Kant perceived the nature of popular philosophy. We will find that instead of according it an inferior place in philosophy, Kant intends to give it an honored place. Kant believes it is not only philosophy, but also noble philosophy.

Kant made explicit statements concerning the relationship between anthropology, as he lectured on it, and critical philosophy, as he wrote about it. In various passages, we find him distinguishing between two types of philosophy: the popular or the "cosmological concept" [*Weltbegriff*], and the scholastic concept [*Schulbegriff*]. This distinction was made in practically every lecture course he held: the lectures on metaphysics, ethics, logic, philosophical encyclopedia, and anthropology, even though it is best known from the passage in the *Logic*, where Kant also presents the classic four questions embracing the whole field of philosophy. Kant claims that the scholastic concept of philosophy derives its cognitions out of concepts, but the cosmological concept of philosophy is the "science of the ultimate ends of human reason."[10]

Given the various datings of these lectures, and also the appearance of the distinction in the first Critique, we can safely assume that this was not a distinction tacked onto his architectonic at the end of his life by an aging Kant. In fact, the association of scholastic with "pedantic" while being contrasted to cosmopolitan philosophy [*Weltkenntnis*], in several of his reflections, brings us back to the original impulse which motivated Kant to lecture on physical geography and anthropology as early as 1755 and 1775 respectively. In these courses, Kant was concerned to teach his students how to orient themselves to their final destiny. The popularity of the courses resided in this universal appeal. In addition to orienting the students, Kant needed to be a kind of teacher who was not pedantic. Popular philosophy calls for a different method of teaching. Such a method would teach students to think for themselves, rather than memorize a system of philosophy.

Kant was referring to the discipline of pragmatic anthropology in the distinction he made between scholastic and cosmopolitan philosophy in the *Logic*. A typical reflection from the 1780s illustrates this point:

> (but why is knowledge of the world knowledge of human beings?) Thus, knowledge of human beings itself can be either scholastic knowledge or cosmopolitan knowledge [*Weltkenntnis*]. The latter is pragmatic anthropology. The latter investigates only (in) so far, what the human being is, in order to conclude, what it can make of itself or [how it] can use others; not psychology, which is scholastic knowledge.[11]

Here Kant makes it clear that pragmatic anthropology is a type of cosmopolitan philosophy and he contrasts that with scholastic philosophy which psychology is. Many philosophers want to characterize the distinction between critical philosophy and pragmatic anthropology as the difference between knowledge that is derived a priori and knowledge that is derived a posteriori. In other words, scholastic philosophy is based in reason and is rational and cosmopolitan philosophy is based in experience and is empirical. But this is not how Kant characterized the distinction. Rather than repeat the distinction made by the Wolff and Baumgarten schools, which differentiated philosophy as rational and empirical psychology as empirical, Kant makes the distinction between the interest people have in the two fields of philosophy.

According to Kant, the distinction between critical philosophy and anthropology is characterized by the distinction between philosophy according to the *Schulbegriff* and philosophy according to the *Weltbegriff*. For Kant, these two types of philosophy are not differentiated based on the origin of their concepts, whether they are rational or empirical, rather, they are distinguished according to the interest people have in them. In the *Critique of Pure Reason*, Kant explains:

> By "cosmical concept" [*Weltbegriff*] is here meant the concept which relates to that in which everyone necessarily has an interest; and accordingly if a science is to be regarded merely as one of the disciplines designed in view of certain optionally chosen ends, I must determine it in conformity with scholastic concepts [*Schulbegriff*].[12]

What decisively determines philosophy according to its cosmopolitan concept and its scholastic concept is the reference to the interest human beings have in the two.[13] The interest people have in the two is further determined by the ends that they serve. Namely, scholastic philosophy serves arbitrary ends and cosmopolitan philosophy serves final ends. The two types of philosophy are teleologically differentiated according to the purpose of the two activities for humanity.

Kant frequently contrasted cosmopolitan philosophers with school philosophers, who only appealed to the interest of those in the university and not to all human beings in the world.[14] In an early manuscript, taken from his anthropology lectures, Kant distinguishes between two types of philosophers.

> There are speculative sciences which are useless for human beings, and there are philosophers whose entire science consists in outstripping one another in shrewdness. These are called the *scholastici*; their art was science for the school, but one could not gain any enlightenment for common life from it . . . but that knowledge extends beyond the school and one seeks to extend his knowledge to a general usefulness: this is the study for the world.[15]

The scholastic philosopher makes clever distinctions, which have no use in the public world. The scholastic pedant is laughable because he shows no ability to discern [*judicium discretivum*] what is useful and what is not.[16] Useful knowledge, on the other hand, teaches us how to "get along with human beings, how we educate human beings, or how we want to make ourselves well loved."[17] In order to get along with other human beings, we have to acquire knowledge of human beings [*Menschenkenntnis*], and learn in experience to meditate [*nachdenken*] on human beings. Knowledge of human beings is useful because one is then "in a position to bend them to one's own intentions."[18]

Scholastic philosophy is only of interest for those who are associated with a university or center of learning. The purpose of scholastic philosophy is to develop philosophical skill [*Geschicklichkeit*], that is, the natural talent that nature gave us to think theoretically.[19] Like any skill it must be developed with respect to arbitrary purposes, that is, with respect to any purpose whatsoever, for all such skills belong to the technical predisposition. This skill does not have to be exercised only with regard to the essential or final ends of human life, but can serve other ends as well, and to develop it sufficiently it should not just be restricted to the essential ends of human life. For this reason, scholastic philosophy is of interest only to those human beings who concern themselves with it, and who have the skill for theoretical or speculative thinking.

Cosmopolitan or popular philosophy, on the other hand, is of interest to all human beings since it deals with the final ends of human life, which concern all human beings, regardless of the particular skills they have. In contrast to scholastic philosophy, its purpose is to develop usefulness [*Nützlichkeit*].[20] Usefulness is the application of skill to oneself and to other people. It belongs to the pragmatic predisposition. In order to make any skill useful, it has to be applied to human life in society, and presupposes some concept of the purpose for which that skill is there. What gives this type of philosophy its universal foundation is that it is not just based on the interest of any particular segment of society, but it is based on the interest anyone could have in it. Everyone can compare their experiences to what Kant has to say.

Kant usually refers to the universal interest that pragmatic anthropology arouses by calling it a popular science. In no way, did he mean by popular that it is a watering down of philosophy. Nor does he mean by popular that it condescends to people's trivial intellectual interests. Popular philosophy is not determined by whether it is popular to the masses. Popular philosophy, for Kant, means that it is of relevance to all people, and that it addresses the final ends of human life. Kant believed it was necessary to learn to make popular use of the knowledge learned in the university so that one would know how to get along with other human beings, how to teach them, and how to make oneself likeable. Kant meant by "popular" to refer to cosmopolitan knowledge [*Weltkenntnis*], which normally would mean knowledge of nature, but in "the sense of popular language, that is, knowledge of human beings."[21] The pragmatic anthropology as *Weltkenntnis* was meant to be popular and be of interest and significance to all people. All human beings can feel themselves included in its themes.

Popularity for Kant does not consist in that which catches the fancy of individuals at a particular time in history. The popular character of a science is commendable only when it has been firmly established by scholastic philosophy:

> The popularity does not consist in setting aside scholastic standards
> [*Vollkommenheit*], but only in not letting the form [of scholastic
> philosophy] be seen as the framework (just like one draws a penciled
> line, on which one writes, and later erases it). Everything scientific
> must be according to rules [*Schulgerecht*]; but the technical [quality]
> of popular philosophy should not be seen, rather [the cosmopolitan
> philosopher must] condescend to the power of comprehension [of
> common people] and to the typical expressions.[22]

Popular philosophy must be founded in scholastic principles because without
this foundation it is neither methodical nor thorough. On the other hand, the
scholastic philosopher must condescend to common knowledge and interest,
and not use technical terms that only skilled philosophers can understand.
Popular philosophy, according to Kant, is the "greatest perfection of a beautiful
mind, but only, then, when it is connected with thoroughness."[23] Popular philosophy should, hence, be preceded by scholastic philosophy.

On the other hand, the scholastic philosopher is one who is devoted to
rational, theoretical, or speculative philosophy only. In the *Groundwork*,
Kant calls these philosophers "minute" [*Grübler*] in their methods, because
they are exacting and conscientious.[24] This kind of philosopher is "pedantic" as
a teacher, because, though they are learned, they do not know how to make
their subject interesting to their students and applicable to the world. Pedantry,
according to Kant, is "exactness of rules (making everything much too clear)."[25]

The description Kant gave in the *Menschenkunde* of the scholastic
philosopher is reminiscent of the description of students in the *Nachricht*
(1765–66), where he referred to the "early clever loquaciousness of young
thinkers, which is blinder than any other self-conceit and as incurable as
ignorance."[26] In the *Menschenkunde*, he explains

> One must differentiate between two types of learning: there are
> minute [*grüblerisch*] sciences, which are useless for human beings,
> and formerly there were philosophers, whose whole science con-
> sisted in exceeding each other in ingeniousness, these were called
> *Scholastici*; their art was science for the university [*Schule*], but no
> enlightenment for everyday life could be acquired through this.
> He could be a great man, but only for the university, without giving
> the world some use for his knowledge.[27]

If the students were minute and specious in their reasoning, it is because they
are imitating what they were learning from their scholastic professors. Kant
concluded the problem lay in the pedagogic method itself and not just in the
students. Kant saw what was lacking in this type of attitude toward philosophy
even in the beginning of his teaching career, and he had begun his lectures on
cosmopolitan philosophy [*Weltwissenschaften*], that is, on physical geography

and anthropology, to make up for this lack. In *Von den verschiedenen Racen der Menschen* (1775), Kant announced his lectures on these two subjects and there declared that physical geography was a pre-exercise in cosmopolitan philosophy [*Weltwissenschaften*], and this was "that which serves to give a pragmatic [character] to all otherwise achieved sciences and skill, through which they are not merely useful for the university, but also for life."[28] The twofold field of physical geography and anthropology are viewed cosmologically and pragmatically. In other words, Kant considered these two disciplines, in the way he taught them, to be philosophy, and philosophy that was useful for the world.

Kant was critical of scholastic philosophy [*Schulphilosophie*], like that of Wolff's, in which the tendency was to memorize a whole body of doctrine.[29] Kant differentiated, as a result, between historical knowledge (*cognitio ex datis*) and rational knowledge (*cognitio ex principiis*). Scholastic philosophy that is memorized and imitated is really nothing better than historical knowledge:

> Anyone, therefore, who has learned (in the strict sense of that term) a system of philosophy, such as that of Wolff, although they may have all its principles, explanations, and proofs, together with the formal divisions of the whole body of doctrine, in their heads, and, so to speak, at their finger-tips, have no more than a complete historical knowledge of the Wolffian philosophy.[30]

Kant is not saying here that scholastic philosophy is rational knowledge (*cognitio ex principiis*), and pragmatic anthropology is historical knowledge (*cognitio ex datis*), as we would expect from some contemporary interpreters, but rather he is arguing that learning rational philosophy is historical knowledge. This is a complete reversal of what contemporary philosophers are thinking about rational philosophy and empirical philosophy. The reason that Wolff's philosophy is really historical knowledge is because students are merely memorizing his philosophy. Likewise, the method of pragmatic anthropology requires the use of a priori principles of judgment and hence cannot be simply relegated to empirical philosophy. That is why his students had to think for themselves. Pragmatic anthropology does not lend itself to being memorized. It requires that students take the principles of teleological judgment and apply them to their own experience.

In the lectures on *Philosophische Enzyklopädie*, which Kant most likely gave in the summer semester of 1775, he goes more in depth into a critique of the type philosophy that is only an art of memorization and imitation. There he distinguishes between a "science of learnedness," and a "science of insight." It is adequate to historical method to explicate texts and language, but the philosophy professor "should at the same time instruct the method of doing philosophy."[31] Philosophy should be a science of insight into method, and not just of learnedness [*Gelehrtheit*] for which memorization would be adequate. Kant was teaching his students a science of insight when he expected the students to compare their experience with what he was saying.

Kant repeats a theme here which can also be found in his anthropological reflections [*Reflexionen zur Anthropologie*], and that is of the philosopher as a rational artificer [*Vernunftkünstler*]. The *Vernunftkünstler* increases the number of concepts in the world, but does not give us insight into the final purpose of human life. They appeal mostly to human curiosity, but to that only in a superficial way without going into the final destiny of human beings: "Wolff was a speculative . . . philosopher . . . he was actually not a philosopher at all, but rather a great artificer, like many others still are, for the intellectual curiosity [*Wißbegierde*] of human beings."[32] So instead of it being popular philosophy that condescends to the superficial curiosity of students, it is rather scholastic philosophy that is the culprit. Pragmatic anthropology judges experience based on the final ends of human life and orders all experiences systematically in relation to those final ends. Kant taught his students a method of philosophy in the anthropology lectures; he didn't teach them to memorize concepts.

In the Nachricht (1765), Kant complained that students should not just learn *philosophy*, but that they should also learn to *philosophize*, they should not just learn *thoughts*, but learn to *think*.[33] He regarded the science of cosmological wisdom [*Weltweisheit*] as essential to the balanced education of young people. Kant's claim in the first Critique that we cannot learn philosophy, but only learn to philosophize, was no isolated thought, but a considered position that he held his whole career.[34] He repeated it often in his lectures, and there we see that by philosophizing he did not just mean critical philosophy, not just practical philosophy, but also pragmatic anthropology.

IS POPULAR PHILOSOPHY A NOBLE ENDEAVOR?

Next, to the question of whether or not Kant considered popular philosophy a worthy and noble endeavor, we find that Kant has a lot to say about the incompleteness of scholastic philosophy without popular philosophy. The sciences and scholastic philosophy are necessary for the development of a skillful and cultured human being, but if they are not brought into dialogue with popular concepts and final human purposes through reflective judgment, then they become one-eyed hypocritical monsters:

> But there is also gigantic erudition that is cyclopic, or has one eye missing; the eye, namely, of true philosophy, by which reason could make proper use of this mass of historical science, a load for a hundred camels.[35]

Under Rousseau's influence, Kant suggests that the critique of science lessens pride. Beginning with the Aristotelian tradition, knowledge among scholars and academicians has been valued for the sake of itself, regardless of its practical value and use. Kant, as a young philosopher, also fell prey to this pride in knowledge and science for its own sake. After happening upon Rousseau, however, Kant began to turn from this attitude of superiority:

> The learned are seemingly the only class to observe the beauty which God has placed in the world and to use the world for the purpose for which God made it. . . . They acquire knowledge, and God created the world for knowledge; they alone develop the gifts and talents of mankind. Can they not, therefore, claim superiority over their fellows? But listen to Rousseau; he turns the argument around and says: "Human beings are not made for erudition, and scholars by their learning pervert the end of humanity."[36]

Kant began to doubt the superiority of scholarship over ordinary judgment. Popular philosophy that condescends to ordinary judgment does not pervert the end of humanity. More than likely Kant's scholastic and speculative tendencies would have left him dissatisfied, if it hadn't been for his discovery of Rousseau. Kant, himself, wishes to give Rousseau the credit for a major turning point in his life:

> I myself am by inclination a seeker after knowledge; I thirst for it and well know the eager restlessness of the desire to know more and the satisfaction that comes with every step forward. There was a time when I thought all this was equivalent to the honor of humanity, and I despised the common herd who know nothing. Rousseau set me right. The blind sense of superiority is vanishing. I am learning to honor men and should regard myself as far more useless than a common workingman did I not believe that this occupation [philosophizing] might lend value to all others and help them to establish the rights of humanity.[37]

In the *Reflexionen zur Anthropologie*, Kant refers to a "*anthropologia transcendentalis*" as the "self-knowledge of the understanding and reason."[38] This could be immediately interpreted as another word for epistemology or the critique of reason, since it seems to be concerned only with the faculties of understanding and reason.[39] In the rest of the passage, however, Kant makes clearer what he means by self-knowledge. I will quote the entire reflection 903 not only because of its intrinsic interest, but also because it is not available in English:

> In addition to skillfulness there is that, which the sciences give, that (^{g} they) civilize, that is, they [at least] take away the roughness in social intercourse, if they don't always polish [one] immediately, that is giving the agreeableness and manners of social intercourse,

because the popularity is missing [since the sciences exist] out of a lack of social intercourse with different situations.

But with regard to the modest judgment about the worth of their own science and the gentle restraint of self-conceit and egoism, which a science gives, if it rules alone in human beings, something is necessary, which would give humanity to the scholar, so that he doesn't lose sight of himself, and [by judging his worth over others] trust his powers too much. I call such a scholar a cyclop. He is an egoist of science, and he needs another eye, [so] that he still sees his object from the point of view of other human beings. Upon this is the humanity of the sciences grounded, that is, to give [their capability] the affability of judgment, through which one is subjected to the judgment of others.

The sciences (ᵍ which reason speciously) which one can actually learn, and which are thus always growing, without making it necessary that what is acquired [the science] [be subject to] a test and a public affirmation of its right [*Fiscalsierung*],⁴⁰ is actually the reason there are cyclops. The cyclop of literature is the most defiant; but there are cyclops of theology, law, medicine. Also cyclops of geometry. Each one must be associated with an eye out of a special factory.*

*(ᵍ for the medical doctor critique of our knowledge of nature, for the jurist our knowledge of (ᵍ right and) morality, for the theologian our metaphysic. For the geometrist critique of epistemology itself. The second eye is thus the self-knowledge of human reason, without which we have no measure of the dimensions of our knowledge. Each gives a descending pitch of measurement.

Some of these sciences are so constituted, that the critique of them weakens greatly their inner worth; only mathematics and philology hold their own against [critique], likewise jurisprudence, and for that reason they are also the most defiant. Egoism follows as a consequence since they extend further the use, which they make of reason in their sciences, and then consider it in other fields as sufficient.)

Here it is not the magnitude [of egoism], but the one-eyedness that makes the cyclop. It is also not enough to know many other sciences, but the self-knowledge of the understanding and reason. *anthropologia transcendentalis.*⁴¹

Here we have the context in which talk of a transcendental anthropology can make possible sense. A transcendental anthropology is necessary to correct the one-eyedness, or one-sidedness, of the sciences. Scholars and scientists tend to think that their sciences are complete in themselves and that they can use the perspective that they achieve through their sciences, to make sense of problems and issues within other contexts as well. This makes them a one-eyed monster.

The question is what kind of perspective it is that can correct the one-sidedness of the individual sciences. "The self-knowledge of the understanding and reason" sounds, at first, like the critique of pure reason itself, but this has already been mentioned with respect to geometry as the necessary eye missing from its perspective. The *anthropologia transcendentalis* must also be a science that humanizes and civilizes, as well as providing a missing perspective.

In the first paragraph, we learn that the sciences teach a skill, and that they have a tendency to civilize, in that they smooth the roughness in social intercourse. This theme is repeated often in Kant's *Anthropology* and *Reflexionen zur Anthropologie*, but, for the most part, there Kant makes a clear distinction between the sciences, which provide culture, through the skills that they develop, and society and politics, which civilize through the "prudence" that they develop. In this reflection, however, he means that the sciences civilize in that they make us overcome our own egoism; we are forced to develop a perspective that has a more universal applicability. In a reflection from the 1780s, Kant wrote:

> (^{s} the greatest impediment to the advance of the human race to its destiny is, that they deviate from their natural destiny more and more: 1. In natural impulses (^{g} 1. in enjoyment). 2. science and culture. 3. freedom. Two destinies that are antagonistic to one another. They always have to contend with this difficulty.) Culture makes human beings deviate from their physical destiny, which always remains the same, in order to maintain the animal species.[42]

The sciences are the second step in the path toward our moral destiny, since they help us free ourselves from our animal existence, from our natural drive to simply maintain our existence. They do not humanize though since they do not bring us to talk with others outside of our specialty, and subject our point of view to their judgment.

Further, the individual sciences do not "polish" us and make us capable of civilized discourse because they are not "popular." The individual sciences have their own particular objects, which lead them to develop a perspective that is one-sided and cannot apply to the whole of reality. Since scientists do not have to discourse with scientists from other fields, or with lay people, they are not forced to make their perspective understandable within another perspective. Hence, the one-sidedness develops. Here again Kant emphasizes that the individual sciences are specious reasoning [*vernünftelnd*] sciences, that don't require a test or "*Fiscalsierung*." Although students have to take tests within their own scientific specialization the sciences themselves are not required to submit themselves to the judgment of the "*Fiscal*," or a deputy who would decide their subordination in the hierarchy of experience. Here

Kant hints that it is the mediating function of judgment that is really important to a *anthropologia transcendentalis*, since it is before the *"Fiscal,"* as judge, that the sciences have to present themselves and justify themselves. The sciences, which represent the function of understanding do not present themselves directly to the prince who represents reason, but must go through the *"Fiscal"* who represents the function of judgment.

Yet, unlike Rousseau, Kant did not neglect to assert the importance of scholarship. Both types of philosophy are needed, and without popular philosophy, even practical moral philosophy becomes a theoretical endeavor that fails to further morality. Even moral philosophy can be viewed completely objectively without having any influence on behavior. Doing moral philosophy can have the effect of making us aware of our talents, or it can have an effect on actions. Anthropology is also necessary as a philosophical companion to moral philosophy. As one finds it in the introduction to Kant's ethics lecture (1774–75), ". . . moral philosophy cannot endure without anthropology, for one must first know of the agent, whether he is also in a position to accomplish what is required of him, that he should do. One can, indeed certainly consider practical philosophy even without anthropology, or without knowledge of the agent, only then it is merely speculative or an Idea; so the human being must at least be studied."[43]

The final end and purpose of knowledge is not theoretical knowledge or speculative knowledge, since that too must come into relationship with the final destiny of the human species. The cosmological concept of philosophy "is the science of the ultimate ends of human reason."[44] Philosophy, Kant argues, is not the doctrine of the skillfulness of reason according to rules, but rather the law-giving of human reason.[45] "This high concept," he argues, "gives philosophy its dignity, i.e., an absolute value."[46] The philosopher is not meant to be a rational artificer,[47] but a lawgiver according to the "highest maxims of the use of our reason."[48] The philosopher who truly philosophizes is the one who is a lawgiver and also integrates scholastic knowledge with the final ends of human life:

> The philosopher understands rules of wisdom, the wise person acts accordingly. I can only say, that it is he who [truly] philosophizes, who tries to establish the highest purposes and the destiny of their reason; but if he achieves this, then he is already in the temple of wisdom. The philosopher as a leader of reason, leads human beings to their destiny. His knowledge, thus, concerns the destiny of human beings. As a [rational] artificer he increases our insights and science. (Science is actually not our destiny) . . . If the philosopher connects all his speculation, science, etc. with the ends, with the destiny of human beings, then he is a leader and lawgiver of reason.[49]

Cosmopolitan philosophy or popular philosophy, since it deals with the final purposes of human reason and teaches wisdom,[50] is a noble form of philosophy. Kant sums up the final ends of human life and philosophy in the *Anthropology*,

> The sum total of what pragmatic anthropology has to say about man's destiny and the character of his development is this: man is destined by his reason to live in a society with men and in it to cultivate himself, civilize himself, and to make himself moral by the arts and sciences. No matter how strong his animal tendency to yield passively to the attractions of comfort and well-being, which he calls happiness, he is still destined to make himself worth of humanity by actively struggling with the obstacles that cling to him because of the crudity of his nature.[51]

That Kant admired and respected the type of philosopher who was cosmopolitan is clear from a letter he wrote to Friedrich Heinrich Jacobi on August 30, 1789. Jacobi had sent him a treatise by Graf von Windisch-Grätz concerning the art of ruling human beings. In his return letter, Kant expressed the greatest respect for the count's talent "as a philosopher in connection with the noblest kind of thinking of a citizen of the world."[52] An interesting comment Kant makes in the *Anthropology* may well be a self-revelatory comment about his own venture into popular philosophy. He writes how

> It is pleasant, popular and stimulating to discover similarities among dissimilar things and so, as wit does, to provide understanding with material for making its concepts general. Judgment, on the other hand, limits our concepts and contributes more to correcting than to enlarging them. . . . When wit draws comparison, its behavior is like play: judgment's activity is more like business. . . . A man whose intellectual work combines both in the highest degree is said to be acute (perspicax).[53]

Kant certainly is comparing what our faculties and characteristics are with what they ought to be, and he is evaluating how the purposes are achieved by the various means at our disposal. This seems to bring wit and judgment together.

In another passage in the *Anthropology*, Kant characterizes the true philosopher as one who searches for wisdom, rather than one who is a scholar:

> We cannot think of the *philosopher* as a man who works at building the sciences—that is, a scholar; we must rather regard him as one who *searches for wisdom*. He is the mere Idea of a person who takes the final end of all knowledge as his object, practically and (for the sake of the practical) theoretically too . . .[54]

The *Anthropology* is certainly about wisdom, so it is not unlikely that he is talking about his own search for wisdom. He has concerned himself with the final ends of human life in both the Critique of Teleological Judgment and the *Anthropology*. Is this not what he means by the true philosopher?

It appears, then, that at least Kant thought that popular, pragmatic, and cosmopolitan philosophy was not only worth doing, but also played a role of balancing scholastic philosophy. Both philosophies are necessary and good, and they balance each other. Popular philosophy gives the missing eye to scholastic philosophy; scholastic philosophy gives universality and form to popular philosophy. The philosopher becomes the lawgiver when philosophy relates to the final ends of reason and human life. The pragmatic anthropology as popular philosophy is the result of Kant's work of law-giving in the midst of the myriad experiences of human life.

Clearly, pragmatic anthropology is meant to be philosophy. It is the philosopher who uses teleological judgment in a systematic way. No other science deals with the *nexus finalis*. Biology deals with the *nexus effectivus*, and without thinking it through systematically, also with the purposes of the organism. But it is the task of philosophy to recognize the final ends of human lives and to judge the purposes of the aspects of human life and to relate those secondary purposes to final purposes. This is not a task of memorization, but a task of judgment and method. Certainly, there will be differences in the way that people characterize subordinate purposes, and how those purposes relate to ultimate purposes and final purposes, but that is exactly what the philosophical task is. We don't have to have agreement, and if there were universal agreement, then it would be something that one could again memorize and imitate. Nothing, Kant argues in a reflection on logic,

> is more harmful than to imitate in philosophy . . . rather one must think for oneself, learn to judge for oneself, to reflect on objects oneself, and learn philosophizing to be able to become a philosopher and be a philosopher. Worldly wisdom cannot be learned in the least from books, but merely through one's own reflection [*Nachdencken*] and one's own meditation [*Meditiren*].[55]

Pragmatic anthropology requires judgment and that systematically. Kant understood that the philosophical task is to be systematic. Clearly, Kant believed that pragmatic anthropology was philosophy. It is not critical philosophy, but rather popular philosophy, but calling it popular in no way means that it is not philosophy.

Notes

Chapter 1: The Rise and Origin of Kant's Lectures on Anthropology

1. Immanuel Kant, *Anthropologie im pragmatischer Hinsicht*, in *Kants gesammelte Schriften*, ed. Königlich Preußische [now Deutsche] Akademie der Wissenschaft, vols. 1–29 (Berlin: G. Reimer [now de Gruyter], 1902–); *Anthropology from a Pragmatic Point of View*, trans. by Mary Gregor (The Hague: Martinus Nijhoff, 1974). [now KGS, Anth, VII: 00; p. 00].

2. Compare Kant's notes from the 1770s and 1780s in volume 15 of *Kant's gesammelte Schriften* and the lecture notes written by students in volume 25 of *Kant's gesammelte Schriften*. Reinhard Brandt concurs in his introduction to *Kant's Vorlesungen über Anthropologie*, in KGS: 24. Brandt writes, "Betrachtet man die Struktur der Anthropologie Vorlesungen im ganzen, so ergibt sich eine große Konstanz von den frühesten Nachscriften bis hin zur Buchpublikation von 1798."

3. Benno Erdmann gives the date as winter semester 1773–74, based on his use of the *Fakultätsalbum*, put out by the students of the philosophy faculty at the Königsberg University. Emil Arnoldt has shown conclusively that this date is one year too late, since more accurate information can be found in the *Fakultäts- und Senatsakten* which was published by the Königsberg University. The anthropology lecture was not indicated in the *Lecktions-Katalog* for the year 1772–73, because Kant had planned to lecture about theoretical physics. This lecture was cancelled due to a lack of registered students and he lectured on anthropology for the first time. See Benno Erdmann, "Zur Entwicklungsgeschichte von Kants Anthropologie," in *Reflexionen Kants zur kritische Philosophie*, ed. Benno Erdmann, vol. 1: 37–64, *Reflexionen Kants zur Anthropologie* [(Leipzig: Fue's (R. Reisland), 1882)], p. 48; and Emil Arnoldt, *Gesammelte Schriften*, ed. Otto Schöndorffer, "Kants Vorlesung über Anthropologie," in vol. 4; *Kritische Exkurse im Gebiete der Kantforschung*, part 1, pp. 319–43, (Berlin: Bruno Cassirer, 1908), p. 326ff.

4. Anthropology was also taught at other universities: Gottfried Polycarp Müller (1685–1747) in Leipzig; Johannes Kern (1756–1785); and Christian Daniel Voss (1761–) in Halle. For more details see Mareta Linden, *Untersuchungen zum Anthropologie-begriff des 18. Jahrhunderts* (Bern and Frankfurt: Lang, 1976), p. 17.

5. KGS, Menschenkunde, XXV: 856.

6. Where Kant claims in the *Anthropology* that he had lectured on physical geography and anthropology for some thirty years, KGS, Anth VII: 122fn, it is misleading, since he actually lectured on the physical geography for forty years, and on the anthropology for only twenty-three and one-half years. See Arnoldt, "Kants

Vorlesung über Anthropologie," pp. 329–33, where he lists the twenty-four times Kant actually held the anthropology lectures, including which texts were used.

7. Norbert Hinske follows Paul Menzer in his argument that the Herder papers are a unified collection and, therefore, it can be inferred that the 1765 given form of the metaphysics lectures was also the form held in 1762. See Norbert Hinske, "Kants Idee der Anthropologie," in *Die Frage nach dem Menschen: Aufriss einer Philosophischen Anthropologie. Festschrift für Max Müller zum 60. Geburtstag*, ed. Heinrich Rombach, 410–27 (Freiburg/München: Karl Alber, 1966), p. 412ff.

8. Hans Dietrich Irmscher, *Immanuel Kant, Aus den Vorlesungen der Jahre 1762–1764, Auf Grund der Nachschriften Johann Gottfried Herders, Kantstudien-Ergänzungshefte* Nr. 88 (Köln: n.p., 1964), p. 51.

9. Arnoldt, "Kants Vorlesung über Anthropologie," p. 333.

10. KGS, Racen, II: 443. The translation of this essay is by Holly L. Wilson and Günter Zöller for the Cambridge Edition of the *Works of Immanuel Kant in English*. Forthcoming in volume 7 of that work.

11. Paul Gedan, Introduction to the *Entwürf*, in *Kants Werke, Anmerkungen der Bände I–V* (Berlin and New York: Walter de Gruyter and Co., 1977), p. 455.

12. KGS, Entwürf, II: 4.

13. Arnoldt is of the opinion, "he had, thus, a pure scientific intention in the institution of a new course of lectures." Comparison of the announcements shows a "gradual advance, which found its conclusion in the purposes which were then set up and continually kept in mind." He sees Kant's later purpose as "openness for the world." And this "gradual advance of the tendency completed itself such that as soon as he was aware of it, he transferred [this purpose] from the present to the past as the original purpose." In other words, Kant reinterpreted the meaning of the physical geography lectures given his success with the anthropology lectures. Arnoldt, "Kants Vorlesung über Anthropologie," p. 402. It is impossible to assert that Kant's only intention was scientific in the beginning, since he could not assert his own thesis that physical geography and anthropology were popular in nature without the experience of his students' reactions to his courses. His interest in the nature of human beings, however, is already clear in this announcement.

14. KGS, Entwürf II, 9, trans. Paul Arthur Schilpp, *Kant's Pre-Critical Ethics*, (Evanston and Chicago: Northwestern University, 1938), p. 20. Schilpp believes that "nearly all of Kant's writings of the 1760s show a decided undertone of moral interest," in contrast to the thesis that Kant's interests changed radically from scientific ones with the advent of the critical era, see p. 21. This is also in line with the thesis developed here that the critical era did not usher in a whole new direction, but rather only a critical support of his already well-established interests.

15. KGS, Entwürf, II: 3.

16. KGS, Entwürf, II: 3.

17. KGS, Nachricht, II: 312.

18. KGS, Nachricht, II: 312.

19. G. Gerland, "Immanuel Kant, seine geographischen und anthropologischen Arbeiten," *Kantstudien* 10 (1905): 515.

20. Friedrich Paulsen is one of the first biographers of Kant to recognize the importance of Kant's anthropology lectures. See Friedrich Paulsen, *Immanuel Kant. Sein Leben und seine Lehre*, 6th ed. (Stuttgart: Fr. Frommanns, 1920), p. 36ff. Ludwig Ernst Borowski believed that the *"Nachricht"* was one of Kant's most important works, see Ludwig Ernst Borowski, *Darstellung des Lebens und Charakters Immanuel Kants*, (Königsberg: n.p., 1804), p. 66.

21. KGS, Nachricht, II: 305.

22. KGS, Nachricht, II: 305.

23. For an excellent discussion of the different concepts of experience in Locke and Thomasius, see Rita Widmaier "Alter und neuer Empirismus. Zur Erfahrungslehre von Locke und Thomasius," in *Christian Thomasius 1655–1728: Interpretationen zu Werk und Wirkung*, hrsg. Werner Schneiders (Hamburg: Felix Meiner Verlag, 1989), pp. 95–114.

24. Christian Thomasius, *Einleitung zu der Vernunft-Lehre* (Halle: Salfeld, 1692), p. 76. For further information on how the term was used in the eighteenth century, see also Georg Andreas Will, "Einleitung in die historische Gelahrtheit und die Methode, die Geschichte zu lehren und zu lernen" (1766) published in *Dilthey Jahrbuch: für Philosophie und Geschichte der Geisteswissenschaften*, Bd. 2, hrsg. Frithjof Rudi (Göttingen: Vandenhoeck and Ruprecht, 1984), pp. 222–65. F. M. Barnard discusses this distinction in one of the few articles on Thomasius written in English, "The 'Practical Philosophy' of Christian Thomasius," *Journal of the History of Ideas* 32 (1971): 221–46.

25. Christian Thomasius, *Einleitung zur Hofphilosophie*, in Ausgewälte Werke, Bd. 2 (Hildesheim: Georg Olms Verlag, 1994), pp. 292ff.

26. Thomasius, *Hofphilosophie*, pp. 292ff.

27. Thomasius, *Hofphilosophie*, p. 306.

28. KGS, Nachricht, II: 305–306.

29. Later "prudent" will hold his special attention for the pragmatic anthropology, and it will mean the ability to apply one's knowledge such that the results are beneficial for oneself.

30. KGS, Nachricht, II: 306.

31. Paul Arthur Schilpp, *Kant's Pre-Critical Ethics*, p. 75ff, argues that Kant was very concerned about human nature even as early as the 1760s. His thesis is sympathetic with mine although he is only looking for the origins of Kant's ethical theory. Still, he sees anthropological concepts like "feeling" as playing an essential role in his development of his ethical thought. "Feelings" meant in the *Beobachtungen*, what drives, tendencies, and inclinations meant for his later thinking. They were helpers toward morality, though never considered to be morality itself.

32. KGS, Nachricht, II: 311.

33. Christian August Crusius, "*Anweisung vernünftig zu Leben*," in *Die philosophischen Hauptwerke I*, (Hildesheim: Georg Olms Verlag, 1999), p. 3.

34. KGS, Beweisgrund zu einer Demonstration des Daseins Gottes, II: 76 and II: 77.

35. KGS, Nachricht, II: 312.

36. KGS, Nachricht, II: 312.

37. KGS, Racen, II: 435.

38. KGS, Racen, II: 434.

39. Probably the most striking and certainly the most decisive example of the two opposing positions in terms of the origin of Kant's anthropology lectures is the discussion that took place between Dilthey and Adickes, by way of letters, during the winter of 1904–05, as the two editors of *Kants gesammelte Schriften* expressed their different opinions about the order and grouping of Kant's writings. Almost the entire content of the seven very long letters is the issue of the place of pragmatic anthropology within Kant's overall thought, because this would decide its place in the arrangement of the texts. Dilthey took the very clear position that it was associated with the physical geography and, therefore, the two should be published together. Adickes was against this stance, since he saw the origin of the anthropology lectures in the empirical psychology section of Kant's metaphysics lectures. Lehmann published all seven letters. See Gerhard Lehmann, "Zur Geschichte der Kantausgabe: 1896–1955," in *Beiträge zur Geschichte und Interpretation der Philosophie Kants*, 3–26 (Berlin: Walter de Gruyter and Co., 1969), p. 13.

40. Norbert Hinske, "Kants Idee der Anthropologie," in *Die Frage nach dem Menschen:* pp. 410–27; Paul Menzer, *Kants Lehre von der Entwicklung in Natur und Geschichte* (Berlin: Georg Reimer, 1911); and Arnoldt, "Kants Vorlesung über Anthropologie," argue that the anthropology arose out of Kant's interest in empirical psychology. The weight of proof stands much more clearly on the side of Benno Erdmann, "Zur Entwicklungsgeschichte von Kants Anthropologie," and Gerland, "Immanuel Kant, seine geographischen und anthropologischen Arbeiten," 1–43; 417–547). The latter two philosophers believe that Kant's interests in metaphysical-cosmology and physical geography led to his notion of pragmatic anthropology. His cosmology provided the stimulus for a pragmatic anthropology and the physical geography provided the scientific method of observation. No amount of empirical observations from psychology alone could have led Kant to the notion of a pragmatic being as a "citizen of the world." The empirical psychology provided, then, only the material, that is, the observations, but certainly not the guiding idea.

41. See Gerland, "Immanuel Kant, seine geographischen und anthropologischen Arbeiten," for an in-depth discussion of the development of Kant's physical geography lectures from his early writings, and also for a discussion of the relationship between the physical geography and anthropology lectures.

42. Gerhard Lehmann, "Zur Geschichte der Kantausgabe: 1896–1955," pp. 3–26, especially p. 13.

43. Norbert Hinske, "Kants Idee der Anthropologie"; Benno Erdmann, *Zur Entwicklungsgeschichte von Kants Anthropologie*, p. 48; Emil Arnoldt, "*Kants Vorlesungen über physische Geographie und ihr Verhältnis zu seinen anthropologischen Vorlesungen*," in *Emil Arnoldt Gesammelte Schriften*, pp. 346–73, Bd. 4 (Berlin: n.p., 1908). Currently, Brian Jacobs also agrees that Kant's *Anthropology* only received the basic structure of the lectures from Baumgarten's *Metaphysica*. See Brian Jacobs "Kantian Character and the Science of Humanity," in *Essays on Kant's Anthropology*, ed. Brian Jacobs and Patrick Kain (Cambridge: Cambridge University Press, 2003), p. 111.

44. Reinhard Brandt, "Einleitung," in KGS, XXV: 8–9.

45. Reinhard Brandt, "Einleitung," in KGS, XXV: 24.

46. Reinhard Brandt attempts to show the development of Kant's thought from empirical psychology to anthropology in, "Ausgewählte Probleme der Kantischen Anthropologie," in *Der ganze Mensch: Anthropologie und Literatur im 18. Jahrhundert*, Hans Jürgen Schings (:Stuttgart and Weimer, 1992), pp. 14–32.

47. See Holly L. Wilson, "Kant's Experiential Enlightenment and Court Philosophy in the 18th Century," *History of Philosophy Quarterly*, 18, no. 2 (April 2001): 179–205.

48. Ibid.

49. KGS, Racen, II: 443.

50. Erdmann, "Zur Entwicklungsgeschichte von Kants Anthropologie," p. 39ff.

51. KGS, Entwürf II: 9. *Kant's Pre-Critical Ethics*, trans. Paul Arthur Schilpp (Evanston and Chicago: Northwestern University, 1938), p. 20.

52. J. H von Kirchmann, *Erläuterungen zu Kant's Anthropologie in pragmatischer Hinsicht* (Berlin: Heimann, 1869), p. 1.

53. Mengüsoglu does not recognize that the purpose of the anthropology lectures was to educate young people, Takiyettin Mengüsoglu, "Der Begriff des Menschen bei Kant," in *Kritik und Metaphysik Studien*, 106–119, ed. Heinz Heimsoeth, (Berlin: Walter de Gruyter and Co., 1966), p. 109.

54. See especially the section on empirical psychology in KGS, Philosophische Enzyklopädie, XXIX: 45.

55. Kant writes: "One could raise the objection that I have not previously explained the concept of the faculty of desire or the feeling of pleasure. This reproach would be unfair, however, because this explanation, as given in psychology, could reasonably be presupposed . . . I need no more than this for the purposes of a critique of concepts borrowed from psychology, the rest is supplied by the critique itself," See KGS, KpV, V: 8fn; p. 9 fn.

56. Paulsen, *Immanuel Kant: Sein Leben und seine Lehre*, p. 278.

57. See Edward Franklin Buchner, *A Study of Kant's Psychology with Reference to the Critical Philosophy*, (Lancaster, PA: The New Era Print, 1897), p. 67ff. Buchner claims that faculty psychology also had an influence on the content of his critical philosophy in so far as the relation between the various fields of mental activities is concerned, that is, how the different faculties related to one another.

58. Arnoldt reports this according to the *Lektionskatalog* and the *Senatsakten* of the University of Königsberg, *Gesammelte Schriften*, 4, p. 329.

59. Reported in Aloys Neukirchen, *Das Verhältnis der Anthropologie Kants zu seiner Psychologie. Inaugural-Dissertation München* (Bonn: P. Hauptmann'sche Buchdruckerei, 1914): 29.

60. Hinske "Kants Idee der Anthropologie," p. 418–19. Hinske admits that Kant modifies the two-part division of Baumgarten (416) to add the feeling of pleasure and displeasure, but insists "the fundamental meaning of the beginning point in the theory of powers stayed with Kant his life long." He also argues that Kant follows Baumgarten in the definition of the human being as "rational animal," but Kant distinguished between *"animal rationale"* (rational animal) and *"animal rationabilis"* (capacity for rationality) which is the teleological characterization of the human being according to Kant, see KGS, Anth, VII: 321; p. 183.

61. Arnoldt, *Gesammelte Schriften*, 4: 327. Alexander Gottlieb Baumgarten, *Metaphysica*, 1st ed. (Halle: n.p., 1739). The *psychologia empirica* is also printed in Refl. to Anth, XV, the rest of the text in XVIII.

62. KGS, Entwurf, II: 10.

63. KGS, Vorlesungen über Anthropologie (Menschenkunde), XXV, vol. 2: 859.

64. Vladimir Satura, *Kants Erkenntnispsychologie in den Nachschriften seiner Vorlesungen über empirischen Psychologie, Kantstudien Ergänzungshefte* 101 (Bonn: Bouvier Verlag Herbart Grundmann, 1971), p. 44.

65. Neukirchen, *Das Verhältnis der Anthropologie Kants zu seiner Psychologie*, p. 26.

66. KGS, Nachricht, II, 309.

67. KGS, Letters, X, 225.

68. Paul Menzer, *Kants Lehre von der Entwicklung in Natur und Geschichte* (Berlin: Georg Reimer, 1911), p.151.

69. Menzer does seem rather to support the thesis that is being argued here, but in this one case he is clearly on the side of Hinske, Adickes, and so forth. Menzer, *Kants Lehre von der Entwicklung*, p. 151–52.

70. KGS, Philosophische Enzyklopädie, XXIX, 6,1,1, p. 11. See also BzB, XX: 293.

71. KGS, Meta L$_1$, XXVIII, 5,2,1; pp. 222–23.

72. KGS, KrV, A 343.

73. KGS, KU, V: 461; p. 353.

74. KGS, KrV, B 877. See also KGS, KU ,V: 265–66; KGS, BzB, XX: 26–87. For an in depth discussion of the problem see Theodore Mischel, "Kant and the Possibility of a Science of Psychology," in *Kant Studies Today*, ed. L. W. Beck, 432–55 (LaSalle, IL: Open Court, 1969).

75. KGS, Anth, VII: 119, 285, 292; pp. 3, 151, 157.

76. KGS, Anth, VII: 122; p. 5.

77. KGS, Anth, VII: 132–34, 143, 161–62; pp. 13–15, 23, 39–40. Kant warns: "In observing ourselves, we make a methodical inventory of the perceptions formed in us, which supplies materials for a diary of introspection and easily leads to fanaticism and madness."

78. KGS, Anth, VII: 125, 283; pp. 7, 149. See also Mischel, "Psychology," p. 454ff.

79. KGS, Anth, VII: 161; p. 39.

80. KGS, Anth, VII: 142; p. 23.

81. KGS, Col 80, XV: 801, Refl. 1502a. The small ^{s} and ^{g} in the reflections refer to insertions: "s"—is a later insertion, from another period than the reflection, "g"—is a contemporaneous insertion, which belongs to the same period as the reflection. See XIV: pp. lviiff.

82. KGS, Col 70, XV: 661, Refl. 1482.

83. Hinske, in "Kants Idee," claims that "every observation is anthropologically of equal interest, and so is every behavior or property of human beings equally justified" (p. 418), though he does claim later that pragmatic anthropology is not mere observation (p. 421).

84. KGS, Letters, X: 145, see also KGS, Menschenkunde, XXV: 856.

85. KGS, Zum ewigen Frieden, VIII: 374.

86. KGS, Menschenkunde, XXV: 857.

87. KGS, Menschenkunde, p. 857; also KGS, Anth, VII: 120; p. 4.

88. KGS, Menschenkunde, XXV: 857.

89. KGS, Letters, X: 145, see also KGS, Anth VII: 121–22; pp. 4–5.

90. KGS, Nachricht, II: 305–306.

Chapter 2: The Character and Content of the Anthropology

1. KGS, Letters, X: 145f.

2. See Theodor Litt, *Kant und Herder als Deuter der geistigen Welt* (Leipzig: n.p., 1930). Litt remarked that Kant "disappeared as a person in the machinery of the ever developing reason," but, we see that in his lifetime, he never disappeared as a person. He had an active social life, and was very concerned about his students. We can see this person even in his writings, if we do not limit ourselves to the three critical writings.

3. KGS, Ed, IX: 444; p. 7.

4. KGS, Ed, IX: 446; p. 11.

5. KGS, Ed, IX: 443; pp. 6–7.

6. KGS, Ed, IX: 444; p. 7.

7. KGS, Ed, IX: 446; pp. 10–11.

8. According to Klaus Weyand "Weltbürger" is a borrowed translation from the Greek *kosmopolith* and was frequently used in the seventeenth century. Kant was probably influenced by August Ludwig von Schlözer in the use of this term. For more, see Klaus Weyand, *Kants Geschichtsphilosophie. Ihre Entwicklung und ihr Verhältnis zur Aufklärung, Kantstudien Ergänzungshefte* 85 (Köln: Kölner Universitäts-Verlag, 1963), p. 49fn3.

9. In the *Beobachtungen über das Gefühl des Schönen und Erhabenen*, Kant sees "moral feeling" as an incentive to moral behavior. Although he later insists, in the *Groundwork to the Metaphysics of Morals*, that the only true incentive to morality is the moral law itself, which is sufficient in itself, he never meant by that that human beings do not need other incentives, or that feelings, or dispositions could not help in leading the human being to becoming more moral. As we will see in the next chapter, even in his later works, Kant was convinced that nature provides drives and feelings which help us to become more civilized if not more moral. This is, at least, a necessary presupposition for the moralization of the whole species, if not for the individual. For the argument about Kant's emphasis on "moral feeling" see Schilpp, *Kant's Pre-Critical Ethics*, p. 57ff.

10. Ernst Platner, *Anthropologie für Ärzte und Weltweise* (Leipzig: n.p., 1772). Marcus Herz reviewed this book and sent the review to Kant. Kant responded sometime in 1773 that he did not want to develop an anthropology from the physiological point of view like Platner did. Briefe 10: 138.

11. KGS, Anth VII: 119.

12. KGS, Anth, VII: 176; p. 52.

13. KGS, Anth, VII: 170; p. 46.

14. KGS, Anth, VII: 214; p. 84.

15. KGS, Anth, VII: 246; p. 113.

16. KGS, Anth, VII: 299; p. 163.

17. KGS, Anth, VII: 312; p. 175.

18. KGS, Anth, VII: 303; p. 166–67. And Anth, VII: 306; p. 169.

19. See Holly L. Wilson, "Kant's Integration of Morality and Anthropology," *Kantstudien* 88 (1997): Jahrg., 87–104.

20. KGS, Anth, VII: 119; p. 3.

21. KGS, Anth, VII: 119; p. 3.

22. Ibid., 260.

23. Hauptvorlesung, 242.

24. KGS, Anth VII: 272.

25. KGS, Col 80 XV: 801, Refl. 1502a.

26. KGS, Anth VII: 120.

27. KGS, Anth VII: 201; p. 72.

28. KGS, Anth, VII: 266; p. 134.

29. KGS, Anth, VII: 198; p. 70, and Anth, VII: 205; p. 76.

30. KGS, Anth, VII: 244.

31. KGS, Anth, VII: 204–205; 198.

32. Ibid.

33. Hauptvorlesung, 83.

34. This formulation is used often. See KGS, Anth VII: 201; Menschenkunde, p. 4.

35. Hauptvorlesung, 4.

36. KGS, Anth VII: 286.

37. KGS, Gr, IV: 416 fn.

38. Pride, for instance, causes others to resist us. KGS, Anth VII: 210–11; 272.

39. KGS, *Collegentwürfe aus den 80er Jahren*, in GS, vol. XV/2, pp. 799–980, here XV: 800, Refl. 1502a. [now KGS, Col 80] See also *Kritik der Urteilskraft* V: 172.

40. Ibid., 873, Refl. 1518. Goethe complained in a letter to Schiller (12.19.1798) that it was a "bad joke to declare the rest of his life as foolish." See "Anhänge," by Rudolf Malter in *Immanuel Kant—Anthropologie im pragmatischer Hinsicht*, ed. Karl Vorländer, intro. Joachim Kopper (Hamburg: Felix Meiner Verlag, 1980), p. 335–36.

41. KGS, Letters, X: 145146.

42. KGS, Anth VII: 244.

43. KGS, Anth VII: 246.

44. KGS, Anth VII: 265.

45. KGS, Anth, VII: 291–92.

46. KGS, Anth VII: 294.

47. Menschenkunde, p. 7. See also *Critique of Pure Reason*, trans. Norman Kemp Smith (New York: St. Martin's Press, 1965), B 776 [now KrV], where Kant refers to the tendency to disingenuousness in human nature, by which we conceal ourselves in order to look good in appearances. This contributes to civilization and moralization.

48. KGS, Anth VII: 210.

49. Max Horkheimer and Theodor W. Adorno, *Dialectic of Enlightenment*, trans. John Cumming (New York: Herder and Herder, 1944). We may have to reconsider whether we can characterize the German Enlightenment in the same way as the French and English Enlightenment. If Kant is the definer, along with Mendelssohn, of the German Enlightenment, and the *Anthropology* along with the *Critique of Judgment* represent its highest achievement, then German Enlightenment also succeeded in giving us a concept of pragmatic reason as well as technical reason. The affinities between moral reason and pragmatic reason are closer than moral and technical reason.

50. Ibid., 209.

51. Hauptvorlesung, 2.

52. KGS, Anth VII: 165, 170.

53. KGS, Anth VII: 171.

54. KGS, Anth, VII: 324–25; 186.

55. KGS, RzA, XV: 2,801, Refl. 1502a.

56. KGS, Racen II: 443, The essay *Von den verschiedenen Racen der Menschen* was published in 1773 as an announcement for his lectures.

57. KGS, Col 70, XV: 659, Refl. 1492.

58. KGS, Anth, VII: 324–25; 186.

59. KGS, Anth, VII: 328; pp. 188–89.

60. KGS, Anth, VII: 331; p. 191.

61. KGS, RzA, XV: 645–46, Refl. 1467. This is not a theory of determination, since it is perfectly compatible with human freedom. Nature's mechanisms still require that human beings respond through choice.

62. KGS, Anth,VII: 328; p. 189. "That is, they expect it [development toward a constitution] from a wisdom that is not theirs , but is yet the Idea of their own reason."

63. KGS, Anth, VII: 321; p. 183.

64. Morality here means perfection in the entire species and does not refer to a moral act.

65. KGS, Anth, VII: 329; p. 189.

66. Weyand, *Kants Geschichtsphilosophie.*

67. Menzer sees the relationship between history and anthropology in Kant, but does not acknowledge that the two have the same developmental history in Kant's thought. According to Menzer, Kant's theory of history developed out of his cosmological and cosmogonical views. Therefore, this must also hold for anthropology, see *Kants Lehre von Natur und Geschichte*, pp. 1 and 120–22.

68. KGS, RzL, XVI: 804, Refl. 3376. See also Anth, VII: 120; p. 3.

69. KGS, Col 70, XV: 659, Refl. 1482. According to Adickes this was written around 1785–88, exactly the time that Kant was writing his treatises on history. See also KGS, RzA, XV: 645–46, Refl. 1467.

Chapter 3: Kant's Theory of Human Nature

1. Norbert Hinske, "Kants Idee der Anthropologie," pp. 410–27. See also Benno Erdmann, *Zur Entwicklungsgeschichte von Kants Anthropologie*, in *Reflexionen Kants zur Anthropologie*, p. 48; Emil Arnoldt, "*Kants Vorlesungen über physische Geographie und ihr Verhältnis zu seinen anthropologischen Vorlesungen*," in *Emil Arnoldt Gesammelte Schriften*, pp. 346–73, Bd. 4 (Berlin: n.p., 1908).

2. Gerhard Funke, "Kants Frage nach dem Menschen," *Jahrbuch der Albertus-Universität zu Königsberg/Pr.* 25 (1975): 5–21.

3. For a good article that attempts to show the development of Kant's thought from empirical psychology to anthropology see Reinhard Brandt, "Ausgewählte Probleme der Kantischen Anthropologie," in Jürgen Schings, ed., *Der ganze Mensch: Anthropologie und Literatur im 18. Jahrhundert*, ed. Jürgen Schings (Stuttgart and Weimer, 1992), pp. 14–32.

4. Gerhard Funke, "Kants Stichwort für unsere Aufgabe: Disziplinieren, Kultivieren, Zivilisieren, Moralisieren," in *Akten des 4. Internationalen Kant-Kongreß*, ed. Gerhard Funke 3: 1–25 (Mainz: n.p., 1974).

5. Monika Firla, *Untersuchungen zum Verhältnis von Anthropologie und Moralphilosophie bei Kant* (Frankfurt/Bern: Peter Lang, 1981).

6. Allen W. Wood, "Unsociable Sociability: The Anthropological Basis of Kantian Ethics," in *Philosophical Topics* 19, no. 1 (Spring 1991): 325–51.

7. Immanuel Kant, *Anthropologie im pragmatischer Hinsicht*, in *Kants gesammelte Schriften*, eds. Königlich Preußische [now Deutsche] Akademie der Wissenschaft, vols. 1–29 (Berlin: G. Reimer [now de Gruyter],1902–), VII: 324; *Anthropology from a Pragmatic Point of View*, trans. Mary Gregor (The Hague: Martinus Nijoff, 1974), p. 185. [now KGS, Anth, VII: 324; p. 185].

8. KGS, Anth, VII: 322; p. 183.

9. Immanuel Kant, *Die Metaphysik der Sitten*, in *Kants gesammelte Schriften*, eds. Königlich Preußische [now Deutsche] Akademie der Wissenschaft, vols. 1–29 (Berlin: G. Reimer [now de Gruyter], 1902–), vol. VI: 387; *The Metaphysics of Morals*, trans. Mary Gregor, (Cambridge: Cambridge University Press, 1991), p. 191. [now KGS, MM VI: 387; p. 191].

10. KGS, Anth, VII: 324; p. 185. Kant talks about progress in his passages on the pragmatic predisposition and the moral predisposition, but does not mention it explicitly within the account of the technical predisposition. But later, when he sums up what anthropology teaches, he says human beings will be cultivated, civilized, and moralized. I take this passage to be referring to progress as well, and that means that the technical predisposition whose end is culture also admits of progress. See KGS, Anth, VII: 324–25; p. 186.

11. KGS, Anth, VII: 328; p. 188.

12. Immanuel Kant, *Zum Ewigen Frieden*, in KGS, VIII: 361–62; Perpetual Peace, in *Perpetual Peace and Other Essays*, trans. Ted Humphrey, (Indianapolis: Hackett Publishing Co., 1983) p. 120.

13. Immanuel Kant, *Pädagogik*, in KGS, IX: 446; *Education*, trans. Annette Churton (Ann Arbor, MI: The University of Michigan, 1964), p. 11, [now KGS, Ed, IX: 446; p. 11].

14. KGS, Anth, VII: 321; p. 183.

15. KGS, Anth VII: 201; pp. 72–73.

16. For the different accounts of the predispositions compare KGS, Anth Vol. 322–24; pp. 183–86 with Immanuel Kant, *Religion innerhalb der Grenzen der bloßen Vernunft*, in KGS, VI: 26–28; *Religion within the Boundaries of Mere Reason*, trans. George di Giovanni (Cambridge: Cambridge University Press, 1996), pp. 74–76. [now KGS, Rel, VI: 26–28; pp. 74–76]. I take the predisposition to humanity to be the same as the pragmatic predisposition. Both are aimed at happiness and civilization.

17. KGS, Anth VII: 324; p. 185.

18. Compare KGS, Menschenkunde, XXV: 859, with KGS, Anth VII: 322; p. 183 where Kant says "among the living beings that inhabit the Earth, man is easily distinguished from all other natural beings . . ." See also KGS, Menschenkunde, XXV: 1199–1200; and KGS, Mrongovius, XXV: 1417–18.

19. Immanuel Kant, *Kritik der Urteilskraft*, in KGS, V: 464n; *Critique of Judgment*, trans. Werner S. Pluhar (Indianapolis, IN: Hackett Publishing Co., 1987). [now KGS, KU, V: 464n; p. 356n].

20. Immanuel Kant, *Lectures on Ethics*, trans. Peter Heath (Cambridge: Cambridge University Press, 1997) p. 212–13. [now LoE, p. 212–13].

21. KGS, KU, V: 431; p. 318.

22. KGS, KU, V: 435–36; p. 323.

23. KGS, KU, V: 431; p. 319.

24. KGS, KU, V: 431; p. 318.

25. Kant writes in the *Grounding*, "Thus a free will and a will subject to moral laws are one and the same." This does not mean that one is free only when one acts morally. It does mean that the human being is free when it is subject to a moral law, whether the maxim is consistent with duty or not. If only moral actions were free then people could not be held responsible for immoral actions. It is the capacity to act on a maxim that makes humans free. This is consistent with Henry Allison's position in *Kant's Theory of Freedom* (Cambridge: Cambridge University Press, 1990); Immanuel Kant, *Grundlegung zur Metaphysik der Sitten*, in KGS, IV: 447; *Grounding for the Metaphysics of Morals*, trans. James W. Ellington (Indianapolis, IN: Hackett Publishing Co., 1993), p. 49. [now KGS, Gr, IV: 447; p. 49].

26. KGS, Ed, IX: 441; p. 1.

27. KGS, Gr, IV: 412; p. 23.

28. KGS, Menschenkunde, XXV: 1199–1200. See also KGS, Mrongovius, XXV: 1419–20.

29. KGS, Menschenkunde, XXV: 1198. See also KGS, Mrongovius, XXV: 1427, and KGS, Pillau, XXV: 847.

30. Immanuel Kant, *Critique of Pure Reason*, trans. Norman Kemp Smith (New York: St. Martin's Press, 1965), B 828 (now KrV B 828).

31. KGS, Ed, IX: 455; p. 30.

32. KGS Gr, IV: 417; p. 27. Kant writes, "Whoever wills the end, wills (so far as reason has decisive influence on his actions) also the means that are indispensably necessary to his actions and that lie in his power."

33. KGS, Anth, VII: 321; p. 183.

34. KGS, Ed, IX: 449–50; pp. 18–20.

35. KGS, Ed, IX: 455, p. 30.

36. KGS, Anth, VII: 324; p. 185.

37. KGS, Anth, VII: 325; p. 186.

38. KGS, Anth, VII; 325; p. 186.

39. KGS, Anth, VII: 322–25.

40. Reinhard Brandt recognizes that it is not easy to see how they are to be ordered in his writing, but he does not give an interpretation as to their significance. Indeed it is not self-evident what sections A, B, and C are apart from Kant's lectures on anthropology. Careful attention to Kant's wording as he introduces the passage reveals their meaning. See Reinhard Brandt, *Kommentar zu Kants Anthropologie*, Kant-Forschungen Band 10 (Hamburg: Felix Meiner Verlag, 1999), p. 487.

41. KGS, Friedländer, XXV: 682.

42. KGS, Menschenkunde, XXV: 1196.

43. KGS, Menschenkunde, XXV: 1197.

44. KGS, Mrongovius, XXV: 1417 and 1417–18.

45. KGS, Mrongovius, XXV: 1418.

46. KGS, Mrongovius, XXV: 1419.

47. KGS, Mrongovius, XXV: 1420.

48. KGS, Anth, VII: 325–26; pp. 186–87.

49. KGS, Anth, VII: 329; p. 189.

50. KGS, Anth, VII: 329; 190.

51. KGS, Anth, VII: 325; p. 186.

52. KGS, Anth, VII: 268; p. 135.

53. KGS, Anth, VII; 269; p. 136.

54. KGS, Ed, IX: 442; p. 3.

55. KGS, Ed, IX: 442; p. 3.

56. KGS, Anth, VII: 267–68; p. 135. Both sex and freedom are natural inclinations, not ones proceeding from culture.

57. KGS, Anth, VII: 201; p. 72.

58. KGS, Reflexionen zur Anthropologie, XV: 865, Refl. 1517.

59. KGS, Anth, VII: 325–26; pp. 186–87.

60. KGS, Reflexionen zur Anthropologie, XV: 889, Refl. 1521.

61. KGS, Reflexionen zur Anthropologie, XV: 885, Refl. 1521.

62. KGS, Rel, VI: 27; p. 75.

63. KGS, Anth, VII: 323; p. 185.

64. KGS, Gr, IV: 416; p. 26.

65. KGS, Anth, VII: 201; p. 72.

66. KGS, Ed, IX: 486; p. 94.

67. KGS, Ed, IX: 450; p. 19.

68. LoE, 155.

69. KGS, Anth, VII: 326; p. 187.

70. KGS, Rel, VI: 27; p. 22. See also KGS, KU, V: 432; p. 320.

71. KGS, Reflexionen zur Anthropologie, XV: 527; refl. 1194.

72. KGS, Rel, VI: 27; p. 23.

73. Immanuel Kant, *Kritik der praktischen Vernunft*, in KGS, V: 152; *Critique of Practical Reason*, trans. Lewis White Beck (Indianapolis, IN: Bobbs-Merrill, 1956), p. 156. [now KGS, KpV, V: 152; p. 156].

74. KGS, Ed, IX: 486–87; pp. 96–98.

75. KGS, Ed, IX: 481; p. 84.

76. KGS, Anth, VII: 292; p. 157. In Friedländer, Kant acknowledges that human beings can have an evil character as well as no character at all. See KGS, Friedländer XXV: 630.

77. KGS, Anth, VII: 292; p. 157.

78. KGS, Anth, VII: 294; p. 159.

79. KGS, Reflexionen zur Anthropologie, XV: 865; Refl. 1517.

80. Immanuel Kant, Verkündigung des nahen Abschlusses eines Tractats zum ewigen Frieden in der Philosophie, in KGS, VIII: 418.

81. KGS, Reflexionen zur Anthropologie, XV: 800, Refl. 1502a. For this same triad division see also XV: 659, Refl. 1482.

82. KGS, Reflexionen zur Moralphilosophie, XIX: 112, Refl. 6618.

83. KGS, Mrongovius, XXV: 1211.

84. KGS, Anth, VII: 201; pp. 72–73.

85. KGS, Anth, VII: 327; p. 188.

86. KGS, Anth, VII: 200; p. 72. See also KGS, Anth, VII: 228; pp. 96–97.

87. KGS, KU, V: 431–35; pp. 318–23.

88. KGS, Anth, VII: 269; p. 160.

89. KGS, Anth, VII: 327; p. 188.

90. KGS, Anth, VII: 327; p. 188.

91. KGS, Anth, VII: 328; p. 188.

92. KGS, Anth, VII: 329; p. 190.

93. KGS, Pillau, XXV: 843.

94. KGS, Anth, VII: 130; p. 12.

95. KGS, DoV, VI: 446; p. 240.

96. KGS, Ed, IX: 455; p. 30ff.

Chapter 4: Kant's Theory of Human Nature as Natural Predispositions

1. KGS, Anth, VII: 322; p. 183.

2. KGS, Rel, VI: 26; p. 74.

3. KGS, Rel, VI: 27; p. 75.

4. KGS, Anth, VII: 323; p. 185.

5. KGS, Anth, VII; 326; p. 187.

6. KGS, Rel, VI; 26; p. 75.

7. KGS, Anth, VII: 306; p. 169. The preservation of the species belongs to the character of women.

8. KGS, Anth, VII: 254; p. 122.

9. KGS, Anth, VII: 262; p. 129.

10. KGS, Anth, VII: 255; p. 123.

11. KGS, Anth, VII: 164; p. 41.

12. KGS, Anth, VII: 170; p. 47.

13. KGS, Anth, VII: 231; p. 100.

14. KGS, Anth, VII: 262; p. 129.

15. KGS, Anth, VII: 281; p. 146.

16. KGS, Anth, VII: 275; p. 141.

17. KGS, Anth, VII: 274; p. 141.

18. KGS, Anth, VII: 268; p. 135.

19. KGS, Anth, VII: 267; p. 134.

20. KGS, Anth, VII: 268; p. 136.

21. KGS, Anth, VII: 268, p. 135.

22. KGS, Anth, VII: 269; p. 136.

23. KGS, Anth, VII: 269; p. 136.

24. KGS, Anth, VII: 269; p. 136.

25. KGS, Gr, IV: 447; p. 49.

26. KGS, Anth, VII: 307; p. 170.

27. KGS, Anth, VII: 307; p. 168.

28. KGS, Anth, VII: 304-305; p. 168.

29. KGS, Anth, VII: 309; p. 172.

30. KGS, Anth, VII: 308; p. 171.

31. KGS, Anth, VII: 269; p. 136.

32. KGS, Anth, VII: 271; p. 138.

33. KGS, Anth, VII: 267; p. 135.

34. KGS, Anth, VII: 270; p. 137.

35. KGS, DoV, VI: 277; p. 96.

36. KGS, DoV, VI: 278; pp. 96–97.

37. KGS, DoV, VI: 287; p. 97.

38. See Holly L. Wilson, "Kant's Evolutionary Theory of Marriage," in *Autonomy and Community: Readings in Contemporary Kantian Social Philosophy*, ed. Jane Kneller and Sidney Axinn (New York: State University of New York, 1998), pp. 283–306.

39. KGS, Anth, VII: 304; p. 168.

40. KGS, Anth, VII: 325; p. 186.

41. KGS, Anth, VII: 303; pp. 166–67.

42. KGS, Anth, VII: 305; p. 168.

43. KGS, Anth, VII: 308; p. 171.

44. KGS, Anth, VII: 306; p. 169.

45. See Wilson, "Kant's Evolutionary Theory of Marriage."

46. KGS, Anth, VII: 308; p. 171.

47. KGS, Rel, VI: 26; p. 75.

48. KGS, Anth, VII: 303; p. 167.

49. KGS, Anth, VII: 323; p. 184.

50. KGS, DoV, VI: 420; p. 82.

51. KGS, KGS, Ed, IX: 441, 442; pp. 2 and 3.

52. KrV, B 737.

53. Michael Ruse, "Evolutionary Ethics: A Phoenix Arisen," Zygon, vol. 21, no. 1 (March 1986): 96.

54. KGS, Ed, IX: 443.

55. KGS, Anth, VII: 323; p. 184.

56. KGS, Anth, VII: 323; p. 185.

57. KGS, Anth, VII: 323, p. 184.

58. KGS, Ed, IX: 441.

59. KGS, Ed, IX: 452.

60. KGS, Col 80, XV: 820, Refl. 1508.

61. KGS, Col 80, XV: 865, Refl. 1517, and DoV, VI: 444, p. 10.

62. KrV, B 737, and LoE, p. 218.

63. KGS, Ed, IX: 449–50.

64. KGS, Rel, VI: 4 fn; p. 3 fn.

65. KGS, Ed, IX: 449–50; pp. 18–20.

66. KGS, Gr, IV: 415; p. 25.

67. KGS, KU, V: 172, p. 11.

68. The subordination of scholastic philosophy under the function of the technical use of our reason is important to the distinction I will show later between the scholastic idea of philosophy and the pragmatic idea of philosophy.

69. KGS, Ed, IX: 455,486.

70. KGS, Ed, IX: 455.

71. KGS, Ed, IX: 475.

72. KGS, Ed, IX: 470.

73. KGS, Ed, IX: 480.

74. KGS, Anth, VII: 201; p. 72.

75. KGS, KU, V: 383; p. 264.

76. KGS, KU, V: 431; p. 319.

77. KGS, Ed, IX: 446; p. 58.

78. KGS, Ed, IX: 446; p. 59.

79. KGS, KU, V: 432; p. 319.

80. KGS, Anth, VII: 325; p. 180.

81. KGS, Anth, VII: 329; p. 189.

82. KGS, Anth, VII: 325; p. 186.

83. KGS, Anth, VII: 323; p.185.

84. KGS, Anth, VII: 322; p. 183.

85. KGS, Rel, VI, 27; p. 75.

86. KGS, KU, V: 432 and 433; pp. 320 and 321.

87. KGS, KU, V: 432; p. 320.

88. KGS, KU, V: 433; p. 320.

89. KGS, KU, V: 433; p. 320.

90. KGS, Anth, VII: 309; p 172.

91. KGS, Anth, VII: 276; pp. 142–43.

92. KGS, Anth, VII: 303ff; pp. 167–68.

93. KGS, Anth, VII: 309; p. 172.

94. KGS, Rel, VI: 27; p. 75.

95. KGS, Col 70, XV: 659, Refl. 1482.

96. KGS, Anth, VII: 201; p. 72.

97. KGS, KU, V: 430ff.

98. LoE, p. 43.

99. LoE, p. 43.

100. KGS, Anth, VII: 249; p. 116. Kant writes, "luxury (*luxus*) is excessive comfort in the social life of the community (so that its comfort works against its welfare), when this excess is associated with taste."

101. KGS, Anth, VII: 201; p. 72. Anth VII: 271; p. 138. Anth VII: 312; p. 175.

102. KGS, Anth, VII: 198; p. 70.

103. KGS, Rel, VI: 27; p. 76.

104. KGS, Anth, VII: 324; p. 185.

105. KGS, Rel, VI: 27-28; p. 76.

106. KGS, KU, V: 376; p. 255.

107. See Sidney Axinn, "Ambivalence: Kant's View of Human Nature," Kantstudien 72 (1981): 169–74, and Wayne Paul Pomerleau, "Kant's Theory of Human Culture as the Meaning of History," *Logos* (USA) 4 (1983): 25–38. "Human nature," according to Kant, should not be characterized as ambivalent. Human nature refers to the character of the species as nature has constituted it, and this is good in itself. Inclinations, however, are also "natural" and ambivalent.

108. KGS, Anth, VII: 324; p. 185.

109. KGS, Anth, VII: 324; p. 185.

110. KGS, Rel, VI: 28; p. 76.

111. KGS, Ed, IX: 448; p. 15.

112. KGS, Rel, VI: 28; p. 76. By "original" Kant is not referring to the definition given in the KrV, that by "*original* is meant that this determination of these limits is not derived from anything else, and therefore does not require any proof; for if it did, that would disqualify the supposed explanation from standing at the head of all the judgments regarding its objects," KrV, B 756fn. The predispositions are not original in this sense since they can be explained in terms of the conditions of their possibility: the predispositions to humanity and morality, for instance, are both rooted in practical

reason (KGS, Rel, VI: 28; p. 76). The predispositions are nevertheless original in the practical sense, not for constitutive judgment, but for regulative judgment. For regulative judgment, we do not need to go any further back in the series of causes than the four original predispositions. They are original teleological causes of all the phenomenon of human experience in society with other human beings.

113. KGS, Col 80, XV: 865, Refl. 1517.

114. KGS, Col 80, XV: 820, Refl. 1508.

115. KGS, Col 70, XV: 716, Refl. 1486.

116. KGS, Anth, VII: 201; p. 73.

117. KGS, Anth, VII: 326; p. 187.

118. KGS, KU, V: 430; p. 318.

119. KGS, Anth, VII: 326; p. 187.

120. KGS, Anth, VII: 325–27; pp. 186–88.

121. KGS, Anth, VII: 324 and 329; pp, 185 and 189.

122. KGS, Anth, VII: 325; p. 186.

123. KGS, Anth, VII: 325–26; pp. 186–87.

124. KGS, Anth, VII: 327; p. 188.

125. KGS, Anth, VII: 333; p. 193.

126. KGS, Anth, VII: 328; p. 189.

127. KGS, Ed, IX: 444; p. 8.

128. KGS, Ed, IX: 445; p. 9–10.

129. KGS, Ed, IX: 445; p. 9–10.

130. KGS, Ed, IX: 447; p. 14.

131. KrV, B 597.

132. KGS, Ed, IX: 444, p. 8.

133. KGS, Ed, IX: 449–50; p. 18–19.

134. KGS, Ed, IX: 449–50; p. 18–19.

135. KGS, Ed, IX: 445; p. 30.

136. KGS, Ed, IX: 445; p. 30.

137. KGS, Ed, IX: 450; p. 19.

138. KGS, Ed, IX: 455; p. 30.

139. KGS, Ed, IX: 469–70; p. 66–67.

140. KGS, Ed, IX: 475; p. 77–78.

141. KGS, Ed, IX: 487; p. 98–99.

142. KGS, Ed, IX: 470; p. 67.

143. KGS, Ed, IX: 470; p. 67.

144. One of the important aspects of education is appeal to the learner's reason by pointing out a plan in everything. Kant writes: "If we wish to form the characters of children, it is of the greatest importance to point out to them a certain plan, and certain rules, in everything." (KGS, Ed, IX: 481; p. 85). Seeing a plan in nature is also essential to the development of character and wisdom in adults.

145. KGS, Anth, VII: 201; pp. 72–73.

146. KGS, Nachricht, II: 305. Kant calls it "the early clever loquaciousness of young thinkers, who are blinder than any other conceited person and more incurable than ignorance."

147. One of the indispensable features of the education to moral character is the knowledge that all people are subject to the same laws of necessity. This holds true for adults too. see KGS, Ed, IX: 482; p. 86.

148. KGS, Anth, VII: 269; p. 136.

149. KGS, Anth, VII: 328; p. 189. Kant talks about the "education from above" which is nature's plan for the development of the human species to humanity. We can expect the species to develop toward a constitution that is based on the "principle of freedom, but at the same time on the principle of constraint in accordance with law," from "a wisdom that is not [our] own, but is yet the Idea of [our] own reason."

150. KGS, Ed, IX: 481; p. 85.

Chapter 5: The Critical Foundations of the Anthropology

1. KGS, KU, V: 387; p. 267.

2. KGS, KU, V: 360; p. 236.

3. KGS, First Intro, XX: 221; p. 409.

4. KGS, KU, V: 379, 404, and 412; pp. 259, 287, and 297. KGS, First Intro, XX: 204; p. 393.

5. KGS, KU, V: 411; p. 295.

6. A. Pfannkuche poses the essential question concerning the methodology of reflective judgment: "what is its purpose?" He writes: "Here a difficult question is raised. That Kant wanted to know the purposiveness in nature only as a principle of observation, as an applied maxim of research, is very clear. But a principle of observation from what point of view?" It seems clear to me that not only does Kant intend the pragmatic *Anthropology* but also the biological sciences. See A. Pfannkuche, "Der Zweckbegriff bei Kant," *Kantstudien* 5 (1901): 51–72, esp. p. 61. Cf. Klaus Düsing, *Die Teleologie in Kant Weltbegriff*, *Kantstudien Ergänzungshefte* 96 (Bonn: H. Bouvier u. Co., 1968), p. 215ff.

7. KGS, First Intro, XX: 210; p. 399.

8. KGS, First Intro, XX: 210; p. 399.

9. Kant writes that we judge the purpose of the eye to be seeing in order to investigate the eye and its lens but also so that we can "devise means to further that effect [seeing]" if the natural lens does not work as it should. KGS, First Intro XX: 236; p. 425.

10. KGS, First Intro, XX: 240; p. 429.

11. KGS, First Intro XX: 240; p. 429.

12. KGS, First Intro, XX: 240; p. 429.

13. KGS, RzA, XV: 800, Refl. 1502a.

14. KGS, Col 70, XV: 661, Refl. 1482.

15. KGS, Friedlander, XXV: 472.

16. Robert Louden, *Kant's Impure Ethics*, emphasizes the empirical character of the anthropology lectures, but then does recognize its teleological nature: "The strong teleological thrust of these descriptions of the destiny of the human species within the anthropology lectures also serves as a correction to the view that Kantian Anthropology is simply empirical science, however broadly conceived one takes 'empirical science' to be." However he locates the teleology only in the account of the human species, which occurs in the Characteristic instead of seeing it also in the Didactic, p. 92.

17. KGS, Anth, VII: 121; pp. 4-5.

18. KGS, First Intro, XX: 238; p. 427. This judgment is certainly evidenced in contemporary psychology, where one finds cognitive, evolutionary, behavioral, and psychoanalytic explanations all claiming to be the right way to explain human behavior. In addition to that, there are all kinds of different therapies claiming to be the right way to heal mental problems. This is not to mention the fact that psychiatrists think that chemical intervention is really needed.

19. KGS, First Intro, XX: 236; p. 425.

20. KGS, KU, V: 373; p. 252.

21. KGS, KU, V: 375; p. 255.

22. KGS, First Intro, XX: 236; p. 425.

23. Kant clearly thinks the *Anthropology* is systematic. See KGS, Anth, VII: 121; p. 5.

24. Klaus Düsing, *Die Teleologie in Kants Weltbegriff*. Kantstudien Ergänzunghefte 96 (Bonn: H. Bouvier u. Co., 1968), p. 116, sees the critical move in Kant's argument precisely here: "The unfolding of the teleological concept of the world in the *Critique of Judgment* begins above all from organisms, since they show us most clearly a purposiveness of nature. . . . Organisms are only *recognizable* for us, according to Kant, in their specificity, when the reflective judgment sees them as natural purposes."

25. KGS, KU, V: 376; p. 255.

26. KGS, KU, V: 371; pp. 249-50.

27. KGS, First Intro XX: 217; pp. 405–406.

28. KGS, KU, V: 425; p. 312.

29. KGS, KU, V: 367–68; p. 245.

30. Kant is not falling back into a position of mere natural teleology. He has argued against the external purposiveness of a utility teleology and critically founded his concept of internal purposiveness. Rudolf Eisler classifies the philosophy of Socrates, the Stoics, and Christian Wolff within the tradition of a "*Nützlichkeitsteleologie*" which "has as a rule an anthropocentric character." They "refer everything to the use of human beings around whom everything in the world turns." See Rudolf Eisler, *Der Zweck. Seine Bedeutung für Natur und Geist,* (Berlin: Ernst Siegfried Mittler und Sohn, 1914), p. 3. Eisler is convinced that Kant's interpretation of teleology is new, since Kant judges things according to their inner form as a natural purpose, rather than judging the existence of the thing as a natural purpose. "The formal concept of purpose is a product of the 'judgment' and at the same time a regulative idea of reason. It is not a 'category' and not a condition of objective experience, not a constitution of empirical reality, but of highest fruitfulness for the interpretation of happenings and for research into causes, especially in Biology.", p. 23.

31. KGS, Idea, VIII: 25; p. 35.

32. KGS, KU, V: 379; p. 258.

33. KGS, KU, V: 380–81; pp. 260–61.

34. KGS, KU, V: 445; p. 334.

35. KGS, KU, V: 442; p. 331.

36. KGS, KU, V: 435; p. 323.

37. KGS, Parow, XXV: 437–38.

38. KGS, Anth, VII: 131; p. 13.

39. KGS, Anth, VII: 133; p. 14.

40. KGS, Anth, VII: 133–134; p. 15.

41. KGS, Anth, VII: 161; p. 39.

42. KGS, Anth, VII: 202; p. 74.

43. KGS, Anth, VII: 219; p. 88.

44. KGS, Anth, VII: 219; p. 88.

45. KGS, First Intro, XX: 228; p. 417. Kant writes: "But if I speak of a perfection ([so that] a thing may, under the same concept of it, have many perfections), then I always presuppose the concept of something as a purpose."

46. KGS, Anth, VII: 144; p. 24.

47. KGS, Anth, VII: 119; p. 3.

48. KGS, Anth, VII: 324; p. 185.

49. KGS, Anth, VII: 145; p. 25.

50. KGS, Anth, VII: 156; p. 35.

51. KGS, Anth, VII: 158; p. 36.

52. KGS, Anth, VII: 165; p. 42.

53. KGS, Anth, VII: 165; p. 43.

54. KGS, Anth, VII: 165; p. 43.

55. KGS, Anth, VII: 165; p. 42.

56. KGS, Anth, VII: 149; p. 28.

57. I have always wondered why Kant objects so much to habits when he is said to have had the habit of taking a walk everyday at the same time. He did break the habit one time, however, and appropriately so, since he had just discovered Rousseau and was eager to continue to read.

58. KGS, Anth, VII: 208; p. 79.

59. KGS, Anth, VII: 167; p. 44.

60. KGS, Anth, VII: 181; p. 56.

61. KGS, Anth, VII: 181; p. 55.

62. KGS, Anth, VII: 182; p. 57.

63. KGS, Anth, VII: 182; p. 57.

64. KGS, Anth, VII: 215; p. 85.

65. KGS, Anth, VII: 236; p. 104.

66. KGS, Anth, VII: 239; p. 107.

67. KGS, Anth, VII: 239; p. 107.

68. KGS, Anth, VII: 287; p. 153.

69. KGS, Anth, VII: 250; p. 117.

70. KGS, Anth, VII: 244; p. 111.

71. KGS, Anth, VII: 244; pp. 111–12.

72. KGS, Anth, VII: 244; p. 112.

73. KGS, Anth, VII: 246; p. 113.

74. KGS, Anth, VII: 251; p. 119.

75. KGS, Anth, VII: 252; p. 120.

76. KGS, Anth, VII: 260; p. 127.

77. KGS, Anth, VII: 270; p. 137.

78. KGS, Anth, VII: 255; p. 123.

79. KGS, Anth, VII: 253; p. 121.

80. KGS, Anth, VII: 266; p. 133.

81. KGS, Anth, VII: 268; p. 134.

82. KGS, Anth, VII: 265; p. 133.

83. KGS, Anth, VII: 266; pp. 133–34.

84. KGS, Anth, VII: 270; p. 137.

85. KGS, Anth, VII: 200 and 271; pp. 72 and 138.

86. KGS, Anth, VII: 234; p. 103.

87. KGS, LoE, Collins XXVII: 466; p. 218.

88. KGS, Parow, XXV: 244.

89. KGS, Anth, VII: 152; p. 31.

90. KGS, Anth, VII: 179; p. 54.

91. KGS, Anth, VII: 328; p. 186.

92. KGS, Anth, VII: 274; p. 141.

93. KGS, Anth, VII: 276; p. 142. In contrast to Reinhard Brandt who thinks this passage is about a theodicy, I would simply interpret it to be the result of the teleological principle that nature does nothing in vain, which is a scientific not theological principle.

94. KGS, Ed, IX: 448.

95. KGS, Anth, VII: 305; p. 169.

96. KGS, Anth, VII: 303; pp. 166–67.

97. KGS, Anth, VII: 329; p. 189.

98. KGS, Anth, VII: 321–22; p. 183.

99. KGS, Anth, VII 324–25; p. 186.

100. KGS, LoE, Collins, XXVII: pp. 2–3.

101. KGS, Friedlander, XXV: 471.

102. KGS, Idea VIII: 18; p. 30. I specifically translated *Naturanlagen* as natural predispositions and not as capacities.

103. KGS, Anth, VII: 328; pp. 188–89.

104. KGS, KU, V: 431; p. 319.

105. KGS, KU, V: 430; p. 318.

106. KGS, KU, V: 430; p. 318.

107. Yirmiahu Yowel uses the concept of the "cunning of nature," to talk about nature's provocations, which seems to me a misconception of what Kant is intending. It can probably be represented as an hegelization of Kant. At one point, Kant does talk of the "*Kunstanstalten*" (KGS, VIII: 360; p.120) or artistic or intricate designs of nature, but as we have seen this is only meant to be referring to the analogy with human art or technology. It does not mean that nature is cunning [*listig*] or clever [*klug*], for Kant almost always talks of the wisdom of nature. Also translating it as "cunning" misleads us to think that nature is in some way manipulating our history to arrive at her designs. It immediately throws our freedom in question. The wisdom and

providence of nature is a concept easily reconcilable with our freedom, and our wisdom. Further, in the *Grounding* (KGS, IV: 416; p. 33), Kant differentiates between prudence [*Klugheit*] as "knowledge of the world," and "private prudence." If a person has the former without the latter, then that person is clever [*gescheut*] and cunning [*verschlagen*], but imprudent. Clearly, Kant uses this term to refer to human beings, and not to nature. See Yirmiahu Yovel, *Kant and the Philosophy of History* (Princeton, NJ: Princeton University Press, 1980).

108. KGS, Col 80, XV: 897, Refl. 1524. See also Funke, "Kants Stichwort," pp. 9–10. According to Funke, the civil society is only possible in an urban society where human beings live closely next to each other.

109. KGS, LoE, Collins XXVII: 219; see also KGS, Ed IX: 448; p. 16.

110. KGS, RzA XV: 235, Refl. 536. Also KGS, RzA XV: 636, Refl. 1454.

111. KGS, KU, V: 433; p. 283.

112. KGS, Ed IX: 442; p. 3.

113. KGS, KU, V: 433; p. 321.

114. KGS, Anth, VII: 333; p. 193.

115. KGS, Ed IX: 442; translation is mine. See also Düsing, *Die Teleologie in Kants Weltbegriff*, pp. 217ff. He agrees that the overcoming of the despotism of the natural instincts is not accomplishable by the goodwill, but only by the "mechanism" or "plan" of nature.

116. KGS, KU, V: 432; p. 319. I have not focused, in this account of the argument in the Methodology, on the a priori principle of "human beings under moral laws," because I wanted to clarify Kant's concept of the last purpose of nature. This concept is anything but clear, especially here in the Methodology. Nevertheless, we must understand this term and what Kant means by it, since it is central to his *Anthropology*, writings on history, his *Religion*, and also his *Metaphysik der Sitten*. Here are just a few places Kant talks about the last purpose, KGS, DoV VI: 420; p. 82; KGS, LoE XXVII: 252; KGS, Rel VI: 20; p. 70; KGS, Col 80, 886, Refl. 1521 and 888; KGS, Idea VIII: 27; KGS, RzA XV: 168, Refl. 1418.

Chapter 6: Kant's Pragmatic Anthropology as Popular Philosophy

1. Kant lectured on anthropology consistently for twenty-three and one-half years until he retired from teaching. He averaged thirty to fifty students a semester with a high of seventy in 1791–92. See Arnoldt, *Gesammelte Schriften*, ed. Otto Schöndorffer, "Kants Vorlesung über Anthropologie," in vol. 4: *Kritische Exkurse im Gebiete der Kantforschung*, part 1, pp. 319–43, (Berlin: Bruno Cassirer, 1908), pp. 326ff.

2. KGS, Letters, XII: 219.

3. KGS, Letters, XII: 202.

4. For further information concerning the reviews of Kant's contemporaries see Rudolf Malter, "Anhang II. Zu Kants Vorlesungen über Anthropologie," in

Immanuel Kant: Anthropologie in pragmatischer Hinsicht, ed. Karl Vorländer, 315–70, (Hamburg: Felix Meiner, 1980), pp. 338–43.

5. Reinhard Brandt, *Kommentar zu Kants Anthropologie,* Kant-Forschungen Band 10 (Hamburg: Felix Meiner Verlag, 1999), p. 7.

6. Ibid., p. 8; Reinhard Brandt/Werner Stark, "Einleitung" in Kant's Vorlesungen über Anthropologie in *Kant's gesammelte Schriften,* vol. XXV (Berlin: Walter de Gruyter and Co., 1997), p. 11.

7. Reinhard Brandt, "The Guiding Idea of Kant's Anthropology and the Vocation of the Human Being," in *Essays on Kant's Anthropology,* ed. Brian Jacobs and Patrick Kain (Cambridge: Cambridge University Press, 2003), p. 85.

8. Brian Jacobs and Patrick Kain, ed. *Essays on Kant's Anthropology* (Cambridge: Cambridge University Press, 2003), p. 3.

9. KGS, Reflexionen zur Logik, XVI: 862, Refl. 3479. See also KGS, Gr, IV: 409, p. 21; and KGS, Reflexionen zur Logik, XVI: 782, Refl. 3329.

10. Immanuel Kant, *Logic,* trans. Robert S. Hartman and Wolfgang Schwarz (New York: Dover Publishing Inc., 1974), p. 27.

11. KGS, RzA, XV: 800, Refl. 1502a. See also XV: 801, Refl. 1502a.

12. KrV, B 868fn.

13. See also KGS, Racen, II: 443.

14. KGS, Logic, IX: 23–25.

15. F. C. Starke, *Immanuel Kants Menschenkunde and Immanuel Kants Anweisung zur Menschen- und Weltkenntnis* (Hildesheim/New York: Georg Olms, 1976), p. 1.

16. Starke, *Immanuel Kants Menschenkunde,* p. 2.

17. Starke, *Immanuel Kants Menschenkunde,* p. 3.

18. Starke, *Immanuel Kants Menschenkunde,* p. 4.

19. KGS, Logic, IX: 27–28.

20. Ibid.

21. Starke, *Immanuel Kants Menschenkunde,* 2.

22. KGS, Reflexionen Zur Logik, XVI: 862, Refl. 3479. See also *Grounding,* 409, p. 21; and Reflexionen zur Logik XVI: 782, Refl. 3329.

23. KGS, Reflexionen zur Logik, XVI: 782, Refl. 3329.

24. KGS, Gr, IV: 388; p. 2.

25. KGS, RzA, XV: 659, Refl. 1482, and XV: 669, Refl. 1482.

26. KGS, Nachricht, II: 305.

27. Starke, *Menschenkunde,* p. 1.

28. KGS, Racen, II: 443.

29. KrV B 864. See also KGS, Nachricht II: 306.

30. KrV, B 864. See also KGS, Metaphysic L2, XXVIII: 531; and KGS, Logik Blomberg, XXIV: 47.

31. KGS, Philosophische Enzyklopädie, XXIX: 5 and 6.

32. KGS, Philosophische Enzyklopädie, XXIX: 8. See also KGS, Logic, IX: 24; KGS, Metaphysic L2, XXVIII: 532: "the philosopher has to be differentiated from the rational artificer [*Vernunftkünstler*]."

33. KGS, Nachricht, II: 306.

34. KrV, B 806.

35. KGS, Anth, VII: 227; p. 95.

36. KGS, LoE, XXVII: 242.

37. KGS, BzB XX: 44. Translated by Karl Jaspers in, *Kant*, ed. by Hannah Arendt and trans. by Ralph Manheim (New York: Harcourt, Brace and World, Inc., 1962), p. 5.

38. KGS, RzA, XV: 395, Refl. 903.

39. Volker Simmermacher, "Kants Kritik der reinen Vernunft als Grundlegung einer Anthropologia Transcendentalis," (Phd diss., Heidelberg, 1951), for instance, uses this passage to claim that because the *Kritik der reinen Vernunft* is the grounding of a *subjektum transcendentale*, it is also the grounding of a transcendental anthropology: "The only medium, in which the self-interpretation can unfold, is reason taken in its broadest sense, that is, in the faculty of knowledge, which comprises intuition and thinking. Reason is the only faculty of the human subject, which can show itself through itself, and thereby knows how to imagine that which thinks, that is, the subject as subject. For that reason as well, the *anthropologia transcendentalis* has to develop as a self-knowledge of the understanding and of reason, which begins in the Critique of Reason. There, reason undertakes "the troublesome business of self-knowledge" [A, xi] of itself, without thereby being given as an object of appearance." p. 3.

40. "*Fiscalsierung*" is a word Kant has formed out of the old German (middle Latin) word "*Fiscal.*" The *Fiscal* is a "public person, who watches over the right of the *Fisci*, that is, the reigning prince's income, sees to it that the law is followed, and brings to court the violation of both in the name of the reigning prince." See Johann C. Adelung, *Grammatisch-kritisches Wörterbuch der Hochdeutschen Mundart*, (Leipzig: n.p., 1796). Another word for Fiscal is a procurator, which is an agent or deputy for another. By "*Fiscalsierung*," then, Kant must mean that the sciences should be brought before a public judge to see if they are giving their due, and staying within their own justified limits.

41. KGS, RzA, XV: 394–95, Refl. 903.

42. KGS, Col 80, XV: 888, Refl. 1521.

43. KGS, LoE, XXVII: 244.

44. KGS, Logic, IX: 27.

45. KGS, Reflexionen zur Metaphysik, XVIII: 30, Refl. 4925.

46. KGS, Logic, IX: 27.

47. KGS, Metaphysik L2, XXVIII: 532: "The philosopher has to be differentiated from the rational artificer [*Vernunftkünstler*]."

48. KGS, Metaphysik L2, XXVIII: 532.

49. KGS, Philosophisches Enzyklopädie, XXIX: 8. Kant had already asserted in the 1760s that "the ultimate purpose [or reason] is to find the destiny of human beings." KGS, Bemerkungen zu den Beobachtungen, XX: 175.

50. The maxims of wisdom are found at KGS, Anth, VII, 200; 72.

51. KGS, Anth, VII, 324–25; 186.

52. KGS, Letters, XI, 72–73.

53. KGS, Anth VII, 221; 90.

54. KGS, Anth VII, 280fn; 145.

55. KGS, RzL, XXIV, 188f.

Bibliography

Adelung, Johann C. *Grammatisch-kritisches Wörterbuch der Hochdeutschen Mundart*. Leipzig: n.p., 1796.

Albrecht, Michael. "Kants Kritik der historischen Erkenntnis—ein Bekenntnis zu Wolff?" *Studia Leibnitiana* 14 (1982):1-24.

Allison, Henry. *Kant's Theory of Freedom*. Cambridge: Cambridge University Press, 1990.

Arnoldt, Emil. *Gesammelte Schriften*. Edited by Otto Schöndörffer. "Kants Vorlesung über Anthropologie." In vol. 4: *Kritische Exkurse im Gebiete der Kantforschung*, part 1, pp. 319–434. Berlin: Bruno Cassirer, 1908.

———. "Kants Vorlesungen über physische Geographie und ihr Verhältnis zu seinen anthropologischen Vorlesungen." *Gesammelte Schriften*, Bd 4, pp.346–73.

Atkinson, R. F. "Kant's Philosophy of History." in *Substance and Form in History*. Edited by Leon S. Pompa, 15–26. Edinburgh: n.p., 1981.

Auxter, Thomas. *Kant's Moral Teleology*. Mercer University Press, 1982.

Axinn, Sidney. "Ambivalence: Kant's View of Human Nature." *Kantstudien* 72 (1981): 169–74.

Baczko, L. A. F von. "Probe eines Commentars zu Kants Anthropologie." *Vesta* (Königsberg, 1807): 177–90.

Barach, C. S. "Kant als Anthropolog." *Mittheilungen der anthropologischen Gesellschaft in Wien* 2 (1872): 65–79.

Barnard, Frederick. "'Aufklärung' and 'Mundigkeit': Thomasius, Kant, and Herder." *Dtsch. Viertelj. Lit. Geistesg* 57 (1983): 278–97.

———. "The 'Practical Philosophy' of Christian Thomasius." *Journal of the History of Ideas* 32 (1971): 1 221–46.

Bauch, Bruno. "Die Persönlichkeit Kants." *Kantstudien* 9 (1904): 196–210.

Baumgarten, Alexander Gottlieb. *Metaphysica*. 1st Ed. Halle: n.p., 1739.

Berning, Vincent. Art. "Anthropologie." In *Handbuch pädagogischer Grundbegriffe*, 1. Edited by Josef Speck/Gerhard Wehle, 1–37. München: pub, 1970.

Böhme, Hartmut & Gernot Böhme. *Das Andere der Vernunft. Zur Entwicklung von Rationalitätsstrukturen am Beispiel Kants*. Frankfurt am Main: Suhrkamp, 1983.

Böhme, Gernot. *Anthropologie in pragmatischer Hinsicht: Darmstädter Vorlesungen*. Frankfurt am Main: Suhrkamp, 1985.

Bollnow, Otto Friedrich. "Existenzerhellung und philosophische Anthropologie." *Blätter für Deutsche Philosophie* 12 (1938): 133–74.

———. "Die philosophische Anthropologie und ihre methodischen Prinzipien." In *Philosophische Anthropologie heute*. Edited by Roman Rocek und Oskar Schatz, 19–36. München: C. H. Beck, 1972.

Booth, William James. "Reason and History: Kant's Other Copernican Revolution." *Kantstudien* 74 (1983): 56–71.

Borowski, Ludwig Ernst. *Darstellung des Lekens und Charakters Immanuel Kants*. Königsberg: n.p., 1804.

Brandt, Reinhard. *Kommentar zu Kants Anthropologie*. Kant-Forschungen Band 10. Hamburg: Feix Meiner Verlag, 1999.

Brandt, Reinhard and Werner Stark. "Einleitung." *Kants gesammelte Schriften*, Bd. 25.I. Berlin: Walter de Gruyter and Co., 1997.

Buchner, Edward Franklin. *A Study of Kant's Psychology with reference to the Critical Philosophy*. Lancaster, PA: The New Era Print, 1897.

Burger, Hotimir. "Kant und das Problem der Anthropologie." *Synthesis Philosophica* 1–2 (1986): 125–35.

Cassirer, Ernst. *Kant's Life and Thought*. translated by James Hayden. New Haven and London: Yale University Press, 1981.

Crusius, Christian August. "Anweisung vernünftig zu Leben." In *Die philosophischer Hauptwerke*, 1. Hildesheim: Gerg Olms Verlag, 1999.

Despland, Michel. *Kant on History and Religion*. Montreal: 1973–4.

Dilthey, Wilhelm. *Gesammelte Schriften*. Stuttgart: B. G. Teubner Veilagsgesellschaft, 1957.

Dessoir, Max. "Kant und die Psychologie." *Kantstudien* 29 (1924): 98–120.

Dörpinghaus, Wilhelm. *Der Begriff der Gesellschaft bei Kant. Eine Untersuchung über das Verhältnis von Rechts— und Geschichts—philosophie zur Ethik*. Inaugural-Diss. Köln, 1959.

Dorner, A. "Kants Kritik der Urteilskraft in ihrer Beziehung zu den beiden anderen Kritiken und zu den nachkantischen Systemen." *Kantstudien* 4 (1900): 248–85.

———. "Über die Entwicklungsidee bei Kant," in *Zur Erinnerung an Immanuel Kant*, pp. 57-90. Ed. by Universität Königsberg. Halle: Waisenhauses, 1904.

Drescher, Siegfried. "Unsere Zeit und Kant." In *Wer war Kant?* Edited by Neske. Pfulligen: 1974.

Düsing, Klaus. *Die Teleologie in Kants Weltbegriff*. Kantstudien Ergänzunghefte 96. Bonn: H. Bouvier u. Co., 1968.

Duque, Felix. "Teleologie und Leiblichkeit beim späten Kant." *Kantstudien* 75 (1984): 381–97.

Eisler, Rudolf. *Der Zweck. Seine Bedeutung für Natur und Geist*. Berlin: Ernst Siegfried Mittler und Sohn, 1914.

————. art. "Anthropologie," in *Wörterbuch der philosophische Begriffe*. Berlin: 1927.

————. *Kant—Lexicon*. 1930, repr., Berlin: Hildesheim, 1977.

Erdmann, Benno. "Zur Entwicklungsgeschichte von Kants Anthropologie" In *Reflexionen Kants zur kritische Philosophie*. Edited by Benno Erdmann. Vol. 1: Reflexionen Kants zur Anthropologie, 37–64. Leipzig: Fue's (R. Reisland), 1882.

Eschke, Hans-Günter. "Immanuel Kants 'Anthropologie in pragmatischer Hinsicht' und die philosophische Anthropologie." *Wissenschaftl. Ztschr. d. Friedrich-Schiller— Universität Jena* 24 (1975): 221–27.

Firla, Monika. *Untersuchungen zum Verhältnis von Anthropologie und Moralphilosophie bei Kant*. Frankfurt/Bern: Peter Lang, 1981.

Fischer, Norman. "The Concept of Community in Kant's Architectonic." *Man and World* 11 (1978): 372–91.

Forschner, Maximillan. *Gesetz und Freiheit. Zum Problem der Autonomie bei I. Kant*, 47–51,180–85. München/Salzburg: Anton Pustet, 1974.

————. "Reine Morallehre und Anthropologie: Kritische Überlegungen zum Begriff eines a priori gültigen allgemeinen praktischen Gesetzes bei Kant." *Neue Hefte für Philosophie* 22 (Göttingen: 1983): 25–44.

Frierson, Patrick R. *Freedom and Anthropology in Kant's Moral Philosophy*. Cambridge: Cambridge University Press, 2003.

Frost, Walter. "Kants Teleologie." *Kantstudien* 11 (1906): 297–347.

Funke, Gerhard. "Kants Frage nach dem Menschen." *Jahrbuch der Albertus-Universität zu Königsberg/Pr.* 25 (1975): 5–21.

————. "Kants Stichwort für unsere Aufgabe: Disziplinieren, Kultivieren, Zivilisieren, Moralisieren," in *Akten des 4. Internationalen Kant-Kongreß*. Edited by Gerhard Funke, 3: 1–25. Mainz: 1974.

Gause, Fritz. *Kant und Königsberg*. Leer/Ostfreiesland: Gerhard Rautenberg, 1974.

Gehlen, Arnold. *Der Mensch*. 9th Ed. Frankfurt: 1971.

Gerlach, Hans-Martin. "Die ungesellige Geselligkeit oder der Antagonismus von Egoismus und Vergesellschaftung." *Wissenschaftl. Ztschr. d. Martin-Luther-Universität Halle. Gesellschafts- und Sprachwissenschaftl. Reihe* 24 (1975): 17–23.

Gerland, G. "Immanuel Kant, seine geographischen und anthropologischen Arbeiten." *Kantstudien* 10 (1905): 1–43; 417–547.

Goldmann, Lucien. *Mensch, Gemeinschaft und Welt in der Philosophie Immanuel Kants*. Phd. Diss., Zürich. Zürich: Europa, 1945.

Gouaux, Charles. "Kant's view of the Nature of Empirical Psychology." *Journal of the History of Behavioral Sciences* (1972): 237–42.

Gregor, Mary J. *Laws of Freedom*. Oxford: Basil Blackwell, 1963.

————. trans. "Introduction." In *Anthropology from a pragmatic point of view*. The Hague: Martinus Nijhoff, 1974.

Groethuysen, Bernhard. *Philosophische Anthropologie*. München: R. Oldenbourg, 1931.

Gulyga, Arsenij. *Immanuel Kant*. Trans. from Russian by Sigrun Bielfeldt. (Frankfurt am Main: Suhrkampf, 1981.

Heidegger, Martin. *Kant und das Problem der Metaphysik*. 4th Ed. Frankfurt am Main: Klostermann, 1973.

Herbart, J. F. "Vorwort zur gegenwärtigen Auflage." In *Immanuel Kants Anthropologie in pragmatischer hinsicht*. 4th Orig Ed. Leipzig: Immanuel Müller, 1833.

Hill, Thomas E. Jr. "Humanity as an End in Itself." *Ethics* 91 (October 1980): 84–99.

Hinske, Norbert. "Kants Idee der Anthropologie" In *Die Frage nach dem Menschen: Aufriss einer Philosophischen Anthropologie*. Festschrift für Max Müller zum 60. Geburtstag. Edited by Heinrich Rombach, 410–27. Freiburg/München: Karl Alber, 1966.

Hinske, Norbert. *Kant als Herausforderung an die Gegenwart*. Freiburg/München: Karl Alber, 1980.

Höffe, Otfried. *Immanuel Kant*. München: C.H. Beck, 1983.

Horkheimer, Max and Theodor W. Adorno. Dialectic of Enlightenment. Translated by John Cumming. New York: Herder and Herder, 1944.

Irmscher, Hans Dietrich. *Immanuel Kant, Aus den Vorlesungen der Jahre 1762–1764, Auf Grund der Nachschriften Johann Gottfried Herders*. Kantstudien-Ergänzungshefte 88. Köln: 1964.

Jacobs, Brian and Patrick Kain. *Essays on Kant's Anthropology*. Cambridge: Cambridge University Press, 2003.

Kaulbach, Friedrich. "Weltorientierung, Weltkenntnis und pragmatische Vernunft bei Kant." In *Kritik und Metaphysik Studien*. Edited by Heinz Heimsoeth, 60–75. Berlin: Walter der Gruyter and Co., 1966.

———. "Der Zusammenhang zwischen Naturphilosophie und Geschichtsphilosophie bei Kant." *Kongressbericht* (Kantkongreß 1965). Köln: Kölner Universitätsverlag, 1967.

———. "Welchen Nutzen gibt Kant der Geschichtsphilosophie?" *Kantstudien* 66 (1975): 65–84.

Kersting, Wolfgang. "Kann die Kritik der praktischen Vernunft populär sein? Über Kants Moralphilosophie und pragmatische Anthropologie." *Studiana Leibnitiana* 15 (1983): 82–93.

Kirchmann, J. H von. *Erläuterungen zu Kant's Anthropologie in pragmatischer Hinsicht*. Berlin: Heimann, 1869.

Kirschke, Siegfried. "Über Immanuel Kants Beitrag zur Herausbildung der naturwissenschaftlichen Anthropologie." *Wissenschaftl. Ztschr. d. Martin-Luther-Universität Halle. Gesellschafts- und Sprachwissenschaftl. Reihe* 24 (1975): 53–57.

Kopper, Joachim. "Einleitung," in *Immanuel Kant: Anthropologie in pramatischer Hinsicht.* Edited by Karl Voländer, Hamburg: IX–VVI. Felix Meiner, 1980.

Krämling, Gerhard. "Das höchste Gut als mögliche Welt. Zum Zusammen-hang von Kulturphilosophie und systematischer Architecktonic bei I. Kant." *Kantstudien* 77 (1986): 273–89.

Kraft, Michael. "Kant's Theory of Teleology." *International Philosophy Quarterly,* 22 (March 1982): 41–49.

Krüger, Gerhard. *Philosophie und Moral in der Kantischen Kritik.* 2d Ed. Tübingen: 1967.

Kuderowicz, Zbigniew. "Kants Rolle in der Entwicklung der philosophischen Anthropologie," in *Revolution der Denkart oder Denkart der Revolution.* Edited by Manfred Buhr/T.J. Oisermann, 248–50. Berlin: 1976.

Landgrebe, Ludwig. "Die Geschichte im Denken Kants." *Studium generale* 7 (1954): 533–44.

———. "Das philosophische Problem des Endes der Geschichte." In *Kritik und Metaphysik Studien.* Edited by Heinz Heimsoeth, 224–43. Berlin: Walter der Gruyter and Co., 1966.

Lehmann, Gerhard. "Zur Geschichte der Kantausgabe: 1896–1955." In *Beiträge zur Geschichte und Interpretation der Philosophie Kants,* 3–26 (includes letters between Dilthey and Adickes). Berlin: Walter de Gruyter and Co., 1969.

———. "Fragen der Kantedition." In *Beiträge zur Geschichte und Interpretation der Philosophie Kants,* pp. 27–44.

———. "Kritizismus und kritisches Motiv in der Entwicklung der Kantischen Philosophie." In *Beiträge zur Geschichte und Interpretation der Philosophie Kants,* pp. 117–51.

———. "System und Geschichte in Kants Philosophie." pp. 152–70.

———. "Ganzheitsbegriff und Weltidee in Kants Opus Postumum." pp. 247–71.

Lepenies, Wolf. *Soziologische Anthropologie. Materialen.* Munich: Carl Henser, 1971.

Linden, Mareta. *Untersuchungen zum Anthropologiebegriff des 18. Jahrhunderts.* Bern and Frankfurt: Lang, 1976.

Louden, Robert B. *Kant's Impure Ethics: From Rational Beings to Human Beings.* New York: Oxford University Press, 2000.

Löw, R. *Philosophie der Lebendigen.* Frankfurt am Main: Suhrkampf, 1980.

Löwisch, Dieter-Jürgen. "Kants Begründung der Gemeinschaft durch die Idee der Menschheit." In *Rationalität—Phänomenalität—Individualität. Festgabe für Hermann und Marie Glockner.* Edited by Wolfgang Ritzel, 175–88. Bonn: h. Bouvier u. Co., 1966.

Long, David A. "Kant's Pragmatic Horizon." *American Philosophical Quarterly* 19 (October 1982): 229–311.

Lübbe, Hermann. "Philosophiegeschichte als Philosophie." In *Einsichten. Gerhard Krüger zum 60. Geburtstag.* Edited by Klaus Oehler und Richard Schaeffler, 204–29. Frankfurt am Main: Vittorio Klostermann, 1962.

Malter, Rudolf. "Anhang II. Zu Kants Vorlesungen über Anthropologie," *in Immanuel Kant: Anthropologie in pramatischer Hinsicht.* Edited by Karl Vorländer, 315–70. Hamburg: Felix Meiner, 1980.

———. Book Review of Kant as Philosophical Anthropologist. *Kantstudien* 64 (1973): 127–29.

Marquard, Odo. "Zur Geschichte des philosophischen Begriff 'Anthropologie' seit dem Ende des achtzehnten Jahrhunderts." In *Collegium Philosophicum. Festschrift für Joachim Ritter,* 209–39. Basel/Stuttgart: 1965.

———. "Anthropologie." In *Historisches Wörterbuch der Philosophie.* Edited by Joachim Ritter, 1: 361–74. Basel/Stuttgart: 1971.

McFarland, J. D. *Kant's Concept of Teleology.* Edinburgh: University of Edinburgh Press, 1970.

Medicus, Fritz. "Kants Philosophie der Geschichte." *Kantstudien* 7 (1902): 1–22; 171–229.

Mengüsoglu, Takiyettin. "Der Begriff des Menschen bei Kant." In *Kritik und Metaphysik Studien.* Edited by Heinz Heimsoeth, 106–19. Berlin: Walter de Gruyter and Co., 1966.

Menzer, Paul. *Der Entwicklungsgang der Kantischen Ethik bis zum Erscheinen der Grundlegung zur Metaphysik der Sitten.* Inaugural-Diss. Berlin: E. Ebering, 1897.

———. "Der Entwicklungsgang der Kantischen Ethik in den Jahren 1760 bis 1785: Erste Teil." *Kantstudien* 2 (1898): 290–322.

———. "Der Entwicklungsgang der Kantischen Ethik in den Jahren 1760 bis 1785: Zweite Teil." *Kantstudien* 3 (1899): 41–104.

———. *Kants Lehre von der Entwicklung in Natur und Geschichte.* Berlin: Georg Reimer, 1911.

Mischel, Theodore. "Kant and the Possibility of a science of Psychology." In *Kant Studies Today.* Edited by L. W. Beck, 432–55. LaSalle, IL: Open Court, 1969.

Moravia, Sergio. *Beobachtende Vernunft. Philosophische Anthropologie in der Aufklärung.* Trans. (Italian) by Elisabeth Piras. München: Carl Hanser, 1973.

Munzel, G. Felicitas. *Kant's Conception of Moral Character: The 'Critical' Link of Morality, Anthropology, and Reflective Judgment.* Chicago: University of Chicago Press, 1999l.

Neukirchen, Aloys. *Das Verhältnis der Anthropologie Kants zu seiner Psychologie.* Inaugural-Diss. München. Bonn: P. Hauptmann'sche Buchdruckerei, 1914.

Niethammer, Arnolf. *Kants Vorlesung über Pädagogik. Freiheit und Notwendigkeit in Erziehung und Entwicklung.* Frankfurt am Main/Bern/Cirencester/U.K.: Peter D. Lang, 1980.

Pappé, H. O. Art. "Philosophical Anthropology." In *The Encyclopedia of Philosophy.* Edited by Paul Edwards. New York: MacMillan Publishing Co., Inc., and The Free Press, 1967.

Paulsen, Friedrich. *Immanuel Kant. Sein leben und seine Lehre*. 6th Ed. Stuttgart: Fr. Frommanns, 1920.

Pfannkuche, A. "Der Zweckbegriff bei Kant." *Kantstudien* 5 (1901): 51–72.

Pieper, Annemarie. "Ethik als das Verhältnis von Moralphilosophie und Anthropologie. Kants Entwurf einer Transzendentalpragmatik und ihre Transformation durch Apel." *Kantstudien* 69 (1978): 314–29.

Platner, Ernst. *Anthropologie für Ärzte und Weltweise*. Leipzig: n.p., 1772.

Plessner, Helmuth. "Ungesellige Geselligkeit. Anmerkungen zu einem Kantischen Begriff." In *Die moderne Demokratie und ihr Recht. Festschrift f. Gerhard Leibholz z. 65. Geburtstag*. Edited by Karl Dietrich Bracher, 382–92. Tübingen: J. C. B. Mohr (Paul Siebeck), 1966.

Pomerleau, Wayne. "Kant's Theory of Human Culture and History." *Logos* (USA) 4 (1983): 25–38.

Rickert, Heinrich. *Kant als Philosoph von Kultur*. Tübingen: 1924.

Riedel, Manfred. "Die Aporie von Herrschaft und Vereinbarung in Kants Idee des Sozialvertrags." In *Kant: zur Deutung seiner Theorie von Erkennen und Handeln*. Edited by Gerold Prauss, 337–49. Köln: Kiepenheuer, 1973.

———. "Geschichte als Aufklärung. Kants Geschichtsphilosophie und die Grundlagenkrise der Historiographie." *Neue Rundschau* 84 (1973): 289–308.

———. "Geschichtstheologie, Geschichtsideologie, Geschichts-philosophie. Untersuchungen zum Ursprung und zur Systematik einer kritischen Theorie der Geschichte bei Kant." *Philosophische Perspektiven* 5 (1973): 200–26.

———. "The Normative Understanding of History versus Historicism." *Idealistic Studies* 8 (1978): 1–13.

Ritzel, Wolfgang. *Immanuel Kant: Zur Person*. Bonn: Bouvier Verlag Herbert Grundmann, 1975.

———. *Immanuel Kant: Eine Bibliographie*. Berlin, New York: Walter de Gruyter and Co., 1985.

Roithinger, Ludwig. "Moralische Anthropologie und Metaphysik der Sitten bei Kant." In *Ethik und Anthropologie: Zur Analyse und Fundierung der Moral durch die Human- und Sozialwissenschaften*, 55–81. Wien/Köln/Graz: Hermann Böhlaus Nachf., 1985.

Rühl, Franz. "Ueber Kants Idee zu einer allgemeinen Geschichte in weltbürgerlicher Absicht." *Altpreußischer Monatsschrift* 17 (1880): 333–42.

Ruse, Michael. "Evolutionary Ethics: A Phoenix Arisen." *Zygon* 21, No. 1 (March 1986): 96.

Satura, Vladimir. *Kants Erkenntnispsychologie in den Nachschriften seiner Vorlesungen über empirische Psychologie*. Kantstudien Ergänzunghefte 101. Bonn: Bouvier Verlag Herbert Grundmann, 1971.

Schilpp, Paul Arthur. *Kant's Pre-Critical Ethics*. Evanston and Chicago: Northwestern University, 1938.

Schlapp, Otto. *Kants Lehre vom Genie und die Entstehung der 'Kritik der Urteilskraft'*. Göttingen: Vandenboeck & Ruprecht, 1901.

Schleiermacher, Friedrich. "Anthropologie v. Immanuel Kant. Königsb. 98." In *Athenaeum: Eine Zeitschrift v. A.W. Schlegel u. F. Schlegel II*, 300–306. Darmstadt: Wissenschaftliche Buchgesellschaft,   .

Schmucker, Josef. "Die 'Beobachtungen über das Gefühl des Schönen und Erhabenen'." In *Die Ursprunge der Ethik Kants*, 99–142. Meisenheim: Glan, 1961.

Schrader, George. "The Status of Teleological Judgment in the Critical Philosophy." *Kantstudien* 45 (1953): 204–35.

Schultz, Uwe. *Immanuel Kant*. Hamburg: 1965.

Schwartländer, Johannes. "Aspekte einer kritischen Verstehenslehre: Reflexionen zu Kants anthropologischer Philosophie." In *Verstehen und Vertrauen: Otto Friedrich Bollnow zum 65. Geburtstag*, 179–98. Stuttgart: W. Kohlhammer, 1968.

Schwemmer, Oswald. "Begriff und Prinzip der Glückseligkeit bei Kant." In *Philosophie der Praxis*. 2d. Ed. Frankfurt am Main: Suhrkamp, 1980.

Simmermacher, Volker. "Kants Kritik der reinen Vernunft als Grundlegung einer." *Anthropologia Transcendentalis*." PhD Diss., Heidelberg, 1951.

Smith, John. "The Question of Man." In *The Philosophy of Kant and Our Modern World*. Edited by Charles W. Hendel, 3–24. Westport, CT: Greenwood Press, 1981.

Smith, Steven G. "Worthiness to be Happy and Kant's Concept of the Highest Good." *Kantstudien* 75 (1984): 168–90.

Sorell, Tom and Milton Keynes. "Kant's Good Will and our Good Nature." *Kantstudien* 78 (1987): 87–101.

Spaemann, Robert and Reinhard Löw. *Die Frage Wozu?: Geschichte und Wiederentdeckung des teleologischen Denkens*. München: Piper, 1981.

Starke, F. C. [Johann Adam Bergk]. *Immanuel Kants Menschenkunde & Immanuel Kants Anweisung zur Menschen- und Weltkenntnis*. Hildesheim/New York: Georg Oms, 1976.

Tenenbaum, Katja. "Natur und Kultur—Zu einem Aspekt der Kantischen Rousseau-Deutung." In *Wissenschaftl. Ztschr. d. Karl-Marx-Universität Leipzig. Gesellschafts- und Sprachwissenschaftliche Reihe* 23 (1974): 183–89.

Thiel, Manfred. "Das Problem einer Fundamentalen Anthropologie. Ein Anliegen unserer Zeit." In *Konkrete Vernunft. Festschrift für Erich Rothacker*. Edited by Gerhard Funke, 159–77. Bonn: H. Bouvier u. Co., 1958.

Thom, Martina. "Philosophie als Menschenkenntnis: Zur Entstehung und Wertung des philosophischen System I. Kants." *Wissenschaftl. Ztschr. d. Karl-Marx-Universität Leipzig. Gesellschafts- und Sprachwissenschaftliche Reihe* 23 (1974): 131–52.

Thomae, Hans. "Die biographische Methode in den anthropologischen Wissenschaften." *Studium Generale* 5 (April 1952): 163–77.

Thomasius, Christian. *Einleitung zur Hofphilosophie.* Ausgewälte Werke, Bd. 2, Hildesheim: George Olms Verlag, 1994.

Thomasius, Christian. *Einleitung zu der Vernunft-Lehre.* Halle: Salfeld 1692.

Tonelli, Giorgio. "Von den verschiedenen Bedeutungen des Wortes Zweck mässigkeit in der Kritik der Urteilskraft." *Kantstudien* 49 (1957–58): 154–66.

Troeltsch, Ernst. "Das Historische in Kants Religionsphilosophie." *Kantstudien* 9 (1904): 21–154.

van de Pitte, Frederick P. *Kant as Philosophical Anthropologist.* The Hague: Martinus Nijhoff, 1971.

———. "Introduction" to *Anthropology from a Pragmatic Point of View,* Translated by Victor Lyle Dowdell. Revised and edited by Hans H. Rudnick. Carbondale: South Illinios University Press, 1978.

Vorländer, Karl. "Einleitung des Herausgebers: Zur Entstehung und Charakteristik der 'Anthropologie,' in *Immanuel Kant: Anthropologie in pragmatischer Hinsicht.* Fifth Ed. Edited by Vorländer, vii–xviii. Leipzig: Felix Meiner, 1912.

Watkins, Eric, ed. *Kant and the Sciences.* New York: Oxford University Press, 2001.

Weyand, Klaus. *Kants Geschichtsphilosophie. Ihre Entwicklung und ihr Verhältnis zur Aufklärung.* Kantstudien Ergänzungshefte 85. Köln: Kölner Universitäts-Verlag, 1963.

Widmaier, Rita. "Alter und neuer Empirismus. Zur Erfahrungs lehre von Locke und Thomasius." *Christian Thomasius 1655–1728: Interpretationen zu werk und Wirkung.* Hrsg. Werner Schneiders. Hamburg: Felix Meiner Verlag, 1989.

Will, Georg Andreas. "*Einleitung in die historische Gelahrtheit und die Methode, die Geschichte zu lehren und zu lernen.*" In *Dilthey Jahrbuch: für Philosophie und Geschichte der Geisteswissenschaften.* Bd. 2, hrsg. Frithjof Rudi. Reprint 1766, Göttingen: Vandenhoeck and Ruprecht, 1984.

Williams, Forrest. "Philosophical Anthropology and the Critique of Aesthetic Judgment." *Kantstudien* 46 (1954): 172–88.

Wilson, Holly L. "Kant's Views on Human Animality." The Proceedings of the IX International Kant Kongress in Berlin Germany, March 26–31, 2000.

———. "Kant's Experiential Enlightenment and Court Philosophy in the 18th Century." *History of Philosophy Quarterly* 18, No. 2 (April, 2001): 179–205.

———. "Kant's Evolutionary Theory of Marriage." In *Autonomy and Community: Readings in Contemporary Kantian Social Philosophy.* Edited by Jane Kneller. State University of New York Press, 1998.

———. "Rethinking Kant from the Perspective of Ecofeminism." In *Feminist Interpretations of Kant.* Edited by Robin May Schott, 373–99. Penn State University Press, 1997.

——— "Kant and Ecofeminism." In *Ecofeminism: Women, Culture, Nature.* Edited by Karen Warren, 390–411. Bloomington, IN: Indiana University Press, 1997.

———. "Kant's Integration of Morality and Anthropology." *Kantstudien*, 88 (1997): 87–104.

———. "A Gap in American Kant Scholarship: Pragmatic Anthropology as the Application of Kantian Moral Theory" in *Akten des Siebten Internationalen Kant-Kongresses: Kurfürsliches Schloß zu Mainz, 1990*, pp. 403-419. Hrsg. von G. Funke. Bonn: Bouvier, 1991.

Wolandt, Gerd. "Kants Anthropologie und die Begründung der Geisteswissenschaften." *Kant: Analysen, Probleme, Kritik*, 357–78. Königshausen and Neumann: Würzburg, 1988.

Wolff, Christian. *Gesammelte Werke*. Jean Ecole et al. (eds.), 3 series, Hildesheim-[Zurich-] New York: Olms, 1962–.

Wood, Allen W. *Kant's Ethical Thought*. Cambridge: Cambridge University Press, 1999.

———. "Unsociable Sociability: The Anthropological Basis of Kantian Ethics. *Philosophical Topics* 19, No. 1 (Spring 1991): 325–51.

Yovel, Yirmiahu. *Kant and the Philosophy of History*. Princeton, NJ: Princeton University Press, 1980.

Zammito, John H. *Kant, Herder, The Birth of Anthropology*. Chicago: University of Chicago Press, 2002.

Index

www.ingramcontent.com/pod-product-compliance
Lightning Source LLC
Chambersburg PA
CBHW030334270326
41926CB00010B/1619